GRAPES
A Vintage View of Hockey

GRAPES

A Vintage View of Hockey

DON CHERRY
with Stan Fischler

Prentice Hall Canada Inc., Scarborough, Ontario

To Rose and Blue and all the honest
hockey players who played for me.

Canadian Cataloguing in Publication Data

Cherry, Don, 1934-
  Grapes : a vintage view of hockey

ISBN-0-13-363499-X (bound)   ISBN 0-13-110801-8 (pbk.)

1. Cherry, Don, 1934-   . 2. Hockey players -
United States - Biography.   I. Fischler, Stan,
1932-   . II. Title.

GV848.5.C53A3 1982   796.962'092   C82-094867-5

Prentice-Hall, Inc., Englewood Cliffs, *New Jersey*
Prentice-Hall International, Inc., *London*
Prentice-Hall of Australia, Pty., Limited, *Sydney*
Prentice-Hall Hispanoamericana, S.A., *Mexico*
Prentice-Hall of India Private Ltd., *New Delhi*
Prentice-Hall of Japan, Inc., *Tokyo*
Prentice-Hall of Southeast Asia (Pte.) Ltd., *Singapore*
Editora Prentice-Hall do Brasil, Ltda., *Rio de Janeiro*

ISBN 0-13-110801-8

Design: Gail Ferreira
Production Editor: Heather Scott McClune
Artwork: Jo-Ann Jordan and Victoria Birta
Production: Monika Heike / Anna Orodi
Front cover photo: Jim Allen / Courtesy *Saturday Night*

    4 5 W 97 96 95
Printed and bound in Canada

CONTENTS

ACKNOWLEDGMENTS

No championship hockey club could succeed without foot-soldiers who are willing to go into the corners and indulge in heavy checking. Likewise, this work could not have been completed without the grand efforts of a number of literary diggers led by the tenacious Michael Berger who industriously worked with Don's tapes and transcriptions. Michael's management of the flow of information was invaluable and the authors are more than appreciative of his help and diligence.

Many others assisted in the transcription of tapes, the typing of manuscript, and the other duties relevant to the book's production. To them we deliver a deep bow and a large round of applause—Richard Friedman, Paul Fichtenbaum, Phil Davis, Phil Czochanski, Sara Kass, Sharon Kopitnikoff, Debbie Klein, Joel Sherman, Andrew D'Angelo, Don Frumkin, Arthur Bulin, David Hom, Ralph Russo, Steve Ginsberg, George Hall, and Lori Weissman.

It would be an understatement to add that the book would not have come to fruition without the encouragement of Gerry Patterson and Janice Whitford, the latter of whom has been a beacon of literary guidance from the inception of the project. Fifteen years and fifty-five books have passed through this typewriter, and never have I enjoyed working with an editor more than Heather McClune. I have been equally delighted with the work of Gail Ferreira who created the book's terrific design.

Stan Fischler

GRAPES
A Vintage View of Hockey

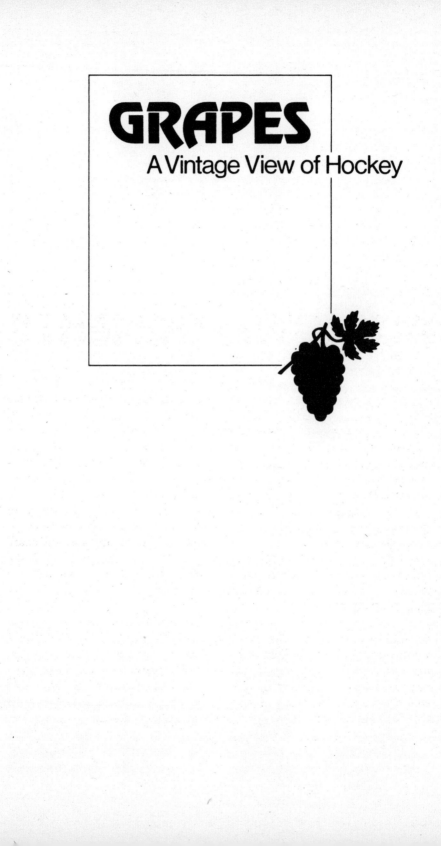

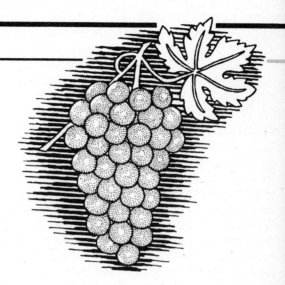

CHAPTER ONE

Close But No Cigar

I died on May 10, 1979; at 11:10 p.m. to be exact.

Two shots killed me. The first, which left me critically wounded, was fired by Guy Lafleur. The one that wiped me out came from the stick of Yvon Lambert.

Had I survived these attacks I have no doubt that I would still be coach of the Boston Bruins today and, quite likely, governor of Massachusetts. But, as my mother always said when she extracted my left *and* right hands from the cookie jar; you can't have everything.

For a time, I did have everything. Early in May, 1979, I was reasonably healthy, only twenty pounds overweight—which is good for me—and I had my family. There was my lovely wife Rose, who had stuck with me through all the battles, (my friends say there's a special place in Heaven for Rose for putting up with me) my beautiful daughter Cindy, my wonderful son Timothy, and most important, my friend and companion Blue—we never call her a dog—who is the Stan Jonathan of Dogdom.

And, of course, there was my job. I was coach of the Boston Bruins. Why, even when I think of it today I find the mere mention of it hard to believe. Me, Donald Stewart Cherry, coach of the Boston Bruins. For my money, there was only one role in history that could surpass running the Bruins and that would be being Lord Nelson commanding the fleet at Trafalgar. He was killed in that action too.

1

I loved coaching the Bruins more than Gretzky and Bossy love scoring goals. Ever since I was a kid growing up in Kingston, Ontario, I dreamed of being a general or admiral directing the troops. Kingston is one of Canada's most beautiful cities, with its preserved historic buildings and lovely waterfront. Also, hockey got started there, so it's not surprising that it's where I decided to enlist.

My luck, the troops I had on the Bruins were special. Very special. The writers liked to call them the Lunchpail Athletic Club. They put in a good day's work and never bitched about it. Anyone who has the good fortune to coach a team like that should count his blessings.

I counted and counted. Not only did I have a team I loved, but there was a constituency to boot. Boston fans are one of a kind. They are blue collar types who come to Boston Garden and give you what-for if you don't give them their money's worth.

There was one guy who always sat in the upper balcony. He had a piercing voice that reminded me of someone pounding on an organ with his elbows. If I was doing badly, he'd yell down, "Hey Cherry, you remind me of a town in Massachusetts. Marblehead!" I think the first time anybody was called Marblehead here was when King Clancy was refereeing. It's one of the classics that's hollered at every coach.

The most famous catcall ever heard in Boston concerned Harry Sinden. The Bruins were having a tough time when Harry was coaching in his first year, and one night a guy hollered, "Sinden! There's a bus leaving for Oklahoma at six a.m. Be under it!" Another time, when Bobby Orr had just joined the club and was skating rings around everybody, the guy hollered, "Sinden! Bench that kid. He makes the rest of the stiffs look bad!"

The trouble with these guys was that they would wait until the whole building was quiet and then start yelling. One night during my first year, when it was very quiet, a guy yelled, "Wake up the coach." I had a running conversation with him. I turned around and hollered, "Have another beer." This got some mild applause from the crowd. In the next period he kept it up, so I yelled, "Aren't you drunk yet?" The crowd gave me a standing ovation for that one.

One day, Terry O'Reilly got into a fight with Dave Schultz, and hurt his hand on Schultz's head. I didn't play Terry for the next game because he couldn't hold a stick, but I dressed him so Schultz wouldn't think he had kept Terry from playing. I forgot how much the Boston fans wanted to see Terry play and they kept giving it to me to play him. Finally I couldn't stand it any longer so at a stoppage of play, I waited until it was nice and quiet, then yelled as loud as I could, "Terry's hurt, but I don't want Schultz to know it." Do you know what reply I got? "Play him anyway, he gets enough dough!"

My first year, one guy was really giving it to Esposito and Cashman. He had Phil in tears of rage one night, and I heard Cash say, "Enjoy the game, you bastard. It's the last game you'll ever see in Boston Garden." I kept my eye on the guy, and after the period he was approached by two guys who looked like Dave Semenko. I never saw or heard from the guy again.

Another time in my first year, we won 3-2 and were booed. I asked one of the writers why the crowd was booing us and he told me that we hadn't covered the spread!

The crowd disliked Don McKenny and Ken Hodge and used to call them "Mary" because they weren't tough enough. But they loved, absolutely adored, Terry O'Reilly. It was said that if O'Reilly shot the puck into his own net, the crowd would boo the goaltender for not stopping the shot.

Tom Fitzgerald once wrote a glowing piece about Terry and someone said to him: "The only reason you people in Boston like O'Reilly is because his name is O'Reilly." Tom answered, "That's not true; we'd like him just as much if his name was Sullivan."

Then there was the media. If there was ever a better bunch of guys around, neither Blue nor I had heard of them. I'll tell you what great guys they were. Many times I would say something in a fit of anger that could really bury me. The sports writers would decide not to print any comments that could hurt me. It must have been the first time in history that writers helped and protected a coach. No wonder I loved them.

I should have been the happiest guy in the world as my Bruins prepared for the seventh game of the Stanley Cup semi-final round against the Canadiens. The series was tied at three games apiece. The writers had picked us to be out in four or five games so already we were away ahead of them. The Canadiens were worried. "Habs on the Ropes," the papers said.

Well, it was true. But Don Cherry was also on the ropes. I had to win this game, and everyone from Boston to Moose Jaw knew why. My manager, boss, and former buddy, Harry Sinden, was after my ass. Harry wanted my skin and the one way he could get me was if we were knocked off by the Canadiens.

Why Sinden wanted me out of my Bruins job is a good question, one I will deal with very shortly. For the moment, suffice it to say that there was a severe personality clash. We had grown farther apart than the Hatfields and the McCoys, and I can guarantee I liked Harry a lot more than he liked me.

All my players were aware of the friction between us. To be unaware they would have to have been spending their days and nights in some distant cave. They were aware, and in a sense, amused by the Cherry-Sinden feud, and they would have fun with it since they never believed I would be fired as long as we kept winning, and we kept winning.

Once, Bobby Schmautz and Gregg Sheppard were marching around in their underwear, singing "Onward Sinden Soldiers." Harry walked into the locker room to hang up his coat and saw the whole scene. Needless to say, Shep was soon gone and Schmautzie followed a little later.

I remember clearly the morning of the seventh game. We were preparing for our morning skate, to loosen up for the game. Somewhere, the team had found a picture of Harry and Tom Johnson, his assistant, and while I was sitting there, putting on my underwear, I saw them putting up this picture and laughing. I knew something was up, but at that point I didn't give a damn. But I thought I should keep the peace for a little while longer, so I went up to see what my little boys had done to piss Harry off today.

Under the picture was written, among other things, "Willard and Ben." For people who haven't seen the movie *Willard*, Willard was a guy who owned a rat named Ben, who was his best friend. I tore down the picture and threw it in the garbage can. But some of the players rescued it and put it back up, when who should come into the dressing room but Tom Johnson. Tom saw the picture, and immediately reported to his boss Harry what *I* had done. "Oh well," I thought, "I'm gone no matter what happens, and besides, it was right on the money."

I remember the players doing something similar during the Pittsburgh series, which we won three games to none. Cheevers was unbelievable in that series. On the morning of the first game, Harry called us all off the ice during our morning skate, and for the first time in five years, really interfered with our game plan. All of a sudden we are going to go over the Pittsburgh lineup, their individual lines and all, the morning of the game. We'd been in the playoffs before and had never done anything like this and all of a sudden, we were doing it for the Penguins.

So, when we all got off the ice, Harry had Pittsburgh's lineup on the blackboard and was telling us how wonderful they were, and how we had to be ready, and sacrifice, and all the bullshit that coaches go through before a game.

Halfway through the speech Harry made such a bad mistake that even I was embarrassed for him. He said "Pittsburgh has a great new winger named Hamilton, who's having a great year. He's scoring a lot of goals and we'll definitely have to watch him." How could Harry make such a blunder? The kid had just come up from the minors and had scored two lucky goals in one game. The players were killing themselves.

Harry left after his performance, and I got up and said, "We're the Boston Bruins; we don't worry about any other team, they worry about us. If we're executing the way we should, they won't win a game. But remember, keep your eye on Hamilton."

I left the locker room and, when I returned, there was Harry, reading the blackboard, only this time the players had written all over the Pittsburgh lineup: "So What? They Suck! Hamilton Who?" And, "Three Straight Games, No Problem!"

I just sighed. (Another nail in the coffin.)

I went back to the Manoir Le Moyne Hotel, where we were staying, and no sooner had I closed the door behind me than the phone started ringing. It was John Zeigler, President of the NHL. He said "Don, I have an article from the *Boston Herald* written by D. Leo Monahan, and it quotes you as saying that the NHL brass does not want a Boston-New York final, they want a Montreal-New York final because they want the big apple and a colourful Canadian team, so watch us get stiffed if it goes seven games."

Ziegler said, "Now I don't mind you calling us stupid among other things, but this article implies we are dishonest. I don't want to put a muzzle on you and your colourful remarks, which are usually good for the league, but we will not mention this again. Is that understood?"

Next thing I knew, I was getting ready for the game at The Forum. I put on my traditional Boston Bruin robe. I walked around, going from player to player, trying to get them relaxed but it was as if they had been in the trenches for too long and were suffering from shell shock.

I walked into the small room where the players fixed their sticks. Bobby Schmautz, my tough little right wing, and Terry O'Reilly, my big right wing were standing there arguing. Schmautz had a hacksaw in his hands and O'Reilly was carrying a blowtorch. Both were working on their sticks. Both wanted to use the vise that holds the sticks while they are being shaved and bent.

I have never in my life experienced anything to compare with the feeling of violence in that room. I honestly thought they were going to go at each other with their weapons, and these guys were, and are, the best of friends. This is just an indication of the fever pitch they were working themselves into for the game.

Take the whole business of deciding which goalie to start. I had used Gerry Cheevers in our quarter-final series against the Penguins and he was terrific. Mind you, I'm talking about an athlete who was 36 years old at the time stopping shots going more than a hundred miles an hour. Now, I didn't want to play him in every game against the Penguins. My other goalie was Gilles Gilbert, a French Canadian and a real stylist. Although he was younger than Gerry, he didn't have Gerry's heart. I had hoped to start Gilbert in Game Three of the Pittsburgh series, but he got so nervous he came down with a case of hives and I had to throw Cheevers into the breach.

I actually didn't have a chance to use Gilbert until the Montreal series. Everyone thought I was nuts to use Gillie because he hadn't played against the Penguins but they didn't figure on the psychological element that is so important in this game. I knew that Gilbert was coming up to the option year of his contract and I knew that if he expected to get a good new contract he would have to excel against the Canadiens.

But, just to be certain, I huddled with Blue. A reporter in Boston once asked me, "How do you pick your goalies?" As a joke I replied,

"Blue picks them for me. We go for walks and she picks which goalie is going to be hot." This really ticked Harry off. So whenever anyone asked me after that, I would say, "Blue says Cheevers is ready," or "Blue says Gillie is going to be hot tonight."

People wonder why coaches have dogs, and I have noticed that athletes often take their dogs for long walks. The reason is that the dog doesn't care whether you win or lose, he just wants to be with you. The joy a dog expresses in solitary walks with you seems to raise your spirits. No dumb questions, no criticisms, a dog just wants to be with you and love you. How could you not feel better?

I could hardly wait, after a game, to get home and take a moonlight walk with Blue. And I really did talk to her. If we had played badly, I'd say, "Well, Blue, we really blew it tonight," or "We really stunk the joint out tonight," or if we played well, "We were smoking tonight." She didn't care, she was always too busy chasing something in the bushes.

One time, the dog-walking idea backfired on me. I thought it would be a good idea to take a walk with Blue in the State Park that bordered our property in Boston. The place had stone fences and deserted mills that were two hundred years old. It was a very warm day and I decided to stop by a beautiful stream. I fell asleep and when I awoke, still a little sleepy, I decided to take a short cut through the woods.

Blue and I wandered for four hours, and she kept looking up at me as if to say, "You jerk." We went through woods and swamps and I got worried when it started to get dark. Finally, I heard tires on a distant highway, so we headed there. I found a piece of rope at a deserted farmhouse to put around Blue and we started along the highway. Two guys drove by and hollered, "Hey, there's Blue." Imagine, they recognized Blue and not me. They picked us up and I found out later that we had walked fifteen miles.

Anyway, Blue was the one who tipped me about playing Gilbert, and Gillie just came up great. We were down to the seventh game and I knew that he would play better than ever in front of the French-speaking crowd. French-Canadian hockey players have a special pride in their culture. Playing in The Montreal Forum is to them what a pilgrimage to Mecca is to a Moslem.

Of course it meant a lot to the English-speaking players as well. I looked at Brad Park and I could have cried. Here he was, 30 years old, should have been in the prime of his hockey life and yet, judging by his wan face, you would have figured he was playing the last game of his life. His knees had had all the cartilages taken out but they never took his heart out.

Park realized that this might be the last time he would get so close to sipping Stanley Cup champagne. He knew in his heart that if we could just get past the Canadiens we would destroy the New York Rangers in the finals.

Timothy and me in Boston Garden, 1975-76.

Rose, Blue, and me.

Cartoon by Bob Alexander that appeared in the Eagle-Tribune, April 29, 1979.

"What I'm thinking," said Park, "is that I have an opportunity here. How many other times will I have that opportunity?"

The Canadiens had won the Stanley Cup more times than anybody, but we sensed that they were tight. "We forced them into a situation where they're in big trouble," said Park. "Now they have to see if they can play loose. It's a first for them in this series. Now they're the team that has to win."

To beat Montreal, we had to get the puck past the big guy, Ken Dryden, who guarded their net. He was the scholar of the National Hockey League. He had a law degree and a great pair of legs; no other goalie could make that statement. He also had a clearer view of the game than most of the players. His professorial approach didn't fool me. Deep down, Dryden was as intense a competitor as anyone else on the ice; maybe more so—especially in the seventh game. Canadiens have never been the same since he left.

"We will gamble more," said Dryden. "We will take more punishment, knowing that there is nothing to save for another game to be played."

Fine. The rhetoric was superb, as it usually is before a seventh game. The question remained: How would it be translated on the ice? Well, it was a hell of a game. My guys were loose and the Canadiens, for some reason that to this day I still can't fathom, couldn't get themselves untracked.

The trick was to stop Guy Lafleur. Sounds easy. About as easy as bottling the Atlantic Ocean. I gave the job of shadowing Lafleur to Don Marcotte. For my money there wasn't a better example of a working guy than Marcotte. (I think it's a joke that he never won the Frank Selke award given to the best defensive forward.) Don's job was to hawk Lafleur on every turn and he was doing it well. I also knew that Scotty Bowman, my counterpart behind the Canadiens' bench, was trying to double- and triple-shift Lafleur to get him away from Marcotte. My answer to that was that if Lafleur could play 60 minutes, Marcotte could play 60 minutes.

"You follow him to the toilet if you have to," I told Donny, "but don't let him out of your sight."

For two periods he followed my orders to a T. Once the two of them collided and were simultaneously cut on the face. They just stood there glaring at each other, like a pair of medieval knights who had nothing but the utmost respect for each other.

After two periods, we led 3-1. Geez, but we could have had at least two more in the second period. Terry O'Reilly and Peter McNab had Dryden beaten but they couldn't put the biscuit behind him.

The trick for a coach between periods of a game like that one is to try to keep everything loose, especially when you have a team of guys who are up for every game. Keep everything loose and in perspective.

Treat it like any other game. What I did was to remind them of their jobs.

To Marcotte I said, "Watch Lafleur, keep with him." To Cashman I said, "Cash, stand in front, don't let him see anything." (This meant I wanted him to screen Dryden on shots from the point.) To Park, "Make sure your shots are on net." To Doak, "Don't run." (This meant that he shouldn't run *at* the Canadiens.) To everybody I said, "Don't get caught." and "Remember now, shoot low." We had found out during the season that if you put a low, soft, screen shot on net, Dryden would miss it.

I told Bobby Schmautz to "waste one." This meant—and very few people in the league have the balls to do this—shoot the puck around Dryden's head. That way, he would be straightened up and unprepared for a low shot.

So, this is the sort of thing a coach says between periods, and it's a funny thing. The players never answer back. They don't even say yes or anything else. They only nod, but they are ready.

We went out prepared for the third period, but Damn! The Canadiens got one at 6:10 and before nine minutes had gone by we were tied up at 3-3.

Then we got a break. Guy Lapointe, one of the best of Montreal's defensemen, hurt his knee and it was the Canadiens' turn to sag. With four minutes left in regulation time my nifty little right wing, Rick Middleton, got the puck behind the Montreal net. He came out front and stuffed it past Dryden to put us ahead, 4-3. There were exactly 3 minutes and 59 seconds separating us from the biggest victory of our lives.

Could we do it? Everybody had his assignment, but I could tell that they were tight. Too tight. I would have liked to call a three day time-out and review all assignments, remind the players that the best defense is a good offense, and return Donny Marcotte to the fray, reasonably well-rested. Under the circumstances, I felt as helpless as a guy trying to catch the gold ring on a merry-go-round while sitting on an inside horse. The game had somehow gotten out of my grasp. It was up and down, fast, faster, fastest. Next thing I knew, Lafleur was going off the ice for the Canadiens and Marcotte had come back to our bench, while the play was still on. I walked over to Donny and gave him a pat on the back. He looked up at me, exhausted, and then looked back onto the ice. Marcotte turned white. I heard him moan, "Oh, no!" Those deathless words will remain with me into my fourth reincarnation.

I looked out onto the field of battle and got that sinking sensation. I didn't have to count the players, I knew. *We had too many men on the ice.* My heart actually hurt then, and remembering now makes it hurt again.

I needed a large—about 40 foot long—invisible hook to instantly haul in my wandering minstrel. (Who will never be mentioned, we made a silent pact never to reveal his name.) If the referee and linesmen wore blindfolds for about a minute I might be able to get somebody's attention and get him the hell back to the bench before we were slapped with a two-minute penalty.

No such luck. Linesman John D'Amico, a hell of a nice guy, noticed that we had six skaters instead of the legal five. I could tell that in his heart of hearts he *didn't* want to blow the whistle on us and that even *he* was hoping that a Bruin would have the good sense to get back to the bench. I could see in his eyes that he was saying to himself, "Don, I hate to do this to you but I have to!"

D'Amico's arm went up and the sound of his whistle cut right through to my bone marrow.

The time of the penalty was 17:26. How did it happen? Why did it happen? I have asked myself these questions so many times!

For starters let me say for now and for an eternity that *I* accept full responsibility for the blunder of blunders. When a team gets caught with too many men on the ice at that stage in a hockey game, it has to be the coach's fault. I deserved to be court-martialed.

The confusion was rooted in the fact that Marcotte had stayed on left wing through three shifts. The other guy was nervous and got carried away. When he finally came back to the bench after D'Amico whistled the penalty he had tears in his eyes. So did my son, Timothy, who had been watching the game at bench level. I imagine I would have been crying, too, but, at that point, I suspect that all my bodily functions had gone on strike. At that moment I took a look at the Canadiens' bench. They looked like a pride of lions about to jump a wildebeest. There was only one thing to do. I called a time-out.

Were we ever in a mess. My trainer, Frosty Forristall, had tears in his eyes and two Bruins fans sitting next to our bench were bawling like babies. I wanted to cry myself but I couldn't. (That would come later.) I told the guys that we had to stop Lafleur, to stay between him and the net as much as possible.

Okay. The time-out was over. There was a face-off and the puck was in motion. I couldn't believe what a terrific job we were doing of killing the penalty. A minute had gone by and we still had the lead. Now it was 70 seconds elapsed and we were *still* ahead.

But the Canadiens mounted a counterattack. Jacques Lemaire, one of the most underrated players on that Montreal team, took a pass near our blue line. Lafleur was moving down the right side like the Japanese Bullet Train. Lemaire dropped the pass over to Lafleur. I figured he was going to try to move in on Gilbert, try a few dekes and get into a really good scoring position.

He was way over to the right, far, far out, sort of where I wanted him. A shot from there would be desperate, but he drew his stick back. He *was* desperate. For a split second I almost felt reassured. Then, his stick swung around the big arc and the blade made contact with the puck.

I can't tell you precisely how fast that puck travelled but anything faster than that shot had to break the sound barrier. Almost in the same moment Lafleur slapped the rubber, it bulged the twine in the left side of the net behind Gillie. There went the lead. *Boom!* Just like that.

We left the ice tied, 4-4, at the end of regulation time. The way my players plodded into the dressing room you would have thought that they had just finished a trek across the Sahara Desert—in uniform. I have seen teams in my eleven year coaching career that were down, but none as thoroughly subterranean as this one.

I knew that getting them to even a reasonable state of battle readiness for the overtime would be the chore of my life.

Before going into the room I had to get my frustrations out. It does no good for the players to see the coach upset, or for the coach to take his frustrations out on the players. So I left them alone for a while. Then I took a deep breath and walked into the room.

It was like a morgue. No jokes this time. I said to them, "Look, when we were down two games to none in this series going back to Boston, if I could have said to you, 'Would you be happy to go into the overtime of the seventh game?' what would you have said?" And they all yelled, "YES!"

I didn't know if I believed it, but they did and that's most important. They were banging at the doors to get going. There never was, nor ever will be, a better bunch of guys. I love them.

And, before you knew it, the buzzer was sounding for the start of sudden-death overtime.

To my surprise, we came out with more drive than I thought we had in us. Marcotte took a pass from O'Reilly when Dryden had one knee down on the ice. Marcotte shot it for the upper corner and started to raise his stick in celebration, as if the puck was going in. But Dryden, who was so damn big, got his shoulder in front of the puck—more by accident than by skill—and my heart was still in my mouth. The rebound came out to O'Reilly and, with an open net waiting to greet his shot, the puck bounced over his stick.

Back and forth the play whirred at a dizzying pace. The clock ticked past the nine minute mark and there was still no tie-breaker. My guys—particularly the older ones—were struggling. Park, Schmautz and Cashman had blood running into their underwear but they kept on going.

At last, Lafleur was off the ice and it seemed as if we might have a respite, but Bowman had some excellent infantrymen. One of them was a kid named Mario Tremblay who had gone into orbit along the right boards. Another was Yvon Lambert, who always looked as if he had two left feet until he put the puck behind your goalie.

Al Sims was alone on defense, with Park coming back, and I could see the fear in Al's eyes as Lambert sped to the goal crease while Tremblay, tantalizingly, waited for the precise moment to deliver the pass. Lambert eluded Park, accepted the puck at the lip of the net and pushed it past Gilbert before the goalie could slide across the crease.

The pain I felt when the red light flashed behind our goal cannot be measured in traditional human terms. To say that a piledriver applied to my stomach would not have created a deeper hurt would simply be minimizing the ache.

A lot of people — and I know that they don't have sadistic tendencies but it feels like they do — ask, "What were your feelings at that exact moment?" I tell you on Blue's head, it was sorrow for my players, especially those who had been given shots of novocaine before the game. The goal doesn't flash in my mind, but somebody's underwear, with blood mixed with the sweat, does.

I felt disgusted with myself for letting it happen. Sometimes when you have too many men on the ice it's the player's fault. But not this time. I hadn't spelled out the assignments plainly enough.

Strangely, I didn't even think of my job until a reporter asked me, "Do you think this will cost you your job?" I said, "My friend, after this loss, I don't really care one way or the other." But I knew I was gone. I had known I was gone as far back as Christmas. There was a slight chance of me staying if we had won the Cup, but at that moment I really couldn't have cared less.

I tried to punish myself by keeping the reporters out of the locker room for fifteen minutes, so they could bombard me with questions and really give it to me. They tried to be kind, but every question was like a knife through my heart.

We flew home on a charter right after the game. I sat with the players, as usual. No sense in changing now. I sat there sipping a beer, and I said to myself, "Well, what now? Do I become a company man? Do I change my principles even though I know they're right?" No sir. I decided then and there, to hell with it, I was gone.

When we landed at the airport the guys were going to the 3B's, their favourite bar. I was feeling so run-down and sick with the flu that I couldn't go. As I think back now, I should have gone, no matter how sick I was. It would have been our last time together.

I could not duck the blame in the disaster. I was captain of the ship, the ship went down, so I was at fault. The temptation was to start feeling sorry for myself but I felt more grief for my players like Park, Ratelle, and Cash — the old warriors — who might never get this close to winning the Stanley Cup again.

And then there was my goalie, Gilbert. We had had our differences before the Canadiens series, but I couldn't quarrel with his effort this time. He faced 52 shots in the last game and was called out onto the ice after the winning goal. He had been chosen star of the game. When Gillie skated out onto the ice to take his bow, his lips were pursed and he had a far-away look in his eyes. If he had been wearing a steel helmet and a tunic I would have guessed that he was a shell-shocked soldier who had just survived a trench bombardment in World War I.

Survival was very much on my mind at this point in time. I knew that Harry Sinden was after my hide and I didn't have to be told that Lambert's goal killed me. Now there was a matter of reincarnation.

I could have been reborn as a yes man. But that would have meant a 180-degree change. If I had to kiss someone's ass to keep my job, I couldn't live with myself—and I couldn't coach either.

Sure, I might fool some people, but I could never fool the players. One thing my guys have always known is that they could count on me to go to bat for them. That's why they were willing to produce for me. You could say I'm crazy but I wouldn't change that for anything in the world.

The question before the house, as well as all of Boston and parts of Canada, was how Harry would dispose of me and no less importantly, how I would dispose of him.

I drove home; Rose was there. She said that it wasn't my fault but I knew better. Blue wanted to go for a walk. "Sorry Blue, no walk this time. Even you couldn't make me feel better." I went to bed, to dream of blood and sweat . . . Sorry guys.

CHAPTER TWO

I'm Not Wild About Harry

There were Frick and Frack, Hope and Crosby, and, finally, Cherry and Sinden. Anything closer than us would have had to be welded together. He was my boss and I was his employee but our relationship had a brotherly quality about it that had all the elements of permanence. (For the first couple of years at least.)

I had heard of Harry long before I met the man. In Canadian hockey circles he was something of a mini-legend. Like me, he had come up through the ranks. At one point he worked as a boilermaker for General Motors and played hockey as a sideline. He was a defenseman and a hell of a good one, at that. On the smallish side, he was reminiscent of Brad Park in size and style. He could really move the puck well but he wasn't rough. (When you think about that it's fascinating because Harry later became the architect of one of the toughest teams of all time, The Big Bad Bruins of the late 1960s and early 1970s.)

Before Harry turned pro he played for a team from Whitby, Ontario, called the Dunlops. It was a senior division club, sponsored by the Dunlop tire people and it was solid enough to be asked to represent Canada in the 1958 World Championships in Oslo, Norway.

Although they were considered a ragtag team, the Dunlops won the whole shebang and Harry, like the other guys on the club, became an instant Canadian hero.

He turned pro in 1960 with Hull-Ottawa of the Eastern Pro League and the following season he was a regular with Kingston in the Eastern League. In 1962-63 he was like the Bobby Orr of the league. He had 10 goals and 56 assists for 66 points, won the leading defenseman award and was the league's most valuable player.

You would figure that the Boston Bruins, who were holding a mortgage on the bottom of the NHL, would have recognized Sinden's talents and given him a break. What they did was invite him to camp and then ignore him.

My first direct contact with Harry was in 1973, my first year of coaching in Rochester, although I had played against him in different leagues for years. In those days we had none of our own players under contract, so the trick was to scrounge around the NHL and get some borderline big-leaguers on a lend-lease basis. Harry was one of the managers I went hustling to and he gave me three guys who helped right off the bat and I liked him for that.

Meanwhile, Harry had won a pair of Stanley Cups for the Bruins, first as a coach in 1970 and then as a manager in 1972. Tom Johnson was coach in '72, then Harry brought in Bep Guidolin to replace Johnson. And although Bep took the team to the finals, he and Harry did not see eye to eye on things, so he departed for Kansas City.

For reasons that I still can't fathom, Harry took a liking to me. Once, he invited me to Chicago for the Stanley Cup playoffs and didn't mention anything about coaching. My early impression of him was favourable. He had an earthy quality about him. When we returned to the hotel there was none of the formality of room service or such sophisticated trappings.

Old School Harry went to the corner grocery store and bought cheese, crackers, and all the beer we could carry and we had a picnic in the suite. I liked that.

The next time I saw Sinden was at the annual hockey meetings in Montreal. It was June 1974 and just about everybody connected with hockey, with the exception of Lord Stanley of Preston, showed up for the annual draft and general search for jobs. Guidolin had been dropped as Bruins' coach. The Bruins were looking for a replacement but I wasn't thinking about the job.

What interested me was Sinden. Somehow I had become intrigued by the man and his style. He seemed to be a cut or two above the run-of-the-mill hockey people. He was easily the classiest operator at the hockey convention.

One night Harry invited me out for a few beers. We talked about the draft, about the NHL generally, about players in particular, about life and sometimes, even, about the distant world outside of hockey. Sometime before the stroke of midnight, Harry leaned back and uttered the unexpected words: "How would you like to coach the Boston Bruins?"

I had the feeling of being ever so slightly electrocuted. Being knighted by Queen Elizabeth was about the only accomplishment that could be equated with an offer to coach in the NHL. And yet, when the feeling subsided I looked Sinden in the eye and wanted to say thanks, but no thanks!

"Look, Harry," I said, "I want a little time to think about it. Lemme talk to my wife."

There was a lot of thinking to be done and not much time in which to do it. My inclination, oddly enough, was to reject the offer. Rochester had become home to me; home in the literal and figurative sense. We had been living there for ten years and had grown to love the city, the people and the hockey community. More than that, I had found myself as a coach and general manager there.

Money was irrelevant in my decision, as it has always been when it comes to hockey matters. I made $4,500 a year for nine years as a player before I got a raise to $5,200. When I came to Rochester, Jack Riley, the boss, increased my salary to $6,000 because that was what the newest rookies were making and he didn't want a man with ten years of pro experience to be getting less than they were.

Another real obstacle to my leaving was the link I had forged with the Rochester Americans hockey club. When I had taken the job of coach and general manager I had said that I wanted to build a dynasty. I had meant it, and I knew that I was getting closer every day.

Better still, management in Rochester left me alone. This has always been vital to me—room to do things my way without the higher-ups interfering—and the Rochester owners knew it and respected my feelings. I never had to worry about them meddling in the team's business.

I had already been fired once in Rochester, in 1972, because I ignored some orders from the front office (since replaced) when they wanted me to play a couple of guys I knew were stiffs. After I came back under a new administration, I was allowed to turn the club around and the people of Rochester appreciated what I had done. Why, one summer three different civic organizations voted me "Citizen of the Year," and I wasn't even a citizen!

I had a good thing going in Rochester. The town was alive hockey-wise; the owners respected me and said that I could stay there as long as I wished. I could have played it safe and simply given Sinden a thanks-but-no-thanks.

Before I made any decision, I phoned my wife, Rose, and told her the situation. "It's your decision, Don," she said. But she also wanted to be sure I realized what a great deal I would be giving up. We had a nice, comfortable home. I was making $30,000-a-year, plus expenses and the use of a car. "You know," added Rose, "you could run for mayor of Rochester—and win."

But she reiterated that I had to make the ultimate decision and—great wife that she was, is and always will be—Rose said she would go along with whatever I chose to do. You have no idea how much easier that makes it for a man. After all, she could have said, "Enough with the travelling; I don't want to move again. We stay!" I knew a lot of other wives who would have said just that.

That night I sat alone in my hotel room, mulling over the options. I remember a pervasive feeling to play it safe and stay in Rochester. But the more I thought about it, the more I became convinced that staying would be the cowardly thing to do. Finally, I said to myself: "For cripes sake, Don. You always wanted to be in the NHL. How many chances do you get to coach the Boston Bruins?" Then, I thought of my dad and what he would have thought of me if I had rejected Harry's offer. *That* did it.

The next morning I met Harry for breakfast. I didn't say a word until we had ordered the bacon-and-eggs. Finally, I said, "Yeah, I'll coach the Bruins."

I was very matter-of-fact about it; so much so that Harry couldn't believe it. With that, he shot back: "Okay, how much do you want, $10,000?"

There was a brief pause. Then Harry burst out laughing and I sailed along with him.

"Harry," I said, "I know you'll be fair." I wasn't going to quibble. All I wanted was the chance to prove myself. I told him to give me what he thought I was worth and as many years as he wanted.

"I'll give you a three year deal," he replied, "at $40,000 a year."

We shook hands and I walked away with a gushing feeling of satisfaction welling within me. It was a good contract, as far as I was concerned, but there was a more important reason for my accepting it and, I'll bet, to this day nobody would guess why. You see, a lot of people think I decided to go to Boston because I had been buried in the minors for so long that I craved the big time and that I couldn't wait to handle superstars like Bobby Orr and Phil Esposito. No way.

I took the Bruins job for one reason and one reason only—Harry Sinden. He had been an excellent coach and I felt that I couldn't just walk into the job without getting some help from a real *NHL* pro. I believed implicitly in Harry's ability to help make me an even better leader than I had been. And I was right.

Another thing. I had a gut feeling of rapport with Harry that I had never experienced before with a boss. I sensed that we could share a special kinship.

There was a lot about us that was similar. We both had had a middle-class upbringing. We came from the same community. Sinden had suffered for years as a minor leaguer, much in the manner that I had. He knew what tough-going was all about. He had scratched and crawled to get to the top, and now I was there with him. Besides, he liked bagpipe music. I had been a tenor drummer in the Rochester pipe band. How could I not be a Harry Sinden fan after that?

As soon as we agreed on the deal I phoned Rose.

"I'm taking the Bruins' job," I said.

"Okay. What time does your flight get in?" was her re

That was Rose! Always taking things in stride. Can yc
for the first time in our lives we owned our own home, ⅃ɩᴇ children
were going to school, and we had friends in Rochester. All this was gone
and all she said was, "What time do you get in?" I have heard that some
hockey wives leave their husbands because their intellectual lives aren't
being fulfilled. I think the song "Stand By Your Man" was written for
Rose. She is one in a million.

On the flight back to Rochester my mind was filled with conflicting
thoughts. I kept saying to myself, "Hey, Don, you're coach of the Bruins."
Then I began reflecting as the clouds rolled by. I was getting $10,000 more
than I was getting in Rochester but I was going to suffer ten times more
pressure. The cushy part of the job I was leaving kept intruding in my
thoughts. I had been general manager. I could come and go as I pleased. I
could get the players I wanted, not the ones someone else ordered me to
get.

The real clincher, the episode that convinced me that I had done the
right thing, occurred when I arrived home and told my nine-year-old son
Timothy that I had accepted the Bruins' job.

Timothy said breathlessly, "You mean I'm going to meet Bobby
Orr?" "Yeah, and so will I," said I, just as breathlessly.

If the truth be known, I was awed by the new job and I hadn't even
started it yet. I signed the Bruins contract without even reading it; that's
how much I trusted Harry. I didn't even have an agent or an attorney look
it over for me. Rose was amused. "You know, Don," she said, "you should
keep a rubber stamp handy for signing all contracts."

Sinden called a press conference in Boston to announce the deal. The
story that I was taking the job broke while I was still in Rochester, but I
flew down to Boston the next day where I was formally introduced in The
Garden Room of Boston Garden. When I walked in, the first thing I
noticed was the huge photo of Eddie Shore hanging on the wall, then the
photos of Dit Clapper and other distinguished Bruins. As I entered the
press conference, the pack of reporters and television people amazed me. I
instantly got the feeling that they were taking a skeptical view of me,
wondering who *is* this jerk up from the minors. To say the least, I was
impressed by the turnout.

I was not so impressed by my debut up at the podium. I made "great"
statements like, "How can we lose with the kind of great players we have
on this team?" And, "If we lose, it'll be my fault." Wonderful. I started
digging my own grave on the first day of the job.

Apparently, some members of the media were impressed. "If you like
honesty and animation with your ice hockey," wrote Joe Gordon in the
Quincy Massachusetts *Patriot-Ledger*, "you'll like Don Cherry."

Actually, I was the original Mr. Naiveté. I had no idea what was going on behind the scenes with the Bruins so, when I talked to the newspaper guys it was without a lot of the facts Harry had at his fingertips.

But more about that later. "I like a tough team," I told them, "and I know I have tough guys on this club and I'll bring out the toughness. They're going to be rough. Every team I've ever been with has been. We intimidated every club in the American League."

Someone asked a good question: did I anticipate having any trouble with the players? "A few," I said, "will probably try to take advantage but when they do I'll step on them and step on them hard."

It sounded good, but I hadn't even met the players yet. That would come just before training camp. In the meantime, my dealings were with Harry and they couldn't have been better. I could hardly wait until the phone rang. When he would say, "Don, Harry here," I would actually get a thrill. And when he told me that he had never considered anyone else for the coaching job I got an even bigger thrill.

The thrill was gone the minute I met the players. This happened at a pre-season bash the Bruins threw at a country club in suburban Boston. They pulled out all the stops; grills with flaming hors d'oeuvres, bloody marys, beer, everything. Starting out the season with a party seemed like a good idea; little did I know that the party would continue for six months. A couple of the players depressed me no end. One guy was so stiff he couldn't talk.

I felt like a jerk and I couldn't imagine how these guys would be able to get in shape eating and drinking the way they did.

All of a sudden it came to me; I was in trouble with this hockey team and I hadn't even coached it yet. I felt I was in trouble and I knew the club was in trouble and so did Harry. Even though I knew most of the guys were winners, some of them had outgrown hockey. Hockey had become a means to an end.

Some of the players were fat, and not only fat physically, but fat in the heart. I could see they had forgotten that hard work had brought them here in the first place. I could feel that the fat cat syndrome had seeped in. This wasn't a hockey club, it was a country club. Some of the guys loved everything about hockey. They loved the limelight, they loved the hours, they loved the adoration, they loved the pay. There was just one thing they didn't love and that was playing the game. We were all in trouble.

Harry's feeling about the partying was, as Al Jolson once said, "You ain't seen nuthin' yet." He knew what the problem was but I took a little longer to appreciate the enormity of it all. I was still a bit too awed and impressed by the big names. "You'll see what I mean," Harry insisted.

Still, Harry didn't put pressure on me in terms of the personnel; at least not in the beginning. I could not have asked for more support if my brother had been general manager of the Bruins. Every so often I would have to pinch myself to believe how well the Sinden-Cherry alliance was going. It was like a marriage made in heaven. I couldn't wait for the game to end just to have the pleasure of sitting down and talking hockey with the man. We usually agreed on *anything*.

Very early on I came to the understanding that Harry was bitter about some of the personnel. I think that he had been burned by some of the players in the past and had come to resent them. That's why he kept telling me that I'd find out what they were *really* like and it helps explain his general attitude toward them. But I give him credit for being democratic; he treated all players alike, even a superstar like Bobby Orr.

Interestingly, Harry and I never got really close, in the personal sense, although we spent a lot of time together during my first season. It was purely a hockey liaison. We didn't socialize together, and hardly ever visited each other's homes. That I left for Harry and Tom Johnson. Their relationship was airtight in every way. Johnson was Sinden's eyes and ears for the team whenever Harry wasn't around. There was a movie around at the time starring Sir Laurence Olivier called *Sleuth*. Well, the players called Tom SuperSleuth, so you can take it from there.

At first I had no problem with Johnson. He just stayed in the background, puffing his big cigar and, since I was getting on famously with Harry, there was no problem with Tom. My problem was with the hockey club. In Rochester, I could rule like Napoleon; I was coach *and* general manager. If a kid didn't follow orders he was benched. And if he still didn't follow orders he was gone. It was a simple formula; play Cherry's way, or don't play for Cherry's team. That formula didn't work in my rookie season with the Bruins. For starters, the team was loaded with fat cats.

Because the war with the WHA was going great guns, every big shot in the NHL knew damn well that if his team gave him any grief, all he had to do was jump to the WHA and make a bundle. You didn't need a Ph.D. in economics to realize that superstars like Bobby Hull and Gerry Cheevers were getting rich, quick, but so were a bunch of wimps who couldn't check their grandmothers or shoot a puck through a pane of glass.

We didn't play nearly as well as we should have that first year. It's easy to look back now and see my mistakes. I should have made the Bruins play my system instead of their wide open style, which is becoming more popular now.

We weren't tough enough. I remember in Detroit a player named Hank Nowak almost took Bobby Orr's head off with an elbow and nobody got upset.

On the subject of Orr, he was, as usual, absolutely fantastic. He had 46 goals and 85 assists that season. He was blocking shots, hitting, fighting. It certainly wasn't his fault we were second to Buffalo. But he was frustrated because he knew I wasn't doing my job. I wanted to put in a system that I knew would work, but some of the players came to me and said they couldn't play that way.

So I said to myself, "Maybe they're right. After all, they've won the Stanley Cup, they've been to the finals, maybe my way is wrong," I knew that way of thinking was wrong, but I went along with it anyway.

Anyway, as we went through the season a lot of players told me not to worry, to wait until the playoffs when they'd make their move. I waited, and I waited. I didn't want to rock any boats, at least not in my rookie season. I kept waiting, and then the playoffs came. We played Chicago in the first round, best of three series. The bell rang and I waited to see my thoroughbreds make their move. And what a move it was. The only thing that could plunge faster than the Bruins did is a supersonic elevator. One, two, three and we were out. I remember after the last game, one of the reporters said to Gillie Gilbert, "Gillie, Esposito was hot, he had 56 shots on him and you had only 18." And Gillie said, "But those 18, there were a lot of good ones in them." Can you imagine how many good ones there were in the 56?

The wipeout left me in a state of shock I had never experienced before. I felt our being ousted was my fault, which it was. Maybe I was just an upstart minor leaguer. I severely questioned my coaching ability, and what I had done to the one man who had confidence in me—Harry Sinden. While I felt badly for myself, I felt worse for Harry. I had let him down, and I told him so. We met after the series at the 3B's Restaurant. I said, "Look, Harry, I know I have two years left on my contract. Forget about 'em. I let you down. As far as I'm concerned you don't have to pay me for the next two years. You can get rid of me right now and I'll have no complaints."

He looked at me as if I was nuts. "Are you kidding? I had never even thought of firing you. But next year, be Don Cherry. You weren't this year." What better vote of confidence could I ask for than the boss saying, "You lost, but don't worry, you're my coach."

I knew we had the nucleus of a good team wih lots of heart. While I washed my car, I played a song by The Who, called "Won't Get Fooled Again." I'd play that record over and over, and I'd say to myself, "They will play my system or else."

One last thing proved to me that I would change the Bruins. The Stanley Cup finals were on television and one of my players came on. He was all tanned since he had just come back from Bermuda, and he was wearing gold beads and everything. The sportscaster asked him, "Why were the Bruins beaten out?" And the guy said, "We weren't mentally prepared." Well, that was my job as coach, and I said to myself, "You son of a bitch, you'll be prepared next year."

It was a tough grind changing the dressing room from a country club to a sweat-shop but gradually the team changed from an undisciplined, doing-it-any-way club, to a tough disciplined grind-you-down team that played just as hard on the road as it did at home, which showed character.

Everything had been going beautifully. We had been in first place for three straight seasons. Earlier, in the second season, Harry had made a dynamite trade, we finished with over a hundred points four seasons in a row, we made the finals, I was coach-of-the-year, and everything was lovely. Life was sweet.

My honeymoon with Harry didn't end abruptly, but rather deteriorated over a series of incidents that took place starting with the fifth season.

Let me say up front, that I was, at the very least, partly to blame for the rift developing. In other words, Harry and I would have stayed friends if I hadn't kept opening my mouth.

Perhaps the best example was The Case of the Phantom Pucks. You have to understand that every team in the league has its official crest laminated on the pucks used in the games. Every team, that is, except the Bruins. Our pucks were black on top, black on the bottom and black on the sides. These pucks looked as if they were on loan from the local street hockey league!

Needless to say, this amateurism seeped down to the players. The rookies, for example, would kid about it. "I only hope I don't score my first goal in Boston Garden," they'd tell me. "If I do, I'll have to put a blank puck on my mantlepiece." Even the fans who normally treasure the pucks that fly into the stands would throw them back at us. Who wants to keep a phantom puck no one knows about?

Everyone made fun of us over the pucks; the opposition, even the refs. I said to Leo Monahan of the *Boston Herald*, "We're being laughed at all around the league. The refs hold these pucks up and look at us and laugh before the games." This was a fatal mistake. Leo put that in the paper the next day, and Harry was really ticked off about it. That was the first straw.

The second straw involved a defenseman named Doug Halward who was the Bruins' first pick in the 1975 amateur draft. When Halward arrived at training camp in September 1975 he was a weak, skinny kid who weighed in at about 175 pounds. Up until then our first round picks had been disasters and this kid, physically at least, didn't look like any bargain to me.

What I wanted from that camp was a big, tough, strong defenseman and I found one—Mike Milbury. Now this kid was a natural. He had been born in Brighton, Massachusetts, and raised in Walpole, just outside of Boston. A graduate of Colgate University, he played football in addition to hockey. Grit could have been his middle name.

Earlier that summer, I had held a hockey school, and John Hoff, who had played with Milbury, mentioned Mike to me and said that he could play my style and that I'd really like him. Weeks later, when we were through in Boston, Harry, the scouts and I were talking about who to invite to camp and I said, "Isn't there a guy named Mulberry or something like that?" And they said, "Oh yeah, Milbury. Okay, we'll invite him too." That's how close Mike came to not being a Bruin.

Mike had spent a year in the minors at Rochester, had picked up 246 minutes in penalties and that, in itself, told me he was a battler. If I had any doubts they were removed in training camp. He wanted desperately to make the Bruins and showed it during the exhibition season. Mike had even worked on his biggest problem, turning into the corners.

I wasn't terribly upset when Mike tailed off in his last exhibition game before the season started. Admittedly, it was a real stinkeroo and he was pretty disturbed by his performance. Mike had got the flu just before the game, but he wanted to make the team so much that he hadn't told me. Consequently, he played a bad game. "Don't worry," I told him, "you've made the team. You've been my best defenseman."

Little did I know that Sinden was eagerly awaiting that bad game. I had no idea how Harry felt about the kid until I began making out my practice roster the next day. As I was pencilling in the names Harry walked over and told me to hold up, there were some names to be scratched because he was sending them down to the minors.

One by one—Doug Gibson, Gordie Clarke—he scratched names. Then, he came to Milbury. "He goes down, too." The words had a distant ring to them. I heard them but I couldn't be sure I heard them right.

When I realized that he did want to chuck Milbury I couldn't believe it. "Hold it," I said, "I don't want him sent down. He's been our best defenseman."

He looked at me, somewhat incredulously. Like, who is this person challenging Harry Sinden? "Milbury goes and Halward stays!"

"Wait a minute," I countered, firing my best shots. "Halward will be good eventually but he's weak now and he can't skate with us. He needs a year in the minors."

This time, Sinden stared at me with a look of finality. "Milbury goes to the minors. Halward stays—AND THAT'S FINAL." He wheeled and walked out of the room.

I was totally bewildered. Obviously, I had been under the mistaken impression that we had been buddies and that we could talk things over in a rational way; that Harry would, at least, hear my arguments and discuss them with reason. Stunned to the core, I sat staring at the dressing room wall when Milbury happened to walk in.

I didn't know what to say to the kid. Everybody on the team from Wayne Cashman to the stickboy, figured that Milbury had made the team. Finally I pulled myself together and took Mike aside. "You're goin' to Rochester, Mike."

He was incredulous. Tears began rolling down his cheeks. "Don," he said, "why?" I didn't have the answer.

Sinden knew deep down that Halward wasn't ready but he was the

With Peter McNab after practice at training camp in Fitchburg.

Tom Johnson, Harry Sinden, and me
—happier times at the Bruins'
training camp in Fitchburg,
Massachusetts, 1976-77.

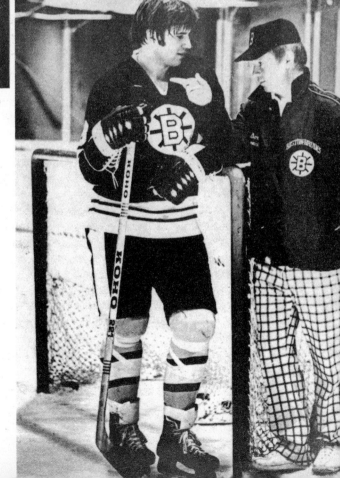

The Boston Globe

"CHEER UP, BLUE, YOUR OLD MAN DID SUPER"

Cartoon drawn by Paul Szep of The Boston Globe, on my leaving the Bruins.
(Paul has won a Pulitzer Prize for political cartooning.)

first draft pick. Well, Halward got his shot and he was on the ice for 13 of the first 15 goals the opposition scored on us.

Meanwhile, Milbury went down to Rochester and had a terrible year because his heart was broken. Harry won the battle of wits but, in the long run, we all lost. It was the first time I ever saw him put a matter of draft choices ahead of winning a hockey game; but it wouldn't be the last. (And, he finally got rid of Halward but kept Milbury.)

The third straw came after we had lost a 2-1 game to the Minnesota North Stars, in Minnesota. We had outshot them by a three-to-one ratio but our shots were ringing off the goal posts and their shots were going in.

Our next game was against the Rockies in Denver. We were late getting out of Minnesota and by the time we got to our hotel I was beat. It was only 9:30 at night but I was so out of it I went straight to bed. All of a sudden the phone rang, It was Harry: "C'mon down, let's have a beer."

Right away I sensed that something was up. The old survival radar machine was working. I didn't want to get up. Harry's voice became more insistent, so I *knew* my radar was right. "No Don," he said emphatically, "c'mon down!"

I got dressed and went downstairs. Harry was at the bar. Just then, a thought came to mind. Something fishy was going on. Suddenly I remembered how, after the Minnesota game, Johnson and I were walking together to the parking lot. I explained one of the problems with the team and he had replied, sarcastically, "Well, that's not the only problem." (His favourite expression.) I blew up. "I know it's not just that," I exploded. "I can list ten problems but I'm starting with one."

Now it dawned on me that Johnson was setting me up for Sinden. In fact Johnson had been talking to him at the bar just before I arrived. When Johnson saw me coming he walked away. I sat down beside Harry at the bar and the next thing I knew he was pounding the bar top. "I WANT TO KNOW WHAT'S GOING ON WITH THIS CLUB."

The tremors must have been recorded on the Richter scale. I answered. "WHADDYA MEAN? WE PLAYED A HECK OF A GAME LAST NIGHT—AND WE SHOULD HAVE WON."

Then he started hassling me about the offense and, right away, I knew Johnson had told him about that. I tried to cool it. I reassured him that the team was coming around and besides, we were in first place. He wouldn't hear me. "I want to know why we have the worst record in the NHL *this* month."

Try as I might, I couldn't get through to him. He kept reiterating that *he* wanted to get to the bottom of the trouble. *He* wanted to call a team meeting and asked me what time would be convenient. I said ten the next morning, but I added that I didn't think we needed a meeting. My hope was that we could handle any of the team's problems quietly but without my knowledge, Harry had gone to Tom Fitzgerald, the veteran hockey writer from *The Boston Globe*, and talked to him before he even talked to me about the team meeting. The story was splashed all over the pages of *The Globe* before we even spoke.

Although the meeting was scheduled for ten, Harry arrived well before I did. He berated the team for 15 minutes. He was so furious that his body was coated with perspiration. After screaming for a few minutes, he would calm down, then he'd start up again. Me, I just sat on the sidelines and took it all in without a word.

Every so often my insides would knot up, especially when he ripped into Peter McNab, our big center. McNab was a good kid we had obtained from Buffalo, and he was turning out to be an asset to the club. Peter was the only player Harry singled out by name; why I don't know. "Your checking, McNab, has not improved by one iota," Harry shouted.

Anyone who knew Peter McNab realized that if you criticized him he would go into an absolute state of shock. So, what happened? Peter turned out to be useless for a month. (He did come out of the incident with a new nickname. For the rest of the season I called him "One Iota.")

After the one-sided discussion at the hotel bar and then the scene at the meeting, I knew things would never be the same between Harry and me. The storm clouds had been threatening for some time but now the lightning and the thunder were pouring down on me.

One day Harry told me I only played—and liked—dumb hockey players like Stan Jonathan and Al Secord, because I was dumb myself. I wasn't so dumb that I couldn't see the kind of image Sinden was trying to create for me. He wanted the hockey world to think that my players were against management; as if it was us against the world. Sure, I did favours for my players. Why wouldn't they be with me? They trusted me. But I didn't turn them against management. Management did that all by itself.

I'll give you an example: We had a right wing named Earl Anderson. He was a nice kid from Roseau, Minnesota, and had gone to the University of North Dakota. He had been suffering from calcium deposits in his left thigh and had to sit out the remainder of the season. He was single and lonely and wanted to be a part of the club even though he was sidelined, so he asked me if he could come along on some of our road trips. The other players also felt he should come, so I asked Harry but he nixed the idea. This bugged me because I knew that the Bruins regularly invited the office help on road trips. "How come office people can make trips and not an injured player?" I asked him.

"You want to know," he replied. "The players want to know, eh! Well I'll tell ya; it's none of your damn business!"

Harry had always said it was a good idea to air our grievances in one-to-one meetings. "You come to me, not the press," he would say. I went to him, we had our one-to-one over Anderson and that was that. So much for one-to-one meetings.

But I'm sure his attitude was a function of a deep-seated resentment.

Every time there was a big story, whether it was in *The Hockey News*, a sports magazine or the local paper, the theme always seemed to be "Don Cherry's Boston Bruins." With every story, Harry would get more steamed. But I loved the members of the media and the feeling, judging by the attention I was getting, was mutual. The more press I got, the angrier Harry got.

One gem from Sinden's Chinese Water Torture manual concerned cars. Every member of Bruins' management was given a Dodge automobile to drive—free. I was told I had to be more and act more like management because I was management, so they said. But when they gave the cars to management, all of a sudden I wasn't management and I didn't get a car. Ricky Middleton and Stan Jonathan quietly went out and did banquets for a car dealer, and one day they presented me with a car. How could you beat these guys?

With each shafting I got from management, I gravitated more to the players, if such a feat were possible under the circumstances. The players wouldn't do anything without me—and for good reason—since I would do *anything* for them. Take performance bonuses as an example.

If Harry had made an arrangement for a player to get a bonus for scoring, say, 20 goals, he wouldn't be disappointed if the guy got 19 and stopped there. Well, one of my all-time favourite players, Don Marcotte, had just such a bonus arrangement for scoring 20 goals. It was late in the season and Donny had 19 goals. Everybody on the club knew about his bonus and the guys were rooting passionately for him to reach the 20-goal plateau.

You see, in hockey, whether anyone admits it or not, as the season draws to a close a team tries to get scoring bonuses for its players. So, we got Marcotte his bonus in our last home game.

But the real example of this concerned Ricky Middleton. Bobby Schmautz, who was always the team spokesman, came to me and said, "Ricky needs three points for a big scoring bonus." I said, "Okay, we'll get his bonus if he has to play all sixty minutes." He was buying a house and needed the money. But then I told Schmautzie, "Don't let on to Harry when he gets his points, don't be jumping around." We were playing in Toronto in the second to last game of the season, and Ricky got his points. When he got the third point, the buggers all jumped off the bench and mobbed Middleton as if he'd just won the Stanley Cup. They were clapping him on the back, ruffling his hair. I thought they were going to carry him off the ice on their shoulders. Harry was sitting up in the stands watching the game, and when he came into the dressing room after the game the guys started chanting, "Ricky, Ricky, Ricky." I swear it was just to piss Harry off. All they were doing was getting me into trouble.

Anyway, in the last home game Marcotte got his twentieth in the first period. Peter McNab turned around on the bench and said to me, "Did you know that Schmautzie has a 20-goal bonus?" When he told me there were only five minutes to go in the game. That's the kind of guy Schmautz is. He hadn't said a word about his own bonus.

With six seconds to go in the game, Schmautzie wanted to come off the ice and I wouldn't let him. Jean Ratelle got the puck back to him and Schmautzie put the puck into the top corner with two seconds to go, making his bonus. Harry was not very happy!

No matter what I did it always seemed that I was deliberately widening the split between myself and management. The truth was, I did anything possible to make my players happier and in a winning frame of mind. This even included finding them better beds in which to sleep.

This actually happened in Montreal. The team had formerly stayed at a hotel called the Chateau Champlain. It was a nice joint except that the beds were so small that a player's feet would dangle over the end. You can't get a good night's sleep that way so I wanted to move the team to a hotel where they had sensible beds, and we moved the team to the Manoir Le Moyne. Harry and Tom remained at Chateau Champlain while we moved to the big bed hotel. Harry did not do cartwheels of joy over that. We found out that they loved the Chateau Champlain because they were provided with two suites that would put the Taj Mahal to shame.

Other incidents that piqued Harry could have been avoided if I had just used my head instead of my mouth.

Once, we had a big game with the Canadiens at Boston Garden on a Sunday night. The game was for first place over-all. Sam Pollock, a hockey genius, was Montreal's g.m. at that time. He changed his schedule so that the Canadiens played on Saturday afternoon before our game, instead of Saturday night. Then they took a charter from Montreal to Boston. They were in bed Saturday night watching the Bruins play Atlanta.

The next morning we had to catch a commercial flight back to Boston at six a.m. There had been a storm warning well in advance and our troubles would have been avoided if Harry had just spent a few bucks and ordered a special charter flight for us.

Harry wouldn't go for the charter so we took the regular flight, ran into a blizzard and had to land in Hartford. From there half the guys rented cars and drove back—all the while saying their prayers—and the others stayed, waiting for airline clearance. We all finally got to Boston Garden an hour-and-a-half before game time, totally exhausted. Still, we were leading 2-1 late in the game when they poured it on and scored the tying goal.

I was really pissed off at Sinden. I didn't mind him stiffing me but when he started to stiff the players, well, that was too much. It so happened that Red Fisher, columnist for *The Montreal Star*, was covering the game. Red was a veteran reporter who didn't miss much that was going on, especially when it was the kind of conflict that existed between Harry and me.

After the game I was boiling mad and who should I run into but Red. "Geez," I said, "we should have chartered home."

Then, I walked into the press area where Harry was talking to some of the other members of the media. After the reporters left it was just Harry and me alone when Red walked in and asked Sinden: "Harry, why didn't you take the charter to Boston the way Cherry wanted?" Red, who I really like as a friend, didn't realize just how much dynamite was in that question. He was just kidding, but Harry didn't take it that way. I almost fell through the floor.

Which brings us to my last season in Boston. My contract was running out and I realized that my $60,000 per year put me in the very lowest echelon among coaches. By this time my colleagues such as Scotty Bowman and Fred Shero were up in the six figure category and they had become the talk of the media. Harry Neale, who had never coached in the NHL, was making $80,000. (Harry kids me all the time now, "Are you finally going to stop talking about my $80,000?" This is the last time, Harry.)

One day I was sitting with some reporters and the subject of coaches' salaries came up. "Y'know," I told them, "I read about guys like Scotty, who has himself a good deal and a farm, to boot. One coach owns a condominium and another coach has a place in Florida." (Mind you, I was kidding with the guys at this point.) I said: "How come I don't have a farm? Or a condo?"

The next day I picked up the paper and there was a headline about me beefing and a quote: "How come I don't have a contract with a lot of money?"

Paul Mooney, president of the Bruins, hit the ceiling when he read that. He figured that I was negotiating my contract in the papers, which was not really the case. But Mooney didn't call me in to find out whether or not the quote was accurate. He didn't ask me anything, just assumed the worst.

By this time Sinden and I weren't even talking. One of the newspapermen mentioned it to Scotty Bowman and he couldn't believe it. "You mean Don's got nobody to discuss strategy, lineup changes, that sort of thing? Amazing. It's hard to believe!"

Not for me it wasn't. At the end of a game Harry would sit in one corner of the dressing room and I would be at the other end and no words would pass between us. The situation became so hairy that Mooney felt obliged to intervene. He flew out to Los Angeles, where we were playing, and said he would come up with a new contract, if . . . .

It was a big "if."

Mooney put it bluntly: "Let's stop all this nonsense. I want you and

Harry to get along." That was fine with me. It was apparent that Paul had also talked to Sinden and Harry had apparently mellowed enough to sit with me on the plane ride back East.

We sat next to each other and it was as if somebody had turned the calendar back to my rookie year. Harry and I were getting along just like in the good old days. After a while I had to get up and go to the can. Meanwhile Fran Rosa of *The Boston Globe* moved in and began talking to Sinden. I had been under the impression, after talking with Mr. Mooney, that any differences we had about the team would be kept between himself, myself, and Harry. Nothing was to go in the papers.

Fine. Except that when we got back to Boston, I picked up *The Globe* and there was a big story by Fran Rosa, based on his conversation with Harry while I was in the can. "SINDEN WANTS TO KNOW 'WHAT'S THE MATTER WITH THE BRUINS'?" It took Harry two minutes to get the feud started again.

We were playing Minnesota, in Boston, coming down to the end of the season. It looked as if we were going to meet Pittsburgh in the first round of the playoffs and I was trying to gear the guys up for them. In the dressing room I had set up the television with a video machine so the players could see replays of a goal or anything else that might be helpful. When we all got together the trainer hit the wrong button and who should come on the screen but Sinden talking about how lousy we were playing and how the Penguins were going to beat us three straight in the playoffs. Now that was great stuff for the players to hear; how their g.m. was "sticking behind" the team. (Later, I discovered we had a squealer in the room and he told Harry that I had purposely turned on the television and purposely picked out the channel he was on. How absurd could Harry get? There was no way for me to know that he was going to be a guest on TV.)

By playoff time, relations between Harry and me had reached the non-existent point again. If I had wanted to bury the Bruins in the media I could have right at that point but I talked to my younger brother, Richard, and he told me to leave with class and not get into a pissing contest with skunks.

Meanwhile, Harry was spreading stories all over town. He wanted to have the press think that the Bruins were paying me $100,000 when it was really $60,000 and that Mooney was ticked off at me, which wasn't the case then. We had beaten Pittsburgh in three straight and had damn near beaten the Canadiens.

When the Montreal series was over I was a wreck. I had had the flu and was thoroughly run-down. Mr. Mooney invited me to meet with him and Harry when I was feeling better. This would be the last attempt at a new peace pact.

Harry, Paul and I met at Paul's private club, one of the oldest in

Boston, called the Indian Club. He had a private room and things went well, but you could feel the tension.

Paul said, "Look Don, you can have your contract, but you have to realize that Harry is the boss. You two just have to get along and stop this constant squabbling." He told me to take a few days to think it over.

I did do a lot of thinking, and I talked it over with Rose. I knew that eventually Harry would get rid of all my buddies. Ricky Smith, the salt of the earth as far as I'm concerned, was going. Schmautzie was going, Secord was going, Wensink, Sims, Miller, a lot more were going. So, it was also time for me to move along. Besides, I knew that Harry was in the wings, and if he didn't get me now he would get me later.

(Incidently, Harry almost got a friend of mine too, but the tables were turned. When I was coaching the Bruins, there was a statistician I would see once in a while, called Richard Chmura. I got to know him and we got close as time went on. Another acquaintance of mine was Joe Skallon, the young man who owns WITS, the radio station that broadcasts the Bruins and Red Sox games.

One night, at a benefit showing of *Rocky II* for the Kidney Foundation, we were all sitting together. Richard and Joe were talking, and Joe offered Richard the job of host in the WITS box at Boston Garden. Richard said he'd take the job, and to make a long story short, Joe and Richard became good friends.

The next year, I went to Colorado, and Sinden started to get rid of anyone who had ever spoken to me. He knew that Richard Chmura was a friend of mine, and he told Nate Greenberg, the P.R. director for the Bruins, not to let Chmura in the building. I heard about it, so I made Richard a scout for the Rockies, just to get him into the Garden.

The president of Joe's radio station resigned, and after one thing and another, Richard got the job. I think Joe forced him into it. He is now president of WITS-Sports. The year before, the two of us couldn't fit into his Pinto, now he has a Cadillac and a Lincoln Continental!

He's making thousands of dollars a year running this station, and not only that, but now Mooney, Johnson and Sinden call *him* up to play golf. The same guys who kicked him out of Boston Garden the year before ask *him* if he'd like to go golfing.)

So, at another meeting at the same club, I told Paul and Harry, "Thanks, but no thanks." I thought I saw Harry give a sigh of relief. This is the first time the real truth, that I quit and wasn't fired, has come out. I left the Bruins at first base, still strong. I left them happy, and I still love the players but I didn't want to be a part of their disintegration.

The day and night of the firing, or resigning, whichever suits you, most of the Bruins, and the press, came to our house. Some brought Chinese food, most brought sad faces. But I knew that I had done the right thing. I told the Bruins, "Don't say anything to the press or you'll get yourselves in trouble. Remember, I'm gone but you're still here." I made this especially clear to Bobby Schmautz. Near the end of the night I heard Schmautzie saying to a television commentator outside my house, "The Bruins have made a big mistake. I've not only lost a great coach, I've lost my best friend."

I told Schmautzie to stop, but he just laughed. Well, the night ended, and everybody went home. I remember I had a splitting headache. As I tried to sleep, a few doubts crept into my mind, but I said to myself, "If he didn't get you now he'd get you later."

So long, Boston. It was great, absolutely the most enjoyable time of my life. But, it was time to move on.

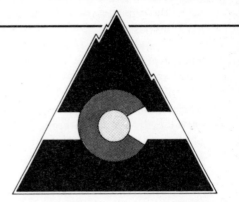

CHAPTER THREE

Sky High In Denver

Once it was official that I had, in fact, decided to cast my lot with a team other than the Bruins, my friends in the media descended on me in droves. They knew that I loved the town and my hockey players, and they couldn't understand my leaving. I had a lot of explaining to do.

So, I explained to them that sometimes my thinking is parallel to Admiral Nelson's. He was his own man, and most important to him were his sailors, who worked and battled for him. He called them his band of brothers and that's what I called my players. But, for me to function as a coach, I also had to feel that I was my own man. So I felt, in fairness to the Bruins, the players, and myself, it would be better for me to move on.

In a sense, I felt the same way about the media and that helps explain the rage they expressed when I took my leave of Boston Garden. Tim Horgan of the *Boston Herald* headlined his column: "IN SIMPLE TERMS IT WAS A MISTAKE." He wondered how Mooney and Sinden could let me go. Horgan expressed the feelings of his colleagues when he wrote: "The basic idea is that a coach who does his job and then some, who produces a winner, controls his players, fills the seats and captivates the media, is doomed to go because he's become more important than upper management, which hired him to do just that in the first place."

Horgan's colleague Joe Fitzgerald was even more cynical. He figured that Sinden had had it in for me as long ago as before the last season. "I've got a hunch," wrote Fitzgerald, "that Harry's mind was made up the first time Cherry told a joke that got a laugh. From the moment Cherry walked on to the center stage at the Garden, Sinden became a forgotten man, and his resentment has been festering for a long, long time."

It was nice stuff, but it didn't take me long to figure out that my two tons of press clippings still wouldn't get me a cup of coffee if I didn't have the four bits to go with them. The time had come to get a job.

I wasn't worried. Throughout the Montreal series there had been stories that at least two teams—the Colorado Rockies and Toronto Maple Leafs— were interested in hiring me. You have to realize that a lot of the stuff you read in the papers is pure bibble-babble. On the other hand, there was some substance to each of the rumours.

I was represented by Alan Eagleson, the Toronto attorney who also heads the NHL Player's Association. The Eagle had an assistant named Bill Watters and it was Bill who phoned me the very day I was fired by the Bruins. He wanted to know how I felt about coaching the Rockies.

At first the idea didn't particularly thrill me. The Rockies had been a bottom rung team almost from day one of their existence. Now they had new owners; a New Jersey trucking magnate, Arthur Imperatore, and his stepson, Armand Pohan, would finance the team. Bill said they would be willing to pay me between $135,000 and $145,000 a season. When I heard those figures my heart started beating out "Rock Around the Clock." Here I was making 60 grand with the Bruins and these guys were willing to more than double it.

That was a good feeling and even better still, other offers began pouring in. Scotty Bowman, who was coaching and managing the Buffalo Sabres asked me to come to Buffalo as his assistant with the understanding that I'd take over behind the bench in a year. "No way, Scotty," I said. "Those owners want you as manager *and* coach."

I got a feeler from Cliff Fletcher, who was general manager of the then Atlanta Flames, and there would be others to come. But the Rockies proved to be the most persistent and, at the same time, the most perplexing. The Rockies' manager was a front office veteran named Ray Miron. He had run farm teams in the Central League and held a number of jobs on lower level clubs until he got the Rockies position. What surprised— and disturbed—me was that once word got around that the Rockies were after me I began getting phone calls from dozens of friends in the business. Instead of congratulating me on my good fortune they began warning me about Ray Miron. The message I got was that it would be a mistake to take the Denver job.

Two of the people closest to me—my mother and my brother, Richard—cautioned me about signing with the Rockies. Maternally-speaking, my Mom wanted me to take a job in the East, closer to home. Richard was more worried about Miron and the effect he would have on me. Even my agent, Bill Watters, was worried. "Do you think you can live with Miron?" he asked me.

Bill must have been figuring that eventually I would want to become general manager of the Rockies and that would mean bumping Miron. There was no way I wanted to be g.m. of the Rockies. I told Bill that I could get along with him because I really thought I could.

I began having delusions of grandeur about the Rockies. They were easily the worst team in the NHL but I figured I could turn them around. This would be the great Cherry crusade, transforming them into a contender.

Rose was ready to go. She had bounced around with me from Hershey to Springfield to Trois-Rivières. Denver wouldn't bother her a bit.

Once I told Bill that I could coexist with Miron, he got the machinery moving on the contract. I had pretty much made up my mind that Denver would be the next stop until Richard began bugging me about what a blunder it would be. He pointed out how tough the contrast would be going from a first-place club to a last-place club. He explained how my reputation as a trouble-maker could be worsened if Miron turned on me. "Miron will have the ear of the owners," said Richard, "you won't. He'll be talking to them after every game. You'll be talking to them once a month."

Normally I listened to Richard and heeded his advice. I figured that, with a three year contract, I could build a winner in Denver by the third year. "We'll develop like the Islanders," I insisted, thanking Richard for his interest; he just shook his head.

Disregarding Richard's advice was the biggest mistake of my life. Bill had completed all the preliminary negotiations and now it was time for me to meet Miron. It so happened that his daughter was getting married in Dallas, Texas, so it was arranged that I would fly there and iron out any details of the contract.

When we got down to the nitty-gritty I stunned Miron. "Before I sign anything," I told him, "you've gotta know in advance that I plan to bring Nate Angello with me."

"Who in hell is Nate Angello?" he wondered.

"He's a skate sharpening genius and I have to have him with me on the team. If he doesn't come, I don't come."

"Are you kidding?"

"Nope."

Miron said he would come up with a two-year deal at $135,000 per year with an additional $35,000 if they decided not to pick up my option. As lovely as it sounded I kept experiencing a gnawing feeling in my stomach and, if I had any brains, I should have realized that I was getting gut messages from my brother about Miron. A feeling that I couldn't ignore was that he was a guy offering me big bucks but his heart wasn't in it. All he was doing was conveying a message from above. My radar indicated that Miron, himself, really didn't want me.

I agreed on the terms in Dallas and then flew to Denver under an assumed name because the Rockies wanted to spring the news as an exclusive story. But they must have leaked stories in advance because the minute I got to town every radio station, television station and newspaper was running stories about how great it would be if I ran the Rockies.

That night I received an upsetting call in my hotel room from Alan Eagleson. "The Maple Leafs want you as coach," he said. "Harold Ballard will give you a three-year deal at $150,000."

It was a hell of a time to find out. At that moment I could have cried. The Toronto Maple Leafs. Ever since I was a kid growing up in Kingston I had been a Maple Leaf fan. I would listen to Foster Hewitt doing the games on radio, and dream of wearing the royal blue and white of the Maple Leafs. Coaching in Toronto would have meant that I'd be only a few hundred miles from my mother's place and close to all my friends. Coaching the Maple Leafs; it was everything I always wanted.

"No," I told Eagleson, "I can't do it."

"Why not?"

"Because," I said, "I gave them my word."

"The hell you did," he snapped, "You haven't signed anything."

"That's true but I gave my word and I can't go back on it."

I wouldn't let the Eagle talk me out of it. My mother had always taught us that if you give someone your word, you keep it. (Looking back at what's happened to me, I have to wonder sometimes if she was right!) From that moment on I was coach of the Colorado Rockies.

The next day they held a formal press conference. I was flanked by Miron on the left and Armand Pohan on the right. Pohan, the boss's stepson, had the title of club president. He was a smooth, good-looking guy who had been a lawyer. He gave me a build-up like you wouldn't believe. When he finished introducing me I figured I would have been underpaid at $600,000 a year.

"We keep saying we're for real," said Pohan. "But people have to see something like this to believe it. This franchise is for real."

When they were through making me sound like Moses, I got up and let them know I wasn't about to part the Red Sea. I said, "I'm not going to fool you and say we are going to win the Stanley Cup in a year. But I can promise a team that will try its best and give an honest effort. If a player doesn't, he will be gone. It's going to take a while, but in the future, we'll be there."

At the June meetings, where we make our draft choices and plan the team for the upcoming season, I began to realize why the Rockies were such persistent losers. The Bruins—give Sinden credit—had always been perfectly organized going into the draft; the Rockies didn't know what they wanted to do. They didn't even have their first draft pick. They had traded it to Montreal for Sean Shanahan and Ron Andruff, guys who never stuck in the NHL.

The draft meeting was the first time I had seen Harry Sinden since our separation. He was with Gary Darling, the Bruins chief scout. I happened to have my old Bruins bag with me and the first thing Darling said was, "Don, you'd better get rid of that bag."

Seeing Harry didn't bother me half as much as the messages I kept getting at the meetings. One hockey friend put it this way: "Watch out for Miron. He's after you already." I hadn't even coached my first game for the Rockies and I was being warned that my g.m. was undercutting me.

Rose and Timothy had flown out to Denver before me, along with our canary named John (after John Wensink), who had caused a mild sensation by singing all the way to Denver on Rose's lap. My friend from Boston, Richard Chmura, drove me out to Denver in two days, with Blue sitting proudly in the back seat. I had taken some Rockies material with me just to get a line on the way things were done and to review some of the players I would be coaching. The first thing that bothered me was the endless number of rules that Miron had imposed on the players—no smoking, no drinking, no skiing; it seemed as if he was dealing with a high school football team.

Then, there was the Rockies' team picture. I kept looking at the picture and thinking to myself that there was something wrong about it but I couldn't quite dope out what. When I got to Denver, Rose picked up the picture and said, "My, what a nice-looking bunch of boys."

Egad. It suddenly came to me; they were a *nice-looking bunch of boys* and not at all the giants I had had in Boston. I needed a team of Lord Fauntleroys like a moose needs a hat rack.

Soon after we arrived in Denver, Ray Miron invited us over for dinner. It was a very enlightening experience. We had a pleasant enough time at the table and then Ray showed me around the house. When we got to his study he pulled out a book. The title read: *All I Know About Hockey* by Ray Miron. He handed it to me, and naturally, I opened it to see what was written. The pages were all blank. There was something very prophetic about that episode which, unfortunately, eluded me at the time.

Superficially, at least, my relationship with Ray was tolerable in my first weeks with the team. But the underlying feeling was different. I sensed that Miron wished I wasn't there, that I was out for his job (which was the last thing I wanted), and that he would rather have hired some unknown from the minors to coach the team.

At last, training camp arrived and my juices were flowing. The guys could skate pretty well. After a week I had them scrimmaging and shooting at the goalies. We had Hardy Astrom, a Swede, Bill McKenzie and Bill Oleschuck. I never thought of myself as the ultimate connoisseur of goaltenders but one look at the guys we had between the pipes convinced me that our goalie problems weren't big, they were colossal. Astrom, if he was at his best, would be lucky to make it in the American League, and he was our number one goalie. When I came home from the first day of training camp I said to Rose, "Either we have the best shooters in the National Hockey League, or the worst goaltenders." Unfortunately for me it was the latter.

One day Miron approached me during a practice. "Don," he said, "would you like us to get you a goalie coach?" I digested that ·for a moment and replied: "No. Get me a goalie."

I was rapidly losing points with Miron and I would lose still more after watching a center named Doug Berry take a few turns for us. He had played for Denver University and was the Rockies' second choice (38th over-all) in the 1977 amateur draft. After the workout I walked into Miron's office. "This guy Berry," I said, "what's he doing here? He can't skate, he can't shoot, and he can't hit."

"Well," Miron answered, "if we send him down, Glen Sather'll pick him up for Edmonton."

I said: "Glen Sather wouldn't pick him up for a million dollars. Why this guy won't score ten goals for us."

Miron had a personal interest in keeping Berry so I had to play him all year and die with him. He scored a big eight goals for me (naturally, he's not in hockey now). Berry wasn't the only lemon they pushed. The Rockies scouts—I could tell they didn't like me either—wanted me to use a kid named Merlin Malinowski, a center and their second choice in 1978.

Somebody once asked me why they called him "Merlin the Magician." I said that was simple: anyone who could stay in the NHL with his talents *had* to be a magician. Miron forced him on me but I didn't want any part of Malinowski. He backed down every time somebody pushed him.

I began to filter through the problems. The Rockies had signed top draft choices, who turned out to be malingerers, and they had lower echelon kids who tried like the dickens and who would be assets to the club in spirit if not in body. When I'd tell Miron that these lazy first-rounders had to go he would say, "Now, Don, wait a minute. This kid (the one I wanted to drop) is on a one-way contract. It wouldn't be a good idea to drop him. This other guy (the one I wanted to keep) is on a two-way contract."

It didn't matter to Miron that the first-round choice was floating, nor did it matter to him that the lower choice was working his ass off. I saw no reason to keep a player on the team who thought he had it made.

That, however, was only one of my problems. A bigger one was Barry Beck. Very big. Like 6-3, 216 pounds worth. Now this was one first-round draft choice who lived up to his notices. He was a rugged defenseman who could have been the most powerful player in the league. He had an excellent shot and could make passes with the best of them. The guys called him Bubba and the word around the NHL was that it was wise—if you valued your health—to leave Bubba alone.

I liked Bubba. He reminded me some of my tough Bruins and I

had big plans for him except that, almost from the start, he was very unhappy. When he had come to the Rockies in 1977, he had signed a five-year contract at $80,000 per year. That was ridiculously low when you take into account the fact that Beck was the most carefully scouted top draft choice in the history of the game.

Bubba knew that there were Rockies-owned players down on the farm in Fort Worth making over a hundred grand. I knew that if Beck was going to be unhappy—and he was easily our best player—then we might as well mail in our resignations for the rest of the season. I went to Miron. "Ray," I insisted, "you gotta give this guy more dough; you gotta negotiate with him. He won't play and I can't blame him."

Miron was adamant. "He signed a contract and that's that. I'm not renegotiating."

I didn't drop the subject. Whenever I got the chance I kept bringing up Bubba. "I know he's going to try," I told Miron, "but he knows that guys are getting double what he's getting. No wonder he's unhappy. But if you're not going to renegotiate, you're gonna have to trade him. You tell him 'He's the franchise,' well, if he is, pay him like he's the franchise."

While I was talking with Miron I kept thinking of my brother, Richard, and his warning—*Don't get into a fight with another general manager.* Here I was fighting another g.m. on behalf of a player who deserved a raise. Pretty soon the Rockies' owner, Arthur Imperatore, got into the act. He was a very impressive hard-nosed Italian gentleman who, for some reason, disliked Beck. I laid it all out for Arthur; Bubba had to get a raise.

"I offered him $100,000 for five years," he said.

"That's not enough," I told him. "The kid will stay unhappy until he gets 180 to 200 grand, so you'd better get rid of him while you can because he's just hurting us going through the motions."

Personally, I hoped that Arthur would come up with the money and that we'd keep Bubba. I liked the kid and figured him for a superstar but Arthur was not impressed with Beck so he phoned his friend, Sonny Werblin, who ran the Rangers, and they put together a deal.

The Rangers got Beck and, in return, we got two forwards—Pat Hickey and Lucien DeBlois—two defensemen—Mike McEwen and Dean Turner—and future considerations. All things considered, I wasn't unhappy over the deal. Hickey could score goals, DeBlois was a kid with promise, McEwen was a good man at the point and Turner was another one with some potential.

Still, when I went over to our practice rink in South Surhuron to give Bubba the news, I felt a twinge of regret. The big guy was in the dressing room when I got there. "Bubba," I said, "I'd like to see you."

I took him into an empty room and said, "I'd like to shake hands with a millionaire."

"What are you talking about?" he said.

"You've been traded to the New York Rangers." (I knew the Rangers would give him at least 200 to 250 grand a year.)

When I told Bubba he was going, his eyes almost popped with glee. He caught himself in time though, and quite properly played the role that he was sorry to leave Denver. But I knew that he could hardly wait to get his Ferrari to the Big Apple. Studio 54, here comes Bubba.

The deal gave us the nucleus for a fair hockey club, but goaltending was still a major problem. Hardy was our main man, as nice a guy as you would ever hope to meet. But we are talking about goaltending here, not personalities. Hardy was making more than $100,000 a year. The team had paid for his family to come to Denver, including his mother and father and a young nanny for his kids. I'm surprised they didn't include the Swedish delegation to the United Nations! Astrom was killing us. For us to get a goal was as hard as climbing Mount Everest, then Astrom would let in a shot that could have been stopped by his kids' nanny.

Astrom was driving the guys nuts. Players would come up to me, almost in tears, saying that in all the years they played hockey, they had never played on a team with a goalie like him.

One of the players who took it especially hard was Mike Christie, a good friend of mine and a veteran defenseman. Unfortunately for Mike, the fates decreed that Mike had to be on the ice every time Hardy let in a soft goal. Finally one night, Mike could take it no longer, like a person who has finally come to the brink of a nervous breakdown. I went into the dressing room, and there was Mike, with his hands over his face, moaning loudly. "Why me, Lord? Why me?" over and over. I couldn't keep myself from laughing, but Mike really expressed the feelings of the team.

It didn't surprise me that we got off to a terrible start. Everything we did was wrong and that just made meat for Miron's insatiable appetite. This was a typical conversation:

Miron: "Don, we're not doing so good."

Cherry: (To myself) "No kidding. No kidding."

Miron: "Do you know we only have five points in 11 games?"

Cherry: (To myself) "The guy is good at arithmetic. He figured out that you get two points for a win and one for a tie. We have one win and three ties. By golly, Ray, you're right. You may not be much of a general manager, but you're a helluvan adder."

Through the years Ray had picked up the nickname Carp. The nickname caused a lot of trouble for a young rookie. One night, Ray went down to Fort Worth to act as g.m. and after the game he went into the Fort Worth dressing room. When the rookie saw him he nudged an old veteran next to him and said, "Who's that?" The veteran, never one to let a practical joke go by, said "Why, that's the Carp." A few minutes later, Ray came over and greeted the young rookie, "Hello son, how are you?" "Fine Mr. Carp. How are you?" said the rookie. The rookie was gone the next day.

Miron was much kinder to Doug Berry, much to my chagrin. Apart from being a useless hockey player, the kid had a distorted idea about the work ethic; he didn't think it existed. I remember distinctly a game against Washington. We had all gone down to the rink for our morning skate. A storm came up as they often do in Denver and we had to stay at the rink for fear that if we went home, we would never get back for the seven-thirty game. Everyone agreed to stay and after the announcement I was in my office with Ray when in came Dougie. He very politely said, "I must go home." Ray said "Why Dougie?" He answered, "Because my girlfriend is at school and needs a ride home." Rockets went off in my mind. I had visions of Orr down at the rink at the Garden at one-thirty in the afternoon for a seven-thirty game, mentally preparing himself. And here was this wimp wanting to drive his girlfriend home. Can you believe it? Naturally I expected Miron to tell him off. I wanted him to say, "Listen you little sonofabitch, you should be getting ready for the game. Never mind driving your girlfriend home."

Instead, Ray, in tones sweeter than honey, said; "Dougie, I wish you could find some other way for her to get home." The kid got away with it.

By contrast, we managed to get a solid, hard-nosed veteran, Rene Robert, in a deal for our defenseman John van Boxmeer. After I got Robert, and looked at some of the guys he had to work with, I'd feel sorry for the guy. He blocked shots, threw his weight around and fought. He played even though he had a broken thumb, a separated shoulder, and a pulled groin. Considering our collection of players, I wouldn't have blamed Robert if he had just thrown in the towel, but he wouldn't quit. Every so often he'd look at me as if to say, "Grapes, how did you ever get me into this?" We gave up a good one to get Robert. Van Boxmeer was a fellow who could double as a forward and a defenseman.

We didn't win a hell of a lot of games with or without Beck or Van Boxmeer but my act was going over big and the gates kept getting bigger and bigger.

The one thing I didn't want to do was deceive the Denver fans into thinking we had a winner. Even a poultry expert wouldn't buy some of the turkeys we had on our roster. "If the people think that all at once we're going to start burning up the league," I warned, "they're mistaken. It's going to be a long, tough grind."

Miron's policies didn't make it any easier. He would pay some flubs 100 to 200 grand a year but then he would chintz on little things like bus rides that would drive the players—and me—up the wall. Once, we were out practising in Nassau County, Long Island, the morning of a game with the New York Islanders. The morning skate was over and it was time to go back to the motel. Any respectable club would have had a bus to whisk the players to their quarters, but Ray wouldn't hire a bus because it would have cost a 100 bucks. We had to go out onto the highway and flag cabs down in the cold; a perfect way to catch pneumonia. Great! After that I began ordering buses on my own because I didn't want my players running out on highways, freezing to death.

Damn it, I still knew that I had to get along with Ray no matter how hard it was, and it was killing me. But there are just so many one-liners a guy can pull with a Hardy Astrom in the net. Instead of improving, he was getting worse. By now the opposition was scoring on shots from center ice. I couldn't take it anymore. One night, between periods of another Hardy horror show, I walked into Miron's office and got down on my knees begging him to make a trade for a goalie. I felt sorry for the players because they were working their asses off. They'd come up with a goal and then, bing, bing, Hardy would let two easy ones go by and we would be finished.

It was truly bizarre. We would lose a game 3-2, and the people in McNichols Arena would give us a standing ovation when we went off the ice. It was really embarrassing, believe me. I'd walk across the ice and people would be hollering, "That's okay, Don, it'll get better" and things like that. Our crowds were climbing to 12,000 then 13,000 (up to 16,000 when the Philadelphia Flyers came to town) and I was convinced that this could be a good franchise if we had a half-decent team.

Needless to say, I didn't harbour any hopes of winning The Stanley Cup, but what I was hoping for was a win when I took the Rockies into Boston Garden. I couldn't wait for December to come when we were to play the Bruins. I got myself a beautiful velvet suit with a waistcoat picked out for the occasion. "We will beat the Bruins," I swore.

When the night finally came I did it up brown; no holds barred. I brought along a bunch of "Cherry Mash" stickers and buttons. The Boston Garden ushers put them on and the stickers were plastered all over the Garden. (I had sneaked out and pasted one on Harry Sinden's bumper.)

I didn't walk across the ice as most visiting coaches do. I walked around the corridor for my grand entrance. (I told you I was a ham.) I really didn't know how the fans would react upon my return. So I peeked out between the doors, and there were what looked like a million TV cameras waiting for me and my grand entrance. And the announcer said, "And here is the coach of the Colorado Rockies, Don Cherry."

I got a standing ovation, but as I was walking around in my ultra-violet suit, some Boston guy said: "Look at that suit he's wearing. He looks like a fag." With that, I looked down and, dammit, I *did* look like a fag.

Anyway, when I got back to the bench I knew they still loved me. They tossed down plastic grapes and chanted "CHER-RY, CHER-RY." The game was beautiful. We fell behind 2-0 but I could hear my guys talking. They didn't quit. (That's the stuff money can't buy.) They began counterattacking, taking the play away from the Bruins, and went on to win 5-3. It was the finest moment of my life. I'll never forget it and nothing in my life can ever equal it. (I understand Harry left the building when we went up two goals.)

For sheer drama the best part was the time-out. My top two defensemen, Mike Christie and Nick Beverly, had played most of the game and they were dead tired. With about a minute to go they came over to the bench and asked me to stall for time. So, I called a time-out.

I gave my guys their assignments and, all of a sudden, a kid reached over and handed me a piece of paper, asking for my autograph. By this time I was just resting, so I signed it. With that, twenty other kids came running down and tried to get autographs. The word went around that I had deliberately called time so that I could sign autographs. That wasn't my idea, but I'll admit it was a good one, so I went along with it.

Arthur Imperatore was there and he just soaked up the whole scene, loving every minute of it. Our room was jammed for more than an hour after the game with the media. When they finally emptied out I yelled to my players: "Everybody get a cab and just tell the driver you're goin' to Kowloon's." That was my favourite Chinese restaurant on Route I outside Boston. Long before I had eaten my specialty, the Moo Goo Gai Pan chicken dish with vegetables, I was saying, "How sweet it is."

And it was. The meal at Kowloon's that night was like The Last Supper.

The next night, we beat the Canadiens in Montreal. Then we flew to Quebec and beat the Nordiques. Life was beautiful. Arthur Imperatore was phoning me three times a day and, at that time, he figured me for a gem of a coach.

But the more we won, the more I got a weird feeling of déjà vu. I kept seeing a funny little look on Miron's face that was strangely similar to the one I had seen on Sinden's. The more I got my name in the paper the more I realized I was digging my own grave. I knew that it was just a matter of time before Miron hanged me.

What I didn't figure on was that I'd be hanged because of a defenseman named Mike McEwen.

CHAPTER FOUR

The Chocolate Cake And McEwen Incidents

If I ever wondered how Rip Van Winkle looked when he awoke from his long nap, I saw him in Mike McEwen. Mike was the most dishevelled person I have ever seen. Unfortunately for me, or for him, this is how I first formed my opinion of him.

He broke in with the Rangers in 1976 after a promising junior career with the Toronto Marlboros. In fact, he made the often difficult jump from the Ontario Hockey Association to the NHL without having played a single game in the minors. He may have been spoiled by what happened in the spring of 1979, when the Rangers rolled over the Los Angeles Kings in the opening round of the Stanley Cup playoffs and then pulled off that colossal upset over the Islanders before blowing the finals to the Montreal Canadiens. McEwen had a hell of a series. His 13 points—two goals and 11 assists—were an all-time playoff record for Ranger defensemen and he was only the third Ranger defenseman to score 20 goals in a season.

There was a lot to like about Mike McEwen. I was hoping that I *would* like him. He had come to me in the blockbuster deal for Barry Beck and, of all the guys we obtained in that package McEwen *looked* like the one who could best flower for us.

His teammates called him "Space Cadet" because he often behaved as if he had a condominium somewhere between Venus and Mars. There was something about him both physically and spiritually that made

46

you think he was residing comfortably on a tract somewhere off our planet.

That the players felt this way was evident from an episode during a game against the Islanders. One of our forwards, Mike Gillis, had his clock rung in a collision with Garry Howatt, a tough little character who loved to run people. Gillis was knocked unconscious and then carried into the dressing room where he was placed on a training table. By the end of the period Gillis had regained his senses and Rene Robert went over to him. "Mike," he inquired, "how are you feeling?"

"Gee, Rene," Gillis replied, "I feel like I'm floating on a cloud."

To which Robert snapped: "You didn't happen to see McEwen up there, did you?"

Once, unknown to me, our trainer, Toby Wilson, had arranged for one of the other defensemen, Trevor Johansen, to room with McEwen on one of our road trips. I didn't know a thing about it for days until, finally, Johansen came over to me one day, very serious, and said: "Grapes, are you mad at me?"

I looked at him and, I have to admit, *I* was puzzled. "No, Trevor," I answered, "you're playing well."

Now, he was concerned. "You mean I haven't done anything wrong?"

After I reiterated that he was in my good graces, Trevor demanded: "Then, why in hell do you have me rooming with McEwen?"

When I think about it, I kind of liked Mike as a person, and I'm sure that he didn't mean any harm; it was just that he caused it; and probably inadvertently at that.

An example of this occurred between McEwen and one of my favourite people, Rene Robert. I had teamed Rene up with my good friend from Boston, Bobby Schmautz, who is sometimes a lot like me, he is his own worst enemy. (For instance, after Colorado had beaten Boston in Boston, Bobby said the reason the Bruins had lost was because I had outcoached the Boston coach. Exit Bobby to Edmonton where we picked him up for Don Ashby.) I was excited as a kid with a new toy at Christmas at the prospect of these two class guys playing together. With these two guys we were coming, or so I thought.

One morning I had the guys out for one of those stupid morning skates and we were doing two-on-ones to help our goalies. This time it was Schmautz and Robert against McEwen. Nobody had his full equipment on and you didn't have to be Einstein to figure out that the idea was not to hit hard or needlessly bring about an injury.

So, there were Schmautz and Robert gliding in on McEwen when, all of a sudden, Mike stuck out his leg—*for no reason at all*—and whipped Rene in the air; when he landed he had ripped his groin. I tell you I just wanted to die on the spot. I had to leave the ice because I had tears in my eyes and I really don't know to this day whether they were for Rene or anger at McEwen.

Whatever McEwen's shortcomings, he had one thing going for him; the boss loved him. Arthur Imperatore had this notion that Mike was the greatest thing that ever happened to hockey since artificial ice. Ray Miron loved him too. Worse, yet, McEwen knew it.

After a game, Arthur would come into the locker room and the first hand he would shake was McEwen's. Mike had a favourite ploy when he knew Arthur and Armand were at a game we had lost. He would sit in the dressing room with his full equipment on after the game, long after the other guys had showered, as if he were heartbroken over the loss. Naturally, when Armand and Arthur came in the dressing room they would see their favourite player seemingly crestfallen and they would go over to him and say, "Come on Mike, you did your best, don't feel so bad, cheer up." They swallowed the act, hook, line, and sinker. Now remember this act was only staged after a loss when Arthur and Armand were at the game. It was beyond the players' belief that two intelligent men like Arthur and Armand could be sucked in time after time.

Arthur had watched Mike in New York and he had the impression that he was the second coming of Bobby Orr. The kid had some good moves; he could handle the puck well and owned a good shot, but he had a number of debits that balanced his assets. For one thing, he had a tendency to stickhandle a bit too much, and, of course, he had this thing about doing as he damned well pleased, no matter what the instructions. That, I figured, came from all the fawning he received. If *you* always had your hand shaken by the boss and the manager, no matter how badly you played, you would figure you had something going.

I knew he wasn't strong, physically, and because of the difficulty breathing the air in Colorado, I wanted him—like the others—to take short shifts. It wasn't right for a player to stay on the ice for two minutes at a time because the thin air conditions would just about kill him.

Short shifts, short shifts; that's what I kept telling my guys and they would all listen—except for Mike. When the others would come off the ice, Mike would stay on. I kept warning him and when Mike did get to the bench, I could tell he was suffering because he was gulping air. I still had the notion that I could make my point with Mike, so I tried before a game we had with the Chicago Black Hawks.

I sat down with him before the game. "Look, Mike," I said, "you're hurting yourself and you're hurting the team by staying out on the ice so long. *I want you to take short shifts like everyone else.* When your partner comes off the ice *you* come off too."

For a moment, I thought the message had seeped through. "Oh yeah," he said, nodding his head. "I'll do it, no problem."

That night, we were winning by a goal when I put Mike on the ice. I remembered how he had assured me about the short shifts. It got past his minute on the ice and I was urging him to get back to the bench. No, Mike had to do it his own way. The minute became a minute-and-a-half and he still wouldn't come off. It got to two minutes and he was so tired he coughed up the puck, the Black Hawks scored and we blew the lead. No matter. We were tied and I would have been quite happy to escape with a point.

The players, meanwhile, were just furious with McEwen. I was fuming and warned him once more. A little while later he went back out for another shift. In my folly, I expected that he'd make an effort to get back to the bench after a minute.

No way. He stayed out for *two minutes and 20 seconds*. Can you believe it? It was as if he were deliberately defying me. He was so tired, he collapsed and gave the puck away for the winning goal. Now was the moment of truth for Don Cherry. I had not taken this kind of defiance from Bobby Orr, Brad Park, or Rick Middleton. A thought flashed through my mind. Do I turn a blind eye to his actions and soberly collect my enormous salary for the next two years? Or do I do what I think is right even though I know he is Arthur and Armand's favourite?

As he returned to the bench, I could see the sweat dripping off his brow. He had now given away the tying and winning goals and he sat down as if it was business as usual. I grabbed him by the front of his jersey and got a hunk of the "C" (as in Colorado) in my hand. "Listen, you little sonofabitch," I shouted, "next time you stay on the ice that long you're gonna have to answer to me. And another thing; you're a selfish little bugger and you're costing this club points in the standings." Then, I pushed him down on the bench. The whole thing took about ten seconds to complete.

Personally, I didn't think much of the incident. As far as I was concerned, McEwen was not physically *harmed* by what I did. Mike wasn't the first player I had grabbed and shaken. I had done it to several of my favourite Bruins—Brad Park, Mike Milbury, you name them. Rick Middleton had once disobeyed me and I shook him for a good ten seconds, yelling my head off. I had done it to Peter McNab, who was a 40-goal-scorer. What I had done to them, I did to McEwen. Just grabbed him, spun him around, and shook him.

McEwen walked out on the team right after the confrontation.

It was one thing to have a beef with me, but to walk out on your teammates is unforgivable. The players were ecstatic, but I knew it was the beginning of the end for me. The next day, the papers jumped on the incident. We left for New York and when we arrived somebody handed me the New York papers—two inch headlines—*Cherry Assaults McEwen*. The players were fit to be tied with laughter. Even *The Hockey News* got into the act, phoning coaches and asking whether I had done the proper thing by shaking McEwen. Everyone had their fun and their pound of flesh, but I knew I had done the right thing. My only regret as it turns out, is that I didn't shake him harder.

It was a tough situation to resolve. I was convinced that I had done the right thing and I had no intention of backing off. A lot of the stories made me look bad and, of course, everybody and his brother were getting into the act—including McEwen's brother, who announced that I had handled Mike all wrong, that the kid had always resented authority, and that there was a special way of treating Mike, which I hadn't known.

What I did know was that the McEwen confrontation was the beginning of the end for me in Denver. Pohan and Imperatore were angry and became even angrier when I brought the team to New York. Arthur had invited several of his friends to see his team play in the Garden and we were beaten, 6-0. The funny thing was that we didn't play too badly, but, as usual, our goaltending was for the birds and, even though we outshot the Rangers, we weren't even close.

Hardy Astrom was in goal for us. After he had given up the fourth score, Kevin Morrison skated over to the bench and said that Hardy "wants to bail out again." I wasn't surprised. Whenever things looked bad Hardy would wave his stick for me to pull him out. I told him to stay in although I knew that all the players realized their goalie wanted out. That's a great feeling for a team!

I had a meeting with the players a few days before Mike decided to return. I warned them to keep their mouths shut and not to give him a hard time if he decided to come back. "This is between McEwen and me," I said, "and there's no sense in you guys putting yourselves in jeopardy." Interestingly, McEwen came back and played the best hockey of his life.

Our initial meeting, when he did come back, was in a hotel coffee shop in New York and I said "Well Mike, you decided to return. What did they say to get you to come back?" I had posed the same question to Miron and they both had the same answer: that he had just decided to come back. I laughed because I knew what they had promised him (my head). As I walked away from Mike and Miron in the coffee shop I said, "Remember Mike ole boy, short shifts."

By the way, later in the year, Mike and I had a joke about the whole situation. We were filming a commercial for a Denver radio station. I was on the ice and I said, "Hi, I'm Don Cherry of the Colorado Rockies, and I listen to Mike Haffner and Woody Paige every afternoon from 4-7. Don't you guys?" The players behind me all said, "No," in unison.

Then I said, "Well, I know one guy who does," and I turned to McEwen. "I know you listen to it." and he said, "No way." So I grabbed him and started shaking him and said, "You will!" and he said, "No," and it went on that way.

I suspect that I was a goner because of what happened between Mike and me and because of the dismal loss to the Rangers in front of Imperatore's friends. But there was one more incident that sealed my fate. It took place in Philadelphia after we had come from behind a 4-0 deficit to pull out a 4-4 tie.

We stayed over in Philadelphia and it so happened that Arthur and Armand did, too. That was okay except that two of my defensemen,

Trevor Johansen and Kevin Morrison arrived back at the hotel at one in the morning, carrying hamburgers and chocolate cake. They had had a few beers and apparently were feeling no pain when they arrived in the hall outside their room.

Morrison wanted a bite of Johansen's chocolate cake and Johansen didn't want him to have it. One thing led to another until chocolate cake began flying around the hall and falling on the carpet.

After the crumbs had settled, the boys realized what they had done—all wrong—got scared and decided they had better clean up before they really got into trouble. They wet some towels and tried to clean up the mess, but all they did was make it worse. By the time they had "cleaned up" the place there were marks on the carpet.

Word got back to Arthur that we had wrecked all the rooms, ruined the carpets, and caused thousands upon thousands of dollars damage. I inspected the damage and it was clear that the only real problem was chocolate cake on the carpet and, if the truth be known, it would cost $150 to clean it all up. That, unfortunately, would have been too easy.

The next day, back in Denver, I got a call from Armand that Arthur was extremely embarrassed about the wrecking of the hotel rooms and the thousands of dollars worth of damage. I said, "Look Armand, I feel bad that Arthur is embarrassed, but sometimes when you get nineteen guys together, things like this happen. Besides, it was only one piece of choco- late cake and the damage was only $150. And Armand, it was the only trouble all year. We have good guys on this team."

I can almost hear the chuckling of other professional coaches. Imagine the uproar caused by one piece of cake! But wait, it gets more unbelievable.

The NHL has a Director of League Security, whose job it is to investigate the possibility of gambling or drugs or some other big threat that might ruin the league. The man's name is Frank Torpey and he was sent to investigate the cake incident. (Two players having a cake fight was a league security problem.)

I could tell that Arthur wouldn't let anyone off the hook so I promised that I'd get to the bottom of the whole thing. There was only one thing to do, have Morrison and Johansen talk to Arthur and explain exactly what had happened. That they did, but Arthur wouldn't listen. When Johansen called, he told me that he could hear Miron's voice in the background, feeding the fire against us instead of trying to douse it with calming words.

The finale was just as I suspected. The bill for shampooing off the chocolate cake mess came to $150 of which each of the two culprits chipped in $75. But that cake turned out to be the straw that broke Imperatore's back, as far as Don Cherry was concerned. The happy phone calls that he had once made earlier in the season stopped coming. Some- how I wasn't his gem of a coach anymore.

Then it happened. I got word that Armand and Arthur wanted to see me at the trucking company office in New Jersey. I had been there before at the start of the season. Then, I had been ushered in like a king. This time I had to stay in the waiting room for half an hour before someone finally tapped me on the shoulder and invited me in.

They sat me down at one end of an enormous fifty-foot table. Arthur sat at the other end of that marble lake, with Armand at his side. Then the meeting began.

I had already decided on my ride from the airport—in a chauffeur-driven limo—that if I was going out, I was going out on my shield.

The inquisition began when Arthur told me we didn't have enough wins. I answered, "But Arthur, when we beat Boston and Montreal and Quebec you said, 'That's all well and good, but we need more asses in the seats in Denver'. Well, Arthur, you have 149,000 more asses in the seats than you had before I was here."

Then the McEwen incident was introduced. I told them my only mistake had been in not correcting him earlier. I brought up the cake incident to prove how things could be blown out of proportion. They admitted that they were a little hasty on that occasion. Too bad the damage to Trevor, Kevin, and me had already been done.

Arthur wanted to know if I had worked hard enough with the team. I told him that I thought I had. I had been at every game, naturally, every practice, and only missed one optional practice. But, that didn't impress Arthur.

He took me to the window and pointed to some truck drivers who were watching their trucks being loaded on the docks and he told me, "See how hard those truck drivers work, even in the rain."

I said, "Arthur, first of all, the drivers are not working in the rain, they are in the cab, second, they don't even load the trucks. I worked for twenty years as a labourer on construction sites, working a jackhammer out in the pouring rain, and if I didn't like it I could go home without pay. So please Arthur, with all due respect, don't give me that bullshit about how hard truckers work."

Since I stopped him on that question he instantly came up with the business about the Rockies lacking leadership. I turned to Armand. "Armand, you can say a lot of things about me but, tell me, do I lead the players or don't I?"

Pohan looked over at his stepfather. "Yeah, Dad, I have to admit that the players would go anywhere with him. If he told them to walk into a roaring fire they'd walk into it."

At least that was one point on which I was supported. Then the phone rang, and Armand had to leave. "Tell me," said Arthur, "what do you think of Ray Miron?"

I said I didn't want to talk about him behind his back.

But Arthur wouldn't buy that. He kept pushing me. "Tell me what you think of him. Tell me." He wanted to know badly. It was his team, so I let him know that I thought Miron was totally inept. And the strangest thing is that Arthur said: "I agree." I looked at him as if to say "Well then, why?" and he said: "I've given the team to Armand and I'm letting him run it as he sees fit."

That really puzzled me. Here was the owner of the club, telling me that I reminded him of himself when he was young; agreeing with me that Miron was for the birds; and *I* was the one he might fire.

While they served me a lunch of celery and cheese, I knew they had made up their minds, or at least Armand had. Arthur wasn't too sure, but he had given the reins of the team to Armand and didn't want to interfere.

The meeting came to a close and Arthur—whom I admired and still do, because he's a man's man—said, "Don, I don't want to destroy you, Rose and Tim, because I like your family." I said , "Arthur, I know you mean that and I appreciate it, but you do what you have to do. Don't worry, you won't destroy us."

I shook hands with Arthur and got into the limo. As I sat looking at the delights of New Jersey, I mused, "Well, Grapes, you just blew 400 big ones and you're being let go two years in a row. What a great reputation you're going to have."

The voice of brother Richard kept haunting me, "Bend a little. You have to get along with this g.m." Sorry Richard. I have to do what I think is right.

So there I was tooling along in a black limo through the Lincoln Tunnel wondering whether or not there would be any light at the end of the Don Cherry Tunnel.

CHAPTER FIVE

The End Of A Rocky Road

Meanwhile, the 1979-80 season had reached the homestretch and we were in the race for the number one draft choice, which annually goes to hockey's worst team. The problem was, we didn't have a number one pick. It had been traded to Montreal for Ron Andruff and Sean Shanahan, and, if you can believe it, Colorado had also given Montreal $110,000. Neither Andruff nor Shanahan made it in the NHL.

I remember distinctly the game I realized we were in deep goaltending trouble. We were playing Boston, and Bill McKenzie—a gutsy little guy—was our goalie. He had most of our wins and was quite capable of putting us in the playoffs. Then it happened. John Wensink took a shot, slipped and fell into McKenzie and tore apart Bill's cartilage and our playoff hopes.

Now we had to rely on Hardy Astrom who, unfortunately for us, had proven he was not an NHL goaltender. Game after game he let in floaters from the red line. With Hardy, I tried a tactic that had worked with Cheevers and Gilbert. I attacked him, verbally. Cheevers and Gilbert would get mad at me and play better to prove that I was wrong. Hardy, on the other hand, believed every word I said.

Once, during a practice, Bobby Schmautz tested Astrom with four shots from the blue line. Each one of them went right along the ice and beat Astrom. I doubt that my wife, Rose, would have missed more than two of them.

Every time we spelled Astrom there was the faint hope that one of our other goalies would suddenly find himself, but such miracles were not our lot. The pity of it all was that we were jelling toward the end of the season, and had one of the league's best lines with Lucien DeBlois on left wing, Rene Robert at center, and Bobby Schmautz on the right side. Everything was going great except the goaltending.

With two games to go in the season we played Edmonton in Edmonton. They had to win the game to make the playoffs. At the end of the first period we had outshot them 10-4, Gretzky and all. The only problem was that the score stood at 2-2. They scored on every other shot, and this was not an unusual happening. After some games, the referee and the linesmen would come over to me and try to make me feel better by saying, "Too bad you fellows don't have a goaltender because you have a good team." This never failed to infuriate me even more.

After the Edmonton game one of the reporters asked Schmautzie what he thought was wrong with the team. He told the newspaperman that he had been in pro hockey for 16 years and had never played in front of worse goaltending. It so happened that Billy McKenzie, who was attempting to come back after the injury to his knee, had played part of the Edmonton game and he read Schmautzie's quotes in the paper the next day. We were on the bus when it happened. McKenzie circled Bobby's quotes, walked over to his seat on the bus and said, "Do you see this?"

Schmautzie, who is a wiry guy not to be tampered with, looked at the story. "Yeah, I see it."

Then McKenzie said, "Do you think something like that makes us feel good?"

Schmautzie looked up and said, "I don't care if you feel good or not, it's the truth. And if you don't like it, come outside and I'll beat the shit out of you." Nothing happened because Schmautzie had merely verbalized what the rest of the guys were thinking.

Now we were down to the last game of the season, against the Winnipeg Jets; the loser to wind up with the worst record of all 21 teams in the NHL. Losing that game meant more to the Jets than it did to us. Except from the point of view of pride, we had little at stake in the game. And, I can assure you, the Jets general manager John Ferguson wanted his club to lose that game in the worst way.

Considering the game they played, the Jets deserved to lose, but their goalie would have none of it. The Jets scored a couple of goals from the blue line and Ferguson was pulling his hair out.

Winnipeg won the game and we won the draft choice, which we had to present to the Canadiens.

Denver fans didn't seem to mind our last place finish. No matter how many games we lost, they kept turning out, and in our last home game, something really unusual took place. Our opponents were the Pittsburgh Penguins, not exactly the greatest draw in the NHL. Denver was engulfed in a terrific snowstorm and, by all odds, we should have been lucky to pull in six or seven thousand fans. Well, this nothing game drew almost 12,000 people—we would have filled the place with 16,000 if it hadn't been for the blizzard—and I was well-dressed for the occasion. The players had given me a cowboy hat and boots for Christmas so I trotted them out for the finale and walked out on the ice before the opening face-off while the players lined up on either side of me with their sticks crossed, the way they do it in the movies. I walked under the umbrella of sticks and the crowd chanted "CHER-RY, CHER-RY." It was a moment I'll never forget, for several reasons. The crowd chanting, the feeling of emotion from the players, the game, but also the pain from the enormous blisters on each heel from the new cowboy boots. But I hardly felt the pain because I was in such ecstasy.

Fred Pietila of *The Rocky Mountain News* described it as "...a delirious, ranting crowd." We wound up getting more standing ovations than goals, but we got five goals to the Penguins' none.

With 5:39 left in the game and the decision beyond Pittsburgh's reach, Rene Robert, who was our team captain, called a time-out. Once again the crowd was chanting "CHER-RY, CHER-RY." But I couldn't figure out what the time-out was all about because I hadn't called it.

"It was to show the people how much we love Grapes," Rene later told Pietila, "and where he stands in our book." (I know how this sounds but please indulge me on this ego trip as it was one of those moments that will live forever.)

What hurt was missing the playoffs. It was the first time in my NHL coaching career that I had ever been out of the playoffs. Same with Schmautzie, Lanny McDonald and Rene Robert. They were all in a state of shock unlike some of the other players who had missed the playoffs throughout their careers.

Bobby Schmautz was the type of person who could help build the Rockies into a top club. After the Winnipeg game, Schmautzie gave a party in his hotel room for the whole team, many of whom he would never see again. The whole thing must have cost him $500. This happens sometimes with teams that make the playoffs, but here was Schmautzie doing it for a team that hadn't even come close. He just did it because he thought it was the right thing to do. This was the kind of player I wanted for the Rockies—Schmautz, McDonald, Robert—quality winning players who are sometimes hard to get along with, but who would be there when the going got rough.

Once the beer at the party started to flow the guys decided that the time had come for a drinking contest. Just about everyone was there with the notable exception of McEwen, who must have been sending out for room service.

My first game back in Boston with the Rockies. I'm pointing out to the ref that Boston had tried to put two men back on the ice after we scored on a powerplay.

This picture was taken after the last game in Denver when we beat Pittsburgh 5-0 before a crowd of 12,000 in a bad snowstorm. The crowd, the players, and I went nuts.

In the backyard with Blue, the day after the Rockies fired me.

I thought what the hell, why not? The season was over and the guys deserved a little fun.

The contest was the Chug-a-Lug variety where the guys had to drink the beer from a full glass right down to the bottom without stopping. Naturally, the one who did it the fastest was the winner. After a lot of preliminaries we got down to a battle between the East and the West. Lanny McDonald, who comes from Hanna, Alberta, represented the West while Kevin Morrison from Sydney, Nova Scotia, represented the East.

By this time we had all been well into the beer and the East-West contest had taken on all the trappings of a Super Bowl bout in the small hotel room. We had cheerleading teams for both sides; guys waving towels for the favourites.

Needless to say, being an Easterner, I was rooting passionately for Morrison. We called him "the Beast" but he really was a super guy. He played a number of games for us even after suffering a separated shoulder. I liked the fact that he was proud to be from the Maritimes. Morrison was always bragging that he was the best drinker in the world so, naturally, we Easterners figured we had it knocked; that we'd win the Great Colorado Rockies Drinking Championship.

So, there was Lanny McDonald, the best goal-scorer on the team, sitting on one side of the table and on the other side sat Kevin Morrison.

"I'm gonna annihilate him," Morrison whispered to us in an aside. We rested assured that our bets had been well placed.

Our cheerleaders launched a "Go Kevin Go" routine and repeated it enough times to convince us there was no way the evil forces of the West could subdue our man. The towels were waving and, if you hadn't known better, you might have figured we were about to start a championship fight.

McDonald and Morrison indicated that they were ready. Three mugs, each filled with a pint of beer, were placed in front of each player. The signal was given and they reached for their respective mugs. Morrison got a grip on his a split-second before McDonald and we cheered lustily, figuring this would give Kevin the edge in a neck-and-neck homestretch drive.

The gulps began and, almost instantly, we knew we were in trouble. Kevin was gurgling but Lanny was pouring the beer down his throat as if he had a water pipe for a throat. Although we didn't clock the bout, Lanny downed the three pints in about ten seconds. Kevin wasn't even half finished when Lanny bounced his third mug off the table. Lanny was the champion. He sat there with a satisfied grin, twirling his handlebar mustache and said, "Schmautzie, another beer for a chaser."

I believe there was a message there, something that summed up my entire Colorado Rockies experience. My drinker couldn't drink, and my best goal-scorer was the best drinker. Of course I wouldn't begrudge Lanny the beer championship. He was a class guy and the proof of that came the next day.

We got up the next morning at five, all hung over from the night before, and feeling sorry for ourselves. When we got to the bus the driver was there with a little kid who wanted some autographs. Most of the guys wanted no part of him. After all, we were out of the playoffs, physically shot to hell, and anxious to get home.

Lanny was the last guy to get on the bus, as usual, and I could tell that the trauma of missing the playoffs had really gotten to him. Just as he stepped onto the bus the little boy approached him.

"Well, hello," Lanny said, as if he had had ten hours sleep and felt like a million dollars. "Who is this now?"

The bus driver interrupted and told McDonald that the kid was his son.

"David," the driver said, "this is Lanny McDonald."

Lanny put his arm around the kid as if the boy was one of his own and spent the next five minutes talking to him. To me, that demonstrated what class and heart Lanny has.

We drove off and, as the bus headed for the highway, I couldn't help but feel a twinge of sadness about the Rockies and myself. As bad as the team was, as lousy as our goaltending had been, I wanted very much to be a part of the rebuilding process of this team. I was convinced that Denver had the makings of a good hockey town, even a terrific one. This had been proven by the support given to a losing team. You can imagine what kind of reaction they would have had for a winner. Til the day I die, I'll always cherish the ovations we got in our finale at the McNichols Arena.

After the season, the reporters began asking questions about the future and one of those questioned was Pohan. Armand said he would assess everyone in the organization. "Does that also mean Don Cherry? " a reporter asked. "Does that mean you're dissatisfied with him?"

Armand hemmed and hawed but the message was clear; there would be no vote of confidence for Don Cherry. There would be no confidence in Don Cherry, at least not from the owners or general manager. Pohan decided to let me dangle in the wind for six weeks while the media did their best to help me keep my job. *The Rocky Mountain News*, one of Denver's two major dailies, launched an opinion poll. They offered readers the opportunity to voice their opinion on three questions:

- Should Cherry be retained as the team's coach?

- Has Pohan caused irreparable damage between himself and Cherry, not to mention himself and the Rockies fans?

- Would the Rockies attendance suffer if Cherry were not retained?

The paper asked readers to phone in their opinions in two days. "The response," said columnist B. G. Brooks of *The News*, "was staggering although none too surprising. *The News* received 3,083 calls over the two-day (16 hours total) period with 3,025 callers saying that Cherry

should be retained and 58 claiming that a coaching change was in order."
(Blue and I went looking for the 58!)

By this time my list of allies was growing, from the columnists like
Woody Paige to talk show hosts to the man in the street.

Pohan had been backed into a corner and didn't like his position a
bit. He kept delaying his decision about my future while dropping snide
remarks here and there. When he finally did come to Denver he phoned
me about 10:30 at night and said, "Well, I think, Don, that this has gone
on long enough."

To that I replied, "You had better believe it has and you can handle
the press conference any way you like—with bare knuckles or the right
way. But I'll tell you this, Armand, if you screw me tomorrow, you can
rest assured that you're goin' to get it back."

"Yes," he said, "I know."

That I was gone as coach of the Rockies was a foregone conclusion.
What I was concerned about was the manner in which Pohan would
orchestrate my dismissal.

As I see it, his plan was to scuttle my coaching career, forever, if
possible. Using his legal background—he was once an assistant prosecutor
in New Jersey—Pohan delivered an elaborate bill of particulars, detailing
my coaching faults. It was so devastating that even I hated myself after
reading it.

For example, he said he could find a coach who would bring more
positive results. That's a laugh. The club didn't improve the year after I
left or the year after that. The only difference was they had smaller
crowds. Then, he blamed the failings of his farm system on me when it
was clearly the work of Miron and himself. Pohan said the Rockies were a
better team than its record indicated, yet, as soon as I was gone he
unloaded half the players.

What hurt most was his reiteration that I couldn't work with
younger players. Although I had done well with the kids in Boston—ask
Mike Milbury, Rick Middleton and Stan Jonathan, to name a few—Pohan
was determined to warp the McEwen incident to suit his purposes. He
insisted that the Rockies were loaded with young potential stars on the
farm and on the big team. The proof of his misrepresentation is in the
standings. The young Rockies did nothing in 1981 after I had gone, and
still worse in 1982.

"We need a coach who can motivate our young players." Pohan also
said. He got Billy MacMillan to coach them in 1980-81 and MacMillan
lasted one year. Then, in one of the superb examples of hockey logic,
MacMillan, who had never been a head coach or a general manager
before, was promoted—after *failing* as a coach—to the job of g.m. If that
isn't the acme of the Peter Principle nothing is. So, MacMillan imported
Bert Marshall as head coach to work with the kids. Marshall lasted half a
season. Next came Marshall Johnston to work with the kids. Ditto.

Finally, said Armand Pohan, "there is no substitute for winning." Pohan and Arthur couldn't produce a winner. They sold the team in 1981, still a loser. Crowds dropped while the Rockies continued losing and have now moved to the Meadowlands. I rest my case.

CHAPTER SIX

Early Life In Kingston

It isn't easy to become a Don Cherry. For starters, you have to have a mother named Maude and a father named Delmar.

Mom was a tailor who worked at the Royal Military College in Kingston. (Canada's answer to West Point.) She specialized in tailoring the uniforms the cadets and military men wore. Mom was meticulously instructed by English tailors and learned early on that if she didn't perfectly tailor a uniform it would be given right back to her to be done over again. Once, she had completed an entire uniform—it took her a month to do the job—and handed it to the chief tailor. The man examined the uniform from top to bottom, found one stitch slightly out of place and demanded that she take the whole thing apart and do it all over again. That was the last time Mom ever made a tailoring mistake.

Dad, at 26, was the best baseball player in town. He had a job, was earning a decent living, and flattered my mother by purchasing chocolates and other nice things for her. When they were married Mom was 23 and Dad 28. Their wedding, at St. George's Cathedral in Kingston, was the major social event of the year; mostly because Dad was a celebrity, having been such a good baseball player.

There were more than 500 people at the wedding and the reception that followed turned out to be a lot wilder than anticipated. My maternal grandfather didn't like liquor, so he made sure that the only beverage served at the reception was non-alcoholic punch.

Dad's friends, who always liked a nip or two, must have been tipped off about the plain punch because they came armed with booze under their coats. As each of Dad's friends came in they slyly poured a bottle of liquor into the punch. By the end of the day, the punch had become pure liquor.

Mom and Dad's honeymoon was out of the ordinary. They went to Montreal, took a suite at one of the hotels and then went to the hockey game at The Forum. The Montreal Maroons goalie, Flat Walsh, was one of Dad's pals from Kingston and after the game Mom and Dad invited him back to the honeymoon suite for a couple of drinks. The trouble was that Mr. Walsh had asked if he could bring a couple of the other players along and Dad had said sure. The next thing they knew the entire Montreal Maroons team showed up. Dad had to order for the whole team—a good one hundred and fifty bucks for booze alone—and the guys stayed and drank all night.

A huge man—he was six feet two, about 234 pounds, with a 17½ inch neck and a 32 inch waist—Dad was a master electrician by trade and the best centerfielder in the Province of Ontario. His size reminded me of Gulliver while the rest of us were Lilliputians. Dad was an intimidating fellow; except when it came to my mother. Her temper could melt him on the best day he ever had. One of those days came along after Dad had complained about the "plain food" Mom had been cooking. "Why don't you make creamed potatoes or creamed onions for a change?" Pop demanded.

Mom didn't say a word, but the next night she made a dish of creamed onions. When Dad came home he was in a bad mood from something that had happened at work. He sat down at the dinner table in a real snit and when Mom put the dish on the table he turned to her and snapped: "I don't like creamed onions."

With that, Mom picked up the plate and poured the creamed onions over his head. To this day I can still see the sauce pouring down his cheeks. I was absolutely terrified. Dad didn't beef about Mom's cuisine after that.

Outside the house, Dad was a veritable lion of a man. He oozed authority from every pore. Every so often he would counsel me about the value of maintaining a positive image. "Donald," he would say, "it's a matter of attitude."

His air was so commanding that people automatically assumed he was a man of authority or one who was due respect. Once we went to a county fair and Dad stopped in front of a girlee show. The manager immediately walked over, believing Dad to be an official of some kind, and said: "Sir, we run a clean show around here. We've never had any problems, no trouble at all." Dad hadn't said a word when the manager added, "How many sons do you have?" Dad told him and the manager gave Dad a handful of tickets. "Take your kids on all the rides for free!" Dad just laughed.

When I walked down the streets of Kingston my heart was often in my mouth. It was like a match being waved near gasoline; with Dad there was always the possibility of an explosion since he gave way to nobody, no matter how tough they might be.

My father's strength was legendary. He liked to go to the Royal Canadian Horse Artillery Club, a private army club in town. He would put ten bucks on the table and wager that nobody could outdo him in a test of strength. If nobody topped him he would get a small barrel of oysters. We ate a lot of oysters at our house because Dad never lost.

Another less violent kick I would get with Dad was going to the movies. The Capital Theatre was our special haunt. It was a nice, big place to watch a movie except that every so often, the projector would break down and a sign saying "Del Cherry, please come to the projection room" would appear on the screen. Dad would excuse himself for a few minutes, return and then the movie would resume. And I'd say, as proud as a kid could be, "That's *my* Dad who fixed it!" I got a special thrill when this happened.

Every once in a while the theatre owner would need Dad to come in early on a Sunday morning to repair the machine. "Only," Dad would tell the manager, "if I can bring my helper." The assistant was me, and for my end of the job I was paid $10. After he fixed the machine, my father would let me sit alone in the middle of the empty theatre (very lonely, very scary) and have the manager show twenty minutes of Looney Tunes cartoons. Bugs Bunny gave Donald Cherry a command performance.

My father had some traits that would be regarded as unusual even by unusual people's standards. He was extremely protective of his own interests; particularly his job. As he approached retirement age, his superiors urged him to teach someone else his job. Dad nixed that. "It took me thirty years to learn the ropes," he snapped, "so let the new guy learn the way I did."

The company finally hired an electrical engineer, paying him twice what Dad was getting. One day the engineer, who was now working alongside my father, wanted to show the bosses how he was going to do something different. He had a pair of bolt cutters and was about to put them around some wires and cut them when Dad interjected:

"I wouldn't do that if I were you."

"Why not?" the guy asked.

"Because that's the primary feed coming in—150,000 volts—and it will go right through you!"

The electrical engineer who was earning twice as much as my father (but who knew half as much) nearly died on the spot along with the bosses.

The point here is that sometimes Dad could be cruel. You see, he knew half an hour before this event that the engineer was going to cut that cable, but Dad waited until the bosses were present and actually let the engineer put the bolt cutters around the cable.

Dad once gave me a beautiful B-B gun. It was gold with a brown handle and had a telescopic sight. Nobody in Kingston had one like it (I think because it came from the United States) and I was extremely fond of the gun. But when my father gave it to me he said in no uncertain terms: "If you ever abuse this, or break anything with it, you'll never see it again."

One day, for reasons that to this day I cannot explain, I took the gun and blasted some holes in the wall of our kitchen. When Dad came home and saw what had happened to the wall he didn't say anything, he just took the gun away, and I never saw it again. (When I was 25 years old I asked my father what he had done with the gun and he *still* wouldn't tell me.) Which is not to suggest that an incident such as that diminished his love for me. Although he always remained as rigid as ever until the day he died, he also had a very positive philosophy especially when it came to mistakes.

I'll never forget the day I was playing a game of Junior B hockey for the Kingston Victorias. It was by far the worst game I had ever played. I was on the ice for all five goals scored against us and was heartbroken because I felt I had lost the game. I mean nobody played as badly in his life as I did on that day. My father was at the game and I know that anybody else's dad would have raised hell over such a terrible game. My father said nothing; not a word. That night, he was sitting in his room reading a book when I went in to see him. I couldn't have been more depressed. "Dad," I said, "I cost my team the game today. I'm just a lousy hockey player."

My father sat and listened; not saying a word until I had finished my harangue. Then, he said, "Yeah, so you had a tough game. But do you remember the time you blocked that shot when the puck was going into the top corner? Remember when you took that guy out of the play on the one-on-one? And how about the time you let that shot go and hit the goalpost?" By the time I left his room I thought I had played the greatest game of my life. I couldn't wait to get on the ice again.

Dad could whistle louder than anyone I've ever heard. He always whistled when he came home from work. He would have something for my brother and me in his lunch pail—a turtle or a frog or even a pigeon—and we'd hear three whistle blasts and come running.

My brother Richard, is three years younger and many years smarter than I am. When we were young he would always get me into trouble. His favourite threat to me if I didn't do his bidding was, "I'm going to tell Momma." Until, one day Mom was listening and I wasn't doing anything when he uttered those words. After that Mom never fell for the threat again.

In effect, I was Richard's guardian. I had to take him everywhere I went which was a great source of annoyance to me. But my Dad would say, "Some day you will rather be with your brother than any other friend in the world." And he was right.

In his own way, Richard was as obsessive as Dad. When he was young my brother was just about the skinniest kid in the world and seemingly weak. One day he and a friend, Billy Kuhn, were out on the lawn. Billy did three push-ups while Richard could hardly lift himself off the grass. It bothered him, and quietly, he began practising. He would do push-ups every night until he was able to do 150, 30 on one hand.

Richard was a defenseman, a better hockey player than I was, and played Junior hockey for the Barrie (Ontario) Flyers under Hap Emms, one of the better junior coaches in Canada.

He turned pro with the Bruins in 1966-67 and then bounced around the minors. While all this was going on he managed to attend university and get his teaching certificate. He played two full seasons with the Philadelphia Flyers in 1968-69 then the Bruins drafted him again and it seemed that he would make the team but he was sent to their Central League farm team in Oklahoma City as an assistant coach.

Richard wasn't especially crazy about the job and he was even less happy about the general manager of the team. This fellow had a bad habit of falling asleep at the games and sending in negative reports about a lot of the young players. He never seemed to know what was going on and always gave the players a hard time, all of which grated Richard no end. When the team was eliminated from the playoffs the g.m. walked into the dressing room, stuck his hand out and began shaking hands with the players.

The sight of him was too much for Richard. He quietly said, "Get out. Get outta here or I'll throw you out the door!"

"You can't do that," said the g.m. "I'm the general manager."

So, Richard picked him up and escorted him out the door.

After the final game, in which the Blazers were eliminated, the club was heading back to Oklahoma City. They were rolling through some town in the Midwest while the anger that Richard had contained over the g.m. kept boiling hotter and hotter inside him. Finally, he couldn't take it anymore and said "STOP THE BUS! STOP THE BUS!"

The bus lurched to a halt and the driver opened the door "I'm retiring," said Richard. "I'm not associating with any organization that has him for a manager." Richard walked out of the bus and out of his hockey career. Impetuous though he may have been, Richard had perceived what was wrong and had said what was wrong. That might be the Cherry syndrome—or is it problem?—and though it might be detrimental to us we wouldn't change for the world.

Richard became a black belt in judo and every time he went to a new tournament he would return home and put a new trophy on the table.

The strange thing was that Dad and I were never allowed to see Richard perform his judo. We found out that, during a match, if someone is being choked or badly hurt, the guy being hurt simply has to tap the other guy on the shoulder and end the match. It was like an S.O.S. to the opponent. The trouble with Richard was that if we had been there watching him and he was being choked—as in being choked to death—he would *never* tap his opponent on the shoulder. He would rather die first and we knew it.

I set a record—unofficially of course—for being strapped by the principal of Rideau Elementary School. Naturally, you would get strapped for misbehaviour and misbehaving seemed to be my major in school. (Learning certainly wasn't.)

In grade four my teacher, Mrs. Arthur, had me up at the blackboard doing multiplication. For me arithmetic was as easy as doping out Einstein's Theory of Relativity. So when I did the problem-solving incorrectly at the blackboard, Mrs. Arthur crisply whacked me on the behind with a ruler. (If she assumed that the blast to my behind would make me a smarter math person she was sadly mistaken.) Once whacked I refused to continue so she would demand that I go to the next room where kid brother Richard was in class. He would be sent to the blackboard, shown the problem and would proceed to do it 100 percent accurately. That vignette accurately sums up my performance in school.

Being whacked by Mrs. Arthur, however, was child's play compared to the strapping that our principal, Mr. Jackson, would apply to my hands. Strapping caused a severe numbing that could only be cured (in winter) by sticking the offending hand deep in the snow.

When Mr. Jackson strapped me he frequently would say, "Donald, this hurts me more than it hurts you." I always regarded that statement as my first introduction to the art of propaganda. Actually, the worst aspect of strapping was psychological. It was like being summoned to the *guillotine* and when it happened just about every one in school knew it. You had to stand with your hands behind your back like a condemned man. My fellow pupils never thought it was very funny. When they walked by while I was being strapped, they would lower their heads, as would the teachers. The kids knew enough not to gloat because on another day they might be standing in my shoes.

Not that Mr. Jackson always held me in disrepute. As a matter of fact, I happened to be one of his favourites because I was the best hockey player in school. For that reason he gave me the honour of caring for the school ice rink.

One day, while putting down the sheets of ice, I was painting the red and blue lines. A couple of guys and two of their girlfriends were watching. They began kidding me, saying that the lines weren't straight. The more they needled me, the angrier I got. What made me angriest was the fact that the line *wasn't* straight. But I kept at it, painting the line and getting closer and closer to them until, when I reached the boards, they unleashed one more blast at my artistic line-painting. I put an end to the criticism by lifting up the can and whipping paint into their faces.

Mr. Jackson gave me the strap for that, too. (And I'm sure it hurt him as much as it hurt me.)

Brutal though my marks had been and bruised though my wrists and hands were, I somehow managed to graduate from public school and enter Kingston Collegiate Vocational Institute, where I maintained my academic consistency—terrible. Fortunately, I had my mother in my corner. "Donald is smart," she would tell her friends. "If only he would apply himself. I know he can do it."

Conservatively-speaking, I must have heard that line a minimum of 400 times.

Much as I disliked school, I can honestly say that I never played hooky and never cheated on exams. Otherwise my marks wouldn't have been as brutal as they were! The one thing I managed to get right in school was the notation in my yearbook: "Ambition—pro hockey player." That was right on. Playing hockey for money was all I ever thought about. I played for my high school team, a Junior B team, a midget team, and a juvenile team, all at the same time.

What seemed odd to a lot of people was the fact that, although I was a loner and did poorly at school, I seemed to have leadership qualities. At school, for example, it was an honour to be voted the person who made sure that the other students got to class on time. The position was voted on by the fellow students and I was the one chosen. This infuriated the teachers who couldn't understand why someone with my low grades could win the approval of his classmates. (I was as surprised as they were.)

(A similar situation developed when I was playing defense for the Rochester Americans 20 years later. The coach, Joe Crozier, had to name a captain and wanted the guys to pick either Bryan Hextall or Teddy Taylor. We voted in secret ballot and I came out the winner, 16-3. Crozier threw the ballots out and called for another vote. This time I won 17-2. Crozier threw out the ballots again, and stalled for a few days. About a week later he got us all together. "I want this business of the captaincy straightened out," he said. Everyone knew he didn't want me as captain because he knew it would be trouble. A third ballot was held and this time the guys put little cherries on the ballot 19 times. Crozier got just as ticked off as my teachers did. Crozier accepted my captaincy grudgingly: "Cherry's your captain, I hope you know what you're doing." P.S. He was right. I was trouble for The Crow.)

Some of my teachers sympathized with me over my hockey aspirations; others didn't. One of them tried to carve me up, verbally, in front of the class. "You're a big deal now," she snapped. "We'll see how you're doing when you're 35 years old. You think you'll be a pro hockey player. We'll see how much money you're making. You won't have a penny in your pocket."

She asked me what I wanted to be when I was 35. I said, "Certainly not a teacher like you."

Needless to say I was shown the door and left the room to a huge round of applause from my insightful classmates.

I know that many people regret not having finished high school and that they never had the opportunity to go on to college. I'm sure they mean every word of it. But I won't kid you. I have absolutely no regrets about going on to the university and "bettering myself." When I left high school I said good-riddance to academia. I was glad to be out.

I wasn't that glad to leave Kingston, although I knew that I would have to leave sooner or later to continue my pursuit of a hockey career. Life was comfortable for me at home. We lived in a nice, middle-class neighbourhood with sixty foot poplar trees lining the street. At night, when there was even the slightest breeze, the trees would rustle in such a way that it put you right to sleep. Dad used to say that they were whispering to one another. I thought it was absolutely beautiful.

When other families were down and out we always seemed to have money, and other good things in life. Dad had built beautiful animal pens in our backyard. We had chickens, rabbits, guinea pigs, bantam roosters and, for a while, even a ferret—a deadly little weasel named Barney— that we had to get rid of when it attacked my dog.

There were still unemployed men who would come around from time to time for a free meal. They would put an "X" on the sidewalk in front of our house. One day, a fellow knocked on the door and said he hadn't eaten for three days and could he please have something to eat. Mom said yes and told him to go around to the back of the house where she made him an egg sandwich. He said, "Egg sandwiches, egg sandwiches, I'm getting so sick of egg sandwiches."

An experience with animals left me in a state of shock. We lived near a fairground and one night some of the horse barns caught fire with the racehorses trapped inside. I was one of the first people to arrive on the scene, along with a guy who had an axe to break the locks on the stable doors. We managed to save fifteen horses, but twenty-five burned to death. I remember one of the men running into a burning barn to get a horse named Blue Boy who was the favourite horse in Kingston. He put a sack over the horse's head and began leading him out. Once Blue Boy had cleared the barn we all started cheering but, suddenly the horse reared— we had startled him—and threw the sack off his head. Then, he wheeled and madly galloped back *into* the burning stall. Before we could do anything Blue Boy had burned to death. It was one of the most horrifying moments in my life.

As I matured, I could tell that many of my father's traits were incorporated in my own behaviour. My passion for good clothes is directly rooted in my Dad's meticulousness about his attire. I will always have a vision of him standing on the corner in front of Pappas' Pool Hall, wearing a black homburg hat (in the Winston Churchill manner), tailor-made suit, tightfitting vest and diamond stick pin glistening in the sun.

Dad lived to the age of 62, when he died of lung cancer.

The doctor told me that if Dad hadn't been so impervious to the pain of the cancer, they might have found out about his illness earlier and might have been able to save him

As it was, Dad got out of bed every morning and went to work, until one morning, two weeks before he died, he couldn't bend over to tie his shoes. That was how much pain he was in.

As close as Dad was to us, he kept everyone else in the neighbour-hood at a distance. Dad was a very impersonal man to all those outside his family, and though he had traits that everyone would like to have copied, he was still pretty much of a lone wolf—with one exception.

I recall that Dad had a special friendship with a chap named Teddy Mateer. Teddy had a disability that hampered his walking; he would sort of hobble rather than walk and his arms would often fly in the air. Everyone made fun of him. My father would buy Teddy hot dogs and soda and cigarettes.

After my father died, my Mom was sitting alone in the back of the funeral home when the door opened and Teddy walked in. Apparently he had never been inside a funeral parlor before, but somehow he had heard about Dad's passing and wanted to pay his respects in his own sensitive way. He walked up to the open coffin and stood before it for several moments and then did something I had never heard of before. Teddy put his hand in the coffin, shook Dad's hand and hobbled out.

CHAPTER SEVEN

Up For A Cup Of Coffee

No less than sixteen years in minor hockey leagues have provided me with the kind of tough adversity that could only be topped by digging trenches in World War I (we got about the same pay). It was a tough life, hedge-hopping from Hershey to Springfield to Three-Rivers, but it also had its rewards. I'm convinced that I came out of it all a better man, well-toughened by what others might interpret as misfortune.

Needless to say, I didn't plan it that way. According to my blueprint, I would move directly from my Junior team, the Barrie Flyers, where we won the Memorial Cup in 52-53, up to the Boston Bruins. Not wanting to be too pushy about it, I was willing to spend a year in the minors but I didn't think more than a year was necessary.

In those days the Bruins number one farm team was located in Hershey, Pennsylvania. The Hershey Bears played in the American Hockey League, a fast league that regularly sent good, young skaters up to the National Hockey League. The Bruins and the Bears held a joint training camp at the Hershey Arena and that's precisely where I headed on a September afternoon in 1954.

Finding Hershey was not easy. Lorne Ferguson and I started by taking the train from Toronto to Buffalo. Then, another train from Buffalo to New York and, finally, a train from New York to Harrisburg, the capital of Pennsylvania. From there, we hopped in a cab and told the driver to take us to Hershey.

As the taxi meandered through Pennsylvania-Dutch countryside, I couldn't help but tingle over the opportunity before me. Here was Donald Stewart Cherry about to become a professional hockey player. By the time I had come out of my reverie, the cab had pulled up in front of a large hotel, The Cocoa Inn, our training headquarters.

"This," said Fergy, "is Hershey."

I looked around and said, "What do you mean 'this is Hershey'? Where is Hershey?"

All I could see was a department store, a bank and the hotel. "My friend," Lorne went on, "you are looking at Hershey."

How, I wondered, could this non-town support an American Hockey League team? How could this non-town be called a city? I would, in time, discover that there was more to Hershey than immediately met my eyes but, for the moment at least, I was unimpressed.

No matter, there was hockey to be played and a job to be won so I marched into the hotel to become a member of the Boston Bruins or, at the very least, the Hershey Bears. Nothing but the best, or second best, for me.

I immediately bumped into some of my buddies from Junior hockey—Skip Teal, Obie O'Brien, Jimmy Robinson and Ralph Willis—and felt right at home. I also met some of the Bruins I had heard so much about but had never seen in person. Bob Armstrong and Bill Quackenbush were on defense. Fleming Mackell, Cal Gardner and Leo Labine were among the forwards.

The first thing they had us do was take a physical (at least that's what they said it was). A guy who was supposed to be a doctor took a look at us. I think he was only interested in seeing whether we were alive and breathing because we all passed without even having to blink.

In the dressing room, at least, there was complete equality but it ended there. A caste system was in vogue and I rapidly learned that, as a newcomer, I was a member of the lower class. All of the established NHL players were in the upper class. They hung out together and, more than that, established their status by generally ignoring the AHL types. This was an unwritten rule just as the "don't-hit-me-and-I-won't-hit-you" rule was enforced on the ice during training camp.

The point of the no-hitting rule was that the guys didn't want to get hurt before the season started so there was an agreement not to hit the other guy if the other guy agreed not to hit you. Usually, this arrangement worked except for oddballs like me. I hit everyone in sight and made a lot of enemies. I had one thing in mind—make the club or die. If I didn't make it somebody would have to pay. One of the Bruins' veterans, Real Chevrefils, came up to me one day and said, "Look, I don't feel good today, how about not hitting me?" I laughed.

There were a lot of laughs in training camp; some of them

unintentional. Like the time we got our "advice" from the higher-ups. Lloyd Blinco, a crusty oldtimer, was general manager of the Hershey Bears, and Murray Henderson, a former Bruins' defenseman, was the coach. One day they called a bunch of us rookies into their office. I assumed, as did my pals Lionel Heinrich and Stan Parker, that we were going to get a lesson on how to play professional hockey, what not to do and all the other wisdom about passing, skating and shooting. This was the kind of learning that appealed to me. "Go ahead, Lloyd," I said to myself, "tell me all about hockey."

Mr. Blinco leaned back in his chair and looked at us very intently. It was obvious to me that he was in no mood for trivialities.

"Listen you guys," said Blinco. "There are three broads in town we want you to stay away from. They're young, only 17 or 18, and they've already got two football players worried right now. So we're warning ya to keep away from them. That's all. Now beat it and remember what I told ya . . . " (Ankles were broken in the rush to get to the phone.)

At that point I wasn't terribly interested in women. I was consumed with the desire to make it as a pro; hopefully with the Bruins. When Lynn Patrick, the general manager-coach of the Bruins, finally called me into *his* office I knew that it wasn't going to be for a lecture on young women. "We like your training camp," he said. "We want you to continue playing the same way you have here; hitting a lot of people."

My heart was flushed with hope until the fateful "but" was delivered. "You're doin' just what we want you to do *but* we've already got six defensemen so we're gonna send you to Hershey to develop."

I was momentarily saddened but not totally depressed. A lot of players are asked to do their basic training in the American League and, deep down, I figured that I could use a year in the minors before I set the NHL on fire. Besides, I was finding Hershey a not-bad town after all. Everything there revolved around the chocolate company which operated as progressive a municipality as you'll find on the continent.

The company supported everything in Hershey, which meant that we could live cheaper than cheap. My room at the Cocoa Inn, a pretty classy place, cost only forty cents a day; and we got fresh towels and sheets daily. What I liked best about Hershey was the aroma. When it rained you could smell chocolate all over the place and I love chocolate. It was very easy for me to adjust to living in Hershey.

The money wasn't bad either. Lynn Patrick signed me for $4,500 and threw in a $1,500 bonus; not bad for a kid who would have been tickled to play for nothing. As soon as I put my name on the dotted line, Lynn took me across the street to the Hershey bank and made sure that I deposited the money. At the rate I planned to improve, my estimation was that I'd be making a five-figure salary in the not-too-distant future. Little did I know that I would be collecting $4,500 for the next nine years!

Once the season started the don't-hit-me-and-I-won't-hit-you agreement was shelved. It was dog-eat-dog in the American League. The teams had an interesting mix of rookies like myself, veterans of the NHL who were on the way down, and a strong nucleus of talented players who, for one reason or another, had not been able to make it to the top. (Many of the latter category were, in fact, of major league calibre but had been overlooked by the NHL people or simply were victims of stupidity or politics.)

The AHL, maybe even more so than the NHL, was filled with characters. One of them was Larry Zeidel, one of my first teammates on the Hershey Bears. Zeidel was a big Jewish kid out of Montreal who had grown up in a gentile neighbourhood and had learned soon enough that if he didn't fight back he wouldn't survive. In my estimation Zeidel was the toughest guy in the American League at a time when it was filled with ornery characters.

To Larry every game was like the ultimate charge of an infantryman over No Man's Land. I never knew a player who could psych himself for a game like Larry. He used to play John Phillip Sousa marches on the phonograph in the afternoon so that by nightfall he was ready to tramp onto the ice and mow down anyone in sight. Larry would fight you on his terms, on your terms; with a stick, without a stick; on the ice, off the ice; it didn't matter to him. When he played for Edmonton, Larry once got into a stick fight with Jack Evans, a tough sonofagun playing defense for Saskatoon. This battle was so bitter that they broke the shafts of their sticks over each other's heads and kept swatting away with the jagged edges of the sticks until they both could hardly be seen for all the blood dripping over their jerseys.

Zeidel's nickname was "The Rock" and he *was* like a rock. Once, during an exhibition game, he had a brutal stickfight with Eddie Shack. This one was so intense that they both were thrown out of the game. After showering and dressing, they each returned to the stands to watch the rest of the game. Shack was sitting in a seat close to the ice with his wife. Larry emerged from the dressing room a few minutes later and took a seat further up in the stands. The fury that had been burning inside him from the fight had not diminished. As he took his seat, Larry's eyes came upon Shack down below. Larry told me later that this thought kept going through his mind: "Shack is going to the NHL and I'm staying in the AHL and I probably won't get another shot at him." All of a sudden Zeidel sped down the stairs and over to Shack, corked him a beauty, and the second best fight of the night was underway; only this time the cops had to break it up.

There wasn't a player in the game who was more involved than Larry, and I speak from first-hand experience because I roomed with him. When he'd get new equipment like shin pads or gloves he would lie in bed and work the gloves in over and over again, getting ready for the game. For some reason he didn't like those gloves so he bugged management for another pair and finally got the kind he liked.

When he got the gloves he had wanted, Larrry acted like a kid on Christmas morning. He wouldn't take them off. At one point he had to go to the doctor for an examination. Obie O'Brien went with him. While Obie was in with the doctor having his knee examined the walls of the doctor's office began to shake. Bottles began falling off shelves and they thought there must be an earthquake. The doctor and Obie ran out to see what the heck was going on and found Larry pounding the walls of the doctor's office, *breaking in his new gloves.*

If you had met Larry off the ice you would never have guessed him to be a hockey player. He was mild-mannered, soft-spoken, and intelligent. Larry was always trying to one-up the opposition. He would sit in the room with me, doping out plays more like a football quarterback than a defenseman. He figured that he and I could invent a secret code that would enable us to produce impromptu plays as we were coming out of our end of the rink. The opposition used to think he was crazy, hearing him shout "X-Y" or "X-C" (a couple of our secret plays) during one of our counterattacks.

Because he was what he was—a fiercely competitive, somewhat eccentric athlete—Larry was often the unfortunate butt of practical jokes. Once, we put bobby pins in his suitcase during a road trip. When he got home his wife opened his suitcase, saw the bobby pins, and almost left him.

Those who trifled with him on the ice usually rued the day they did. Bo Elik learned that lesson. He was a promising forward for the Cleveland Barons who had been rookie-of-the-year in the American League and was earmarked for an NHL career with the Rangers, before he crossed Larry. We were playing the Barons in Hershey one night, and they were beating us. Elik would come to the center red line, dump the puck into our end and yell: "Go chase it, Larry!"

Since it was a loose puck in his end of the rink, Larry went skating in after it and lugged it out before passing it to one of our forwards. But Elik got hold of the puck again, wheeled around, came up to the red line, dumped it in again and snapped: "Go chase the puck, Larry. Chase the puck."

Instead of chasing the puck, Larry drew back his stick like a harpoonist and drove it right up Elik's nose. The blood gushed like water coming out of a whale's spout. As a postscript, Larry shot back: "Now you chase it, Bo." Elik was never the same player after this episode.

I don't want you to think that Larry didn't drive me nuts, because he did. One night I threw thirty bucks on the table during a poker game with the guys and said "Anybody who takes Zeidel as a roommate can have it." There were no takers. Another thing that drove me nuts was that Larry worried about losing his hair and would sit up half the night giving himself hot oil treatments to help save his locks!

The big thing with him was finishing first in penalty minutes. He

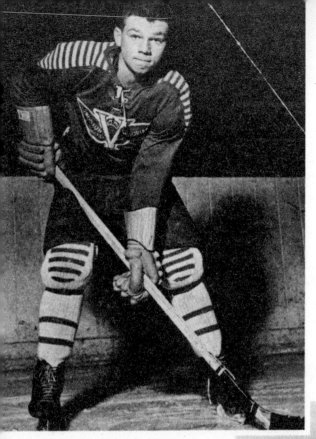

My first year pro with Hershey, age 20.

Me at fifteen playing for the Kingston Victorias, January 1949.

Tootsie and the hockey player,
March 31, 1956.

As a Boston Bruin, 1954-55.

figured that would be a good idea because it would insure that he would get his name in the paper. Even that kind of notoriety was all right with him. He would get mad at me because I was always neck and neck with him in the penalty race.

One night we were playing the Barons and I got into a terrific fight with Ian Cushenan of Cleveland. After the referee sent us to the penalty box, Cushenan and I went at it again; which burnt Larry up because he knew I was taking the penalty lead away from him. So, what did he do? Zeidel skated over to the penalty box, lifted the door off its hinges and threw the whole door on to the ice. That got him the misconduct penalty he wanted!

A couple of hours after the game I went back to our room and fell asleep. Larry, who often went for long walks at night, stormed into the room at five in the morning. He was carrying the late paper and screaming at me: "You said you didn't want to win the penalty race, Don, *but you're ten minutes ahead of me.*"

Well, Larry made up for those minutes the next night in Rochester. Gaye Stewart was the referee. He had been a hell of a good forward in the NHL, first with the Maple Leafs and then the Black Hawks, but he wasn't much of a referee. Midway through the game he handed Zeidel a ten-minute misconduct penalty and the two of them were standing alongside the penalty box arguing. For the life of me, I couldn't figure out what was bothering Stewart. I skated over to the referee and said, "Larry didn't deserve that misconduct." With that, Stewart turned to me and there was a big hunk of spit rolling right down his eye.

Playing alongside Zeidel was a help to me because there was no way I could give less than my best with him as my tailgunner. I played 63 games, got 7 goals and 13 assists for 20 points and had 125 penalty minutes. I knew I wasn't twinkletoes out there so I played it tough and management seemed pleased with the way I handled myself. At the end of our season the Bruins announced that a promising forward named Norm Corcoran and I were being called up as reserves during the Stanley Cup playoffs.

The Bruins were going up against the Montreal Canadiens in the semi-final round and neither Normie nor I figured we'd get to play. Still, it was nice that they thought enough to bring us up as spectators and, besides, we were getting $100 a game just for watching.

Well, what do you know. Fernie Flaman, just about the toughest of the Bruins defensemen, was hurt in the fourth game of the series and Milt Schmidt, who was coaching Boston at the time, decided to dress me for the fifth game. (Montreal was leading, three games to one at the time.)

When Schmidt gave me the news that I was going to dress for the fifth game, I nearly fell out of my pants. Nervous? I had never been so scared in my life. Here I was in Canada's temple of hockey, The Montreal Forum, getting my baptism of fire in the Stanley Cup playoffs. It was all unreal.

This was an exceptional game because Boom Boom Geoffrion and Rocket Richard were to be honoured for finishing one-three in the scoring race. This was the Rocket's first appearance at The Forum since being suspended by Clarence Campbell for hitting Hal Laycoe, the Bruin defenseman, over the head with his stick. Riots, vandalism and mobs had wrecked downtown Montreal because the French-Canadian fans were outraged by the suspension. Hal Laycoe was infuriated at the thought that he had to stand to honour Rocket, who had, after all, creased his head with a stick. Hal threw sticks and gloves all over the dressing room before the game trying to work out his anger.

The strangest thing happened that night. The crowd booed Boom Boom for winning the scoring championship, because he passed the Rocket in the scoring race while the Rocket had been suspended. The Rocket was still God in Montreal, and when he came out on the ice to receive his tribute, you'd have thought he was the second coming. The crowd went nuts cheering him.

As I stood there, watching Laycoe and hearing the fans cheer the Rocket and boo Clarence Campbell simultaneously, I thought to myself, "What a great league. Does this happen all the time?"

The Canadiens went up 4-0 before we even scored and went on to win, 5-1. Naturally, I wasn't happy with the defeat, but I *had* made it to the top and, better still, my mother and my Aunt Tilly were there in The Forum to see their pride and joy in action. And while I didn't get the first-star selection, there was a very encouraging item in *The Hockey News*: "Cherry declared himself in on next season's Bruins' plans by conducting himself ably in the final playoff game."

My mom and aunt rewarded me with a post-game dinner of hamburgers at a local greasy spoon and then gave me two large shopping bags full of homemade cookies and cake. I thanked them, put my mom and Aunt Tilly in a cab and then went looking for my teammates. They had mentioned that they were going to a bar called the Venus de Milo, a hockey players' hangout, also known as a den of iniquity.

I walked up the stairs of the Venus de Milo loaded down with shopping bags filled with homemade cookies. Of course, I was embarrassed just carrying the bags into a place like that, let alone the contents, which I had hoped would remain hidden from view. Finally, through the smoke I spotted my teammates and walked over to their table. Just as I got there, I heard the soft sound of a "rrrppp," looked down and saw a large hole in the shopping bag and a mountain of cookies on the floor. My buddies had fun with that one for three hours.

I woke up the next morning feeling like a million dollars. I was a Boston Bruin. There in the Montreal *Gazette* was my picture. My friends in Kingston had been able to see me on television, playing alongside all-stars like Bill Quackenbush. To top it all off, I returned to Boston with the guys on the train. We sat in the club car, drinking beer all night, talking hockey and eating my mother's cookies. I loved every minute of it.

When I returned to Kingston, I had reason to believe I would be in the NHL the following fall. Despite the pressure of the playoff game, I had played well. No goals had been scored while I was on the ice and management, I believed, liked me. There was only one problem—Lynn Patrick advised me to stay away from baseball during the summer. He knew that I had once broken my ankle and he didn't want me taking any unnecessary chances before I came to training camp.

Baseball meant almost as much to me as hockey did. I weighed Patrick's words and then gave in to my youthful emotion. I wanted to have a good time and, during the summer, baseball gave me those kinds of kicks. I said, "To hell with it, I'm going to play ball," and I did.

I lived to regret it. My idea of playing it safe was to stay in the outfield, to avoid sliding when base running and to keep in mind that the last thing I wanted to do was get hurt.

During one game, someone hit a Texas leaguer over the infield, and I ran and dove for the ball. Unfortunately, I had never learned how to dive properly so as not to get hurt. I landed on my shoulder, didn't roll with the fall, and separated my shoulder.

Worse luck, the separated shoulder required surgery. After the operation the doctor told me that I could not do any running, that I had to take it easy. Consequently, I couldn't run to get in shape for training camp. But everytime I thought of training camp, images of the other guys reporting in mint condition came to mind and I got more and more restless until, at last, I decided to do some running.

That was mistake number two. Running put too much pressure on the incision and the cut opened up and wouldn't heal. If I had been smart I would have stayed home until it did heal but I wanted to make the Bruins so badly I went to camp in a disabled condition. That was mistake number three.

The trip to Hershey didn't help the situation. I remember going to sleep one night and waking up in a pool of blood from the open cut. I had no choice but to see Hammie Moore, the Bruins' trainer. I told him that the cut wasn't staying together and asked him what I should do about it. He gave me twenty Band-Aids and that was it.

At the scrimmages I was practically helpless. I couldn't raise my arm and, consequently, had no power to shoot the puck. But it was a jungle, with every man for himself, and nobody was going to sympathize with me. I remember lining up for shots on goal at the blue line. Bill Quackenbush, the defenseman with whom I teamed in the playoff game, was next to me. Quackenbush was known for his defensive qualities and not for his shot, which was one of the weakest in the league. The puck came out to me and I took my "shot." My shoulder was so weak the puck practically crawled to the net. Quackenbush turned to the coach, Milt Schmidt, and with his words dripping with cruelty said, "Milt, that guy has a shot that's even worse than mine!"

I managed to hang in there until an exhibition game. During the scrimmage I nailed a little forward named Eddie Panagabko with a check. He did a somersault and wound up slicing open the bottom of my skate, right through to my foot. They rushed me to a doctor who would not have been qualified to deal with horses. Before I realized what was happening, he had me on the table and had begun sewing up the bottom of my foot *without anesthesia*.

The pain was so excruciating I thought I would pass out. When the doctor finished, he sent me back to my room at the Cocoa Inn to "recuperate." Some recuperation. As far as the Bruins were concerned, I was a missing person. They didn't want to hear from me or even cared what was happening. If it hadn't been for my teammates bringing me tea and coffee I could have wasted away and my passing would have gone unnoticed.

It was obvious to me that I had blown my chance of making it with the Bruins in 1955-56. Now the question was whether I had lost my shot with the Hershey Bears. Fortunately, the Bears didn't throw me to the wolves. After six weeks off skates, I finally was able to at least get back in action and the Bears put me in the lineup. I still wasn't anywhere near top shape but they bandaged my foot and got me ready for a game against the Providence Reds.

You would think that I would be somewhat discreet in my come-back. I wasn't. On my very first shift I ran into a character named Jimmy Bartlett, a real tough kid off the streets of Montreal who could really throw them. Bartlett had just run over one of our more timid players and I figured it was time I protected my own. Bartlett didn't kill me, but he took the decision. After I returned to the bench my timid teammate, who couldn't have beaten his grandmother in a one-on-one, said to me very disparagingly: "Geez, Don, I was surprised you let Bartlett take you."

Can you believe that! Here's a guy who needs me to protect him and I obliged even though my foot was killing me and I hadn't skated for six weeks, and he gives me this crap about losing the fight. I was learning fast the ways of pro hockey.

After the game my foot felt awful but I left the bandage on, took a shower and then asked the trainer to look at the wound. A callous had developed and a lot of pus had gathered around the bandage. For some reason, which I hope to learn before the century is out, the trainer was in a great big hurry. When I showed him my foot he very angrily ripped off the bandage and, in so doing, ripped off the callus.

As soon as the callus came off the blood gushed out all over the place and nearly over the suit of Frank Mathers, our coach. Mathers looked at my foot and looked at the trainer. "If Cherry isn't ready to play the next game," Mathers said, "you're fired!"

The second time around he patched up my foot with a lot more care and I *was* ready to play the next game and, in no time at all I became one of the two best defensemen on the Bears. I waited for the call from the Bruins but it never came.

I was caught in a situation I was to suffer for years to come. When Boston had an injured defenseman, they would never call me up although I was their top rookie defenseman. You see, I was too valuable for Hershey to lose. Instead, Boston would call up our fifth defenseman who wasn't playing anyway. In reality, it would have been better for me to have been the fifth defenseman, because all Boston wanted was a guy to sit on the bench. At least that guy made the NHL.

Being young, reasonably good-looking, and single, I wasted no time getting into the social swing of things (not that you could go very wild in a town of 7,500 people). Very early on Andy Branigan, one of the oldest players on the team, took me aside and offered this bit of advice: "Don, you can do one of two things: you can drink or you can run around with women but you can't do both because you have to have your sleep."

It was a tough decision but I opted for drink; not to excess, mind you, but quite a bit nevertheless. However, a chance meeting with a fellow named John Martini somewhat changed my plans. Martini was a Hershey native who followed the Bears closely. We became good friends and, one day, his wife, Anne, mentioned that she had a niece she wanted me to meet. Her name was Tootsie.

Tootsie. The only Tootsies I had ever known were bubble dancers. But I was game and, sure enough, a date was arranged and I met my Tootsie. She was no more than five feet tall and couldn't have weighed more than 100 pounds. I soon discovered that her real name was Rosemarie, later to be shortened (by me) to Rose.

I didn't know it at the time but our meeting turned out to be the best thing that ever happened to me; and certainly saved my hockey career. At the time I was following Andy Branigan's advice to a T. I wasn't running around with women but I *was* having a few pints.

Rose and I hit it off immediately although I wasn't exactly overjoyed with the bill of particulars her parents presented. For one thing I had to have Rose home by 11 p.m. which, by my standards, was still afternoon. (What I'd do is take Rose home and *then* go out drinking with the guys. I was a real sweetheart.)

For starters I gave Tootsie (soon to be Rose) the standard hockey player's line: "Are you going to the game Wednesday night?" She said: "I've never been to a hockey game." So, I put two tickets in her hand and hoped for the best.

Whether my best was good enough is a moot point. I don't know if I was trying to impress her or not but on Wednesday night I got into a terrific fight with a guy named Tony Schneider who was as tough as they came. He cut me up pretty good and ripped my sweater off. (Some time later Rose told me that she thought all Canadian hockey players were animals.) I thought it was just great but I realized that my new girlfriend might have been turned off by the bloody scene.

Despite the bloodshed Rose said "yes" when I asked her out again and, despite all odds against it, we hit it off. Why we hit it off is something I couldn't quite understand. I was a big, hotheaded, belligerent Scots-Irish-Protestant attracted to a tiny, frail, quiet Italian-Catholic. We had nothing whatsoever in common but, as they say, opposites attract and no two people in the world were more opposite than Rose and I.

For some reason I never quite cottoned to the name Tootsie, although that was *the* name she was known by at home. One of the first times I phoned her for a date, her father answered. "Is Rose there?" I asked. "Sorry, there's no Rose here," was the answer. Before I could say another word the guy hung up on me.

I phoned again. "Is Rosemarie there?" Again, her father said, "There's no Rosemarie here." *Click.*

Another dime went into the phone. "Is *Tootsie* there?" Her dad said, "Just a minute," and called Rose-Tootsie to the phone.

It was several months before I met her family; a fact that didn't exactly please Rose. After every date she would ask. "When are you comin' to dinner?" For some reason I kept stalling until, finally, she put her foot down. "If you don't come over to my house and meet my family I'm not going to go out with you anymore."

I agreed to come visit the night after our next hockey game. So, what happens? In the next game I got clipped over the eye by a stick and needed 17 stitches to close the wound. Looking in the mirror before I left for Rose's house, I figured my face resembled a needlepoint diagram more than the image of a suitor. Nevertheless, I arrived at the house and was introduced to Rose's mother, father, and sister, Paulette. Each of them seemed to do a double-take when they looked at me

While we were eating dinner, I caught her mother, father, and sister peeking at me, studying the wound over my eye and, undoubtedly, wondering what kind of character Rose had brought home with her. They simply couldn't understand how their darling daughter could go out with a person who made his living in so violent a fashion. But they also figured that if this was what their daughter wanted, it was fine with them. Despite my obvious shortcomings, I was soon made to feel right at home and, as the winter progressed I found that I was looking forward to seeing Rose more each time than I had the previous time, although marriage had yet to enter my mind.

When the season ended I returned to Kingston without having made a commitment to my steady girlfriend. Once I got home I resumed my baseball career and my usual off-season job with Kingston Utilities, but I found I couldn't get Rose out of my mind. It was then that I realized that I was deeply in love with her and decided then and there that I "would make the move." I bought a diamond ring, hopped in my car and began the thirteen hour drive from Kingston to Hershey. Of course, I didn't bother to tell Rose that I was on my way.

By sheer coincidence, I arrived at her house precisely at the moment she was, as women say, "putting a face on." I knocked on the door and Rose answered. There she was, mouth agape, with cream all over her face and not looking at all like the Rose I had left behind. For a second I had a mind to drive back home to Kingston but, of course, I knew all along that Rose was for me. We were engaged on June 12, 1955 and were married on March 31, 1956.

We spent our honeymoon in Miami Beach during a hurricane. I should have known that it was a portent of things to come.

CHAPTER EIGHT

The Siberia Of Hockey

I

With every month in Hershey, the feeling increased that my chances of ever returning to the Bruins were remote. This didn't bother Rose. She thought it was just wonderful living—and me playing—in her home town, and she got the mistaken notion that I would spend the rest of my life on defense for the Hershey Bears.

I didn't find the thought of being a lifetime Hershey Bear very distressing. I had acclimatized myself to life in the American League and found it not bad at all, albeit tough. The NHL was still a six team league in those days so the AHL was jammed full of solid hockey players dying to make it to the bigs but willing to fight it out in our league in the meantime.

When people talk about rough hockey today, they are referring to a brand of sport that is child's play compared to what it was in the AHL during the late 1950's. We didn't wear helmets. We didn't use mouth guards and most of us didn't have our own teeth. Those who ran afoul of my partner, Larry Zeidel, certainly didn't have their own teeth. Needless to say, Zeidel, The Rock, didn't have too many of his own molars either.

Once, when we were playing the Buffalo Bisons, Zeidel sliced Gordie Hannigan so badly that the blood was flowing out of his head to the beat of his heart. Hannigan was so bent on vengeance that he refused to go to the medical room for repairs until he had belted Zeidel. His teammates had to convince him to get stitched up first—he needed 30 stitches to seal the cut—and *then* come back and get Zeidel.

In those days there was hardly a raised eyebrow over such battles. Another time, we were playing Rochester and Zeidel got into a duel, with big Eddie (Spider) Mazur of the Americans. The two of them looked like a pair of gladiators hacking away at each other. They were finally separated and thrown out of the game. As Mazur walked down the corridor to the dressing room, Zeidel plastered him with a punch and the brawl erupted again. Only this time the police came with guns drawn and sent the two fighters on their separate ways.

Not only did the players fight with greater ferocity then but they could also put beer away with unmatched speed. I remember Bobby Solinger, who was a really good American League scorer, walking into a bar in Hershey with another player, Bobby Hassard. When the waitress arrived and asked what they wanted, Solinger said "Twelve beers. And two glasses!"

I was always learning. Watching Zeidel in action, I should have been more aware of the sucker punch but, naturally, I had to learn the hard way. Until my confrontation with Bob Baun of the Rochester Americans, I had always fought my battles fair and square. If someone bothered me or started in with one of our smaller players, I battled by The Marquis of Queensbury rules. No dirty stuff for Don Cherry. Then, Bob Baun came along and altered my hockey philosophy.

A fight had erupted between one of my Hershey teammates and someone on the Rochester team. The rest of us just stood around to watch. I was on the perimeter of the action, minding my own business, when—Pow!—Baun skated up alongside me and punched me in the face so hard I was knocked to the ice. But that wasn't enough, he jumped me and put what seemed like a death grip around my neck. Every time I tried to get loose he'd squeeze even tighter, figuring that I was trying to get away. Actually, I couldn't breathe and was simply trying to keep from dying.

By now there was a pile of players around and I was practically hidden from view. I recall saying to myself, "So this is how it is to die." I figure that I was about one second away from croaking when Baun finally loosened his determined grip and I began breathing again.

After that episode nobody ever suckered me. *I* was the one who did the sucker punching. I reached a point where I became so proficient at it I could sucker a guy sleeping on a bed. (In those days you learned early.)

At the end of the 1956-57 season, two things happened. One was great and the other terrible. The great event was the birth of my daughter Cindy, and the terrible event was a trade that sent me to Eddie Shore's Springfield Indians. That name sent shivers up a player's spine.

Normally, a player expects to be traded at any time and, though most of us don't like to move; we learn to accept it. But in the professional hockey world of the 1950's there was one exception—the Springfield Indians. Nobody, but *nobody*, wanted to be traded to Springfield if he could help it. There was one compelling reason for this: Eddie Shore, the Darth Vader of hockey.

The idea of being traded to Springfield was so scary that when players signed contracts (with other teams) they made sure the contract had a clause stating *that they could not, under any circumstances, be traded to Springfield.*

To understand why, you have to know about Shore, himself. Eddie was born on a wheat farm in Saskatchewan and toughened himself as a kid by hauling harvested grain to town and riding wild horses. When he made it to the NHL he had become one of the most fearless athletes in history. He was an eight-time All Star and four-time Most Valuable Player. Most important, in terms of Shore's machismo, he had accumulated more than 900 stitches in his body as well as fractures of his back, hip, and collarbone. His nose had been broken fourteen times and his jaw had been smashed five times. The man played with all the care of a souped up Ford in a demolition derby. Which is well and good, but Eddie, when he became an owner, wanted all his players to behave the same way.

After Shore retired from pro hockey he bought the Springfield hockey club in the American League and ran it in a manner that would have made Jack Benny seem like a big spender. When Eddie first got the franchise in 1940 he used to park cars outside the arena until about ten minutes before game time. Then, he'd go in, suit up, and play defense for the Indians.

Eddie didn't believe that hockey players should waste money taping their stockings so he would have his men take old tire inner tubes, cut them into rubber bands and put them around the stockings instead of tape. When the Ice Follies came to Springfield Arena, Shore would be up near the rafters, operating a spotlight, just to save a few more bucks.

If there was a way of saving a penny, Shore found it and heaven help the man who tried to take it away from him. Once, he gave a demonstration of the uses of solar energy before anyone had even heard the expression. The Springfield rink was a barnlike structure with rows of windows near the ceiling on either side of the ice. Late in the morning, the sun would shine through the windows giving the rink its only natural light and warmth. That is, *if* the sun came out.

Well, on this day, the Cincinnati Mohawks were in town to play and asked Shore if they could have the ice for a morning practice. Eddie said, sure, fine, nine o'clock the ice would be ready. So, at nine sharp, Emile Francis, the Mohawks goalie, stepped on the ice but there wasn't a light on in the arena; the place was pitch-black. Shore walked in and Francis asked him to turn the lights on so they could start the workout.

Eddie looked at Francis as if he were stupid and said, "Wait a half-hour til the sun rises and comes through the windows. Then, you'll have plenty of light."

The Mohawks had no choice but to wait, but they got the last laugh on Shore. At the game the next night their coach, King Clancy, climbed over the boards before the opening face-off and presented Shore with a lantern.

Those who played for Shore had to contend with more than his frugality. Eddie considered himself the Albert Einstein of professional hockey, and if you didn't believe it, all you had to do was ask him. He had more theories than there are pucks in the world and he was determined to pass these ideas along to his players whether they liked it or not. Usually they didn't, but they really didn't have a choice in the matter.

One of Eddie's theories was that there was an intimate connection between dancing and hockey, so one year he opened training camp by having his players tap dance in the hotel lobby and then execute ballet steps on the ice.

Shore once had a rather low-key defenseman named Don Johns. Donnie had spent a couple of years in the NHL with the Rangers but couldn't quite cut the mustard and now he was back in the minors with Shore who was determined to make a better hockey player out of him.

After a practice one day, Shore called Johns over to the side of the rink. Eddie never called a player by his first name; it was always *Mister* This and *Mister* That. "Mister Johns," he said, "you could be a better hockey player if you made some adjustments in your style."

"Okay," said Johns, "what am I doing wrong?"

"Mister Johns," Shore explained, "*you are not combing your hair right.*"

Shore meant every word of it, *that* was the scary part. He told Donnie to part his hair on the other side. This would help him because "he would have something to think about."

A couple of months under Shore were enough to send some players back to their farms in Manitoba and Saskatchewan; especially when he would inflict one of his special techniques on them. Once, at a practice, Eddie had his players churning up and down the ice taking shots on goal. Suddenly, Eddie blew his whistle and called a rookie over to him. "Young man," he said, "don't you know you should be skating with your legs closer together?" And without waiting for an answer Shore pulled a piece of rope from his pocket, tied the kid's legs together, and then ordered him to skate. Can you imagine what it was like skating with your legs tied?

Since Shore, himself, was virtually immune to pain he assumed that everyone else reacted the same way. After one game, when Donnie Johns had been cut for forty stitches in his leg and was immobilized in a hospital bed, Shore visited him and said, "You ought to be ready to play soon."

"But, Eddie," snapped Johns, "I can't even turn my leg . . ."

Shore would have none of that back talk. "Listen, Mister Johns, when I played hockey I once had a hundred stitches in my leg, and I was out only three—no, two-and-a-half—days."

No club in the history of sports worked on a tighter budget than Shore's Springfield Indians. Eddie considered it extremely generous of him to allow his players fifteen cents to tip taxi drivers. It didn't take long for such notoriety to spread around the league and soon there wasn't a cabby anywhere who would pick up the Springfield Indians.

Another way Shore would stick it to his players was with contract clauses. He had guys on the Indians who would have it written in their contracts that if they scored 30 goals or more a season, they'd get a big bonus from Eddie. But Shore had a way of getting out of that: as soon as the player in question reached 29 goals, Eddie would bench him for the rest of the season.

Many who survived the Springfield Siberia look back on the experience with a mixture of horror and humour and strange as it may seem, from one of Shore's championship teams, fourteen players became professional coaches and another, Brian Kilrea, a great Junior A coach.

There was something funny about the sight of Shore tying a goalkeeper to the net during a practice session. Eddie did this because he wanted to get the message across to the goalie that goaltenders should never fall to the ice.

Goalie Don Simmons was the victim of many a Shore theory. When the goalie was suffering through a particularly long slump, Eddie was convinced that Simmons had developed a mental block about goaltending. Shore insisted that Simmons return to his home in Port Colborne, Ontario, for a rest. "Go home to your mother," Shore suggested. "Help her around the house. Wash the dishes and do the chores for her. That'll take your mind off hockey. While you're at it, find a studio and take some dancing lessons."

The closest a goalie ever came to suffering a nervous breakdown on the ice happened in Springfield because of Shore. The Indians were playing the Cleveland Barons and referee Frank Udvari had called a penalty against Springfield that Shore felt his team didn't deserve. Eddie went bananas and when it became apparent that Udvari would not change his mind—when does a referee *ever* change his mind—Shore called all of his skaters to the bench. All, that is, with the exception of goalie Don Simmons.

When Udvari realized what was happening, he skated over to Shore and said: "I'm giving you ten seconds to put a team on the ice and then I'm dropping the puck."

Eddie looked the referee straight in the eye and ordered his players onto the bench. Except, of course, for Simmons who was dolefully standing in front of the Indians' net.

Udvari watched the ten seconds click off and then moved into the face-off circle where the five Cleveland players were awaiting the start of play. The referee handed the puck to the linesman and he dropped it in front of Bo Elik of Cleveland. As soon as the puck hit the ice Bo pushed it ahead with his stick and along with his four teammates charged in on poor Donny Simmons.

The Barons were so stunned by the no-defense situation that they fought among themselves over who was going to take the shot. Elik finally let the puck go and missed the net completely. The Barons retrieved the puck and fired again . . . and again . . . and again with all their shots going wild. Simmons finally dove on top of the loose puck, stopping play. By this time Shore must have felt some compassion for the goalie because he ordered his other five skaters back on the ice.

Anyone who crossed Shore became a "Black Ace", one of the many extras he kept on the squad—but wouldn't dress—for punitive purposes. The Black Aces had to work extra hard in practice and were always available to play should any of the regulars enrage Eddie even more. In addition to scrimmaging with the team, the Black Aces were required to do odd jobs around the arena such as painting seats, selling programs, making popcorn and blowing up hundreds of balloons before the ice shows. When Kenny Schinkel was a Black Ace, he was helping Shore change a light bulb in the Coliseum's high ceiling. To do so Eddie had to climb on a platform which the players pushed from bulb to bulb. At one point Shore was hanging onto an overhead cable with one hand and screwing in a bulb with his other hand when Schinkel "accidentally" pushed the tower from underneath him. Eddie was just hanging there from the cables like a trapeze artist. Kenny finally thought he would see The Old Man afraid and screaming; but he hung by one hand and calmly looked down and said "Mr Schinkel, would you please return the platform to its rightful place?" (You just couldn't beat him.) Schinkel finally got around to pushing the platform back so he could get down.

Few who crossed Shore escaped without some form of retribution. He had been known to lock a referee in his dressing room if he thought the ref had handled a game poorly or he would grab the loudspeaker microphone and denounce a referee (or an opposing player) for everyone in the arena to hear.

One night, during a game against Cleveland, he went berserk after referee Lou Farelli disallowed a Springfield goal even though the goal judge, Bill Tebone, had flashed the red light signifying the point. Eddie ordered Tebone to leave his post behind the net. He said that if the referee could overrule the goal judge there was no point in having one. When Farelli ordered Shore to get the goal judge back on the job, Eddie just ignored him and the game finally resumed without one important official.

Many of us who played in Springfield learned a lot of hockey from Shore. He was a masterful teacher and would spend as much time on the ice as any player would require, but he had so many quirks it was difficult to determine whether you suffered more from his idiosyncracies or benefited more from his teachings.

Schinkel, who played for Eddie more than most guys, was a classic example. Eddie would pay closer attention to him because he regarded Kenny as a son. If Schinkel didn't feel well Eddie would worry about him and prescribe one of his many instant cures.

One night Shore noticed that Schinkel was sniffling. It was the common cold that has baffled medical science. Eddie suggested that Kenny take twelve drops of iodine. Schinkel took the advice and it worked!

Another time, Schinkel was complaining of feeling lethargic. Eddie looked him over and suggested that Kenny was suffering from yellow jaundice. The Old Man prescribed his special "Marlet Treatment." This was one of Shore's favourites and he used it on several players. It was a laxative made up of a number of oils.

Schinkel tried half the prescription and, almost instantly, lost twelve pounds. He stopped the Marlet Treatment then and there. "If I had taken the whole thing," Kenny said, "I would have been dead!"

I give Shore credit, though. Some people are nuts and never realize it, at least Eddie had an inkling. He once said; "Most of us are a little crazy in some form or other. The thing is some of us admit it."

This was the man who would be my boss for four seasons. I was upset because I realized that my hopes for a big-league career were sinking fast. Poor Rose took it even harder. She had thought we were going to stay in Hershey for the rest of our lives. Now, she learned differently. We packed the car, bundled up our daughter, Cindy, put her in a crib in the back of the car, and headed for Springfield. We hadn't driven ten miles when the canvas ripped off the bags we had tied down on top of the car. Then it started raining and everything was ruined.

I wondered: could anything that happened with Eddie Shore be worse than this? It didn't take me long to discover the answer—in the affirmative!

CHAPTER NINE

The Siberia Of Hockey II

Having heard so much about Eddie Shore before actually meeting him, I had pictured someone large and ominous. That, however, was not the Eddie Shore who shook my hand and welcomed me to the Springfield Indians. Eddie Shore, in living colour, was surprisingly small and bald, but obviously tough. He had many scars on his face and even though he was in his 60's he appeared to be in mint condition.

In no time at all I learned what Shore thought of me. He gave me a nickname—The Madagascar Kid. I think that's where he would have sent me, given the opportunity. One of the things he disliked about my style was my skating. By his standards it was lousy. "Mr. Cherry," he would say, "If you could visualize that in reality your manoeuverability is nil."

For all his idiosyncracies, Shore did have a magnetic quality. While we rebelled against him we also listened to him, if not all the time then most of the time. But we were always trying to go one-up on Eddie whenever possible. I succeeded once during training camp. It was an exceptionally warm day and a dense fog hung over the ice. Every so often the players would skate around holding towels in an attempt to dispel the fog, but it always came back.

During the workout, Shore became displeased with my skating (as usual) and called me over for a private meeting. I skated to the boards, listened to his harangue for about a minute and, even though he hadn't finished, I began to slowly back away while the fog enveloped me. In two seconds I had become thoroughly lost in the fog, but I could hear Shore roaring: *"I know you're there Cherry. You're goin' to pay for this once the fog lifts."*

Of course, the fog lifted and I paid for it. I became one of Shore's favourite targets, but I was in good company. There were always guys on the team who were willing to collaborate in an attempt to get even with The Old Man. Once, he had us on the ice practising two-on-ones—two forwards skating in on one defenseman. Eddie was berating me as usual about my hockey ability or lack thereof, with his back to the drill while I was facing the drill. The defenseman, backing up at full speed, didn't see Eddie. Naturally, Eddie couldn't see what was happening either. I could have warned Eddie, because I was facing the play, but I thought, "What the hell!" I stepped aside just as the big defenseman hit Eddie in the back. Eddie flew six feet in the air and so did the defenseman. Nobody laughed, because it would have meant their lives, but it was a great feeling. As usual, I paid for it later.

One day he had me and another defenseman named Duane Rupp—with whom he had a separate beef—stay on the ice after practice. He had us skate around and around the ice *for four hours and twenty minutes*. Torturous as it was, Rupp and I never gave in. Then Shore had the arena lights turned off and we skated in the dark. By this time, the only way we could keep going was with some sustenance. Fortunately, some of our teammates brought us some tea with honey; without it, we certainly would have collapsed. I asked Eddie the next day why the punishment, and he answered "When I was instructing you yesterday, you glanced at the clock behind my head. When I talk to you, you look me in the eye."

Shore was only half of my problem; the other half was coach Pat Egan. He was a former NHL defenseman, built like a boxcar. Pat had been a tough hombre when he skated for the Boston Bruins, but Shore had completely intimidated him. Whenever The Old Man snapped his fingers, Egan jumped. He did everything Eddie asked him to do, including a paint job on Shore's house.

Egan used to take out his hostility on the players. He liked to make like a tough guy, but those of us who saw him in action with Shore knew different. Once, during a practice Egan said, "I'd like to take you, right now, back to my room and have it out with you."

It was big talk, sounded good, but there was a catch to it—my job. Egan knew that if I did go back to his room and beat the crap out of him, *I* would be the guy who would get suspended for beating up the coach. That stupid, I was not.

I finally nailed Egan in an East-West game with the Black Aces. He wasn't wearing any equipment and he was scrimmaging with us (his first mistake).

He picked up the puck behind his net and roared out of his end. I came running at him. He knew I was coming, but he tried to pretend he didn't know I was after him. What he didn't know was that I knew he was faking, and that he intended to jump in the air at the last minute before I got to him to try and hurt me.

Just as he went to jump, I cross-checked him and broke my stick on his shoulder. He was hurt, but I have to give him credit for one thing: he finished practice.

Even though Egan was the coach, Shore was on the ice most of the time, giving instruction. He loved to trade shoves with the players. He would hit a guy on the shoulder and send him flying backwards. Then, he'd say, "Hit me in the shoulder." The player would hit The Old Man, but Eddie would be ready. He would bend his knees in his favourite stance and could always handle the blow. "You see," he would gloat, "I don't move. I have my skates planted right."

We used to let Eddie get away with this little game because if we didn't, we would all pay; until the day Kent Douglas joined us. Kent was that rare kind of individual who stands up for his rights no matter what. He was tough as nails and wouldn't take anything from anybody.

When I saw The Old Man hit him on the shoulder, I said to the guys, "Uh oh, watch this. This is going to be fun." After Shore hit Kent, Douglas said, "Don't do that Eddie." Eddie said, "Oh yeah? Now you hit me." Before I could get to Kent he had knocked Shore ass over tea kettle. Kent would never play "the game" with Shore.

The Old Man and Douglas loved to argue over hockey points. Whenever we wanted to kill time we'd tell Kent to ask Eddie a question. Then we'd stand around for an hour and a half while the two argued about it.

Shore would argue with anybody. Cal Gardner was another. He had been in the NHL for a number of years with the Rangers, Maple Leafs and Bruins. Now he was winding down his career in Springfield. At this point in time it would have been foolish for anyone to start tampering with Gardner's skating style, but that didn't stop Shore. He bawled out Gardner for not using the Shore technique. Gardner was fuming.

Cal said to Eddie one day, "Eddie, how many years did you play in the NHL?" Eddie said, "Eight." Cal said, "Yeah Eddie? Well, I played twelve." I thought somebody finally had Eddie, but Eddie shot back, "Yes, Mr. Gardner, but if you'd played my way, you'd have lasted sixteen years!" You couldn't top The Old Man.

The way Shore figured it, there was always a better way of doing things—his. Our goalie, Claude Evans, once came up with a shutout in a 5-0 win. After the game Shore walked into the dressing room and fined Evans $50 *because he didn't bend his knees.*

I didn't bend my knees very well either. They were always stiff, like tree stumps and there was nothing I—or Shore—could do to make them more supple. Once, when my knees were particularly stiff, he set a club record by calling me over for a bawling out five times in two minutes.

There were a few rare players who could do no wrong. Bill Sweeney was one of them. He was a smallish center, who was Rangers' property, but never could seem to make it in the NHL. He had the "rep" of being too slow. With us, he was the number one scorer, the number one dart player, the number one golfer and not a bad drinker at that.

Sweeney had a bulbous red nose and, in his own youthful way, bore a striking resemblance to the great comic W. C. Fields. For five years I called Sweeney "W.C." and he had no idea why I had tagged him with the nickname. One day, we were walking down the street and passed a theatre. There was a big billboard in front with a picture of W. C. Fields, his nose redder than ever.

I noticed that Sweeney was looking at the billboard in a funny way, not quite sure what was bothering him. He looked at Fields, then he looked at me, then he stared back at the billboard and it finally hit him. "You sonofabitch," he shouted. "All these years you've been making fun of me and I never knew it."

Sweeney was one of those gifted players who, in the era of the six-team NHL, was buried in the AHL for life. Another like him—who got a reprieve late in his playing career—was Barclay Plager, a hard-nosed defenseman. Barclay was the victim of one of the great fix-the-back capers.

Anyone who played for Shore was liable to be given treatment for a number of ailments and back problems were one of his specialties. The trouble was that Shore's treatments were often worse than the ailment itself, a fact of which we were all well aware.

One day we were sitting in the dressing room, kibitzing around, when Shore came walking down the hall. After a practice, the dressing room door would be left open. There was a mirror on it enabling someone in the dressing room to see who was walking down the corridor. On this day, Brian Kilrea, one of our better forwards who was given to pranks, noticed Shore coming. When The Old Man was within hearing range, Brian spoke loud enough for Shore to hear, "Gee Barclay, is that right—*is your back really hurting you?*"

That's all Plager had to hear. He knew that the Indians had had a defenseman named Bob McCord who had complained about a bad back. Shore got him on the table and ruined his back so badly that he couldn't play. Shore sent him to Three-Rivers. If you were smart, you didn't let Shore hear about your bad back.

The Old Man walked over to Plager. "Your back bothering you?" he asked.

"No, no," said Barclay, "my back's okay."

"Get on the table Mister Plager."

"No, Honestly, Eddie. My back's all right."

"GET ON THE TABLE, MISTER PLAGER."

Barclay had no choice. He climbed on the table and Shore went to work on him, pulling and jerking until poor Plager was a mess.

By this time Kilrea and the rest of us had executed an orderly retreat to a nearby bar and were downing a few when one of the boys walked in. "Did you hear what happened to Barclay?" the guy asked. "They put him in an ambulance and took him to the hospital. His back was so bad he couldn't straighten up. You better look out, Brian. The last thing we heard while they were putting him in the ambulance was Barclay screaming, 'I'm going to kill Kilrea!'"

Shore was always trying to straighten us out in one way or another; sometimes in the most unlikely manner. There was the time when he sent out invitations to the wives of all the players. They were asked to report to our dressing room at 7:30 p.m. Naturally, the women figured that The Old Man was throwing a party for the team. They put on their fanciest dresses, assuming that, for once, Shore would give us a good time.

One by one the women filtered into the smelly, liniment-filled room, jock straps hanging on pegs, smelly underwear (brown from never being washed) on the benches and nothing but ugliness all around. At last, The Old Man walked in. He looked around at the women. "The club is not doing too well and there's a very good reason for this state of affairs. *You ladies are giving your husbands too much sex!* To prove my point, I'm going to ask Floyd Smith, who is newly-married, to send his wife home." That was the end of the "party." Smitty's wife Audrey was devastated. She turned to Rose and said, "It wouldn't be so bad if it were true but it's not. I wish it was."

To say the women were embarrassed would be the understatement of the half-century. But those who played for Shore for more than a year became inured to embarrassment because there *always* seemed to be something that The Old Man would do to inspire red faces. The most obvious was his practices. One day he decided that it would be a good idea if all the players walked around the arena squatting like ducks. Just by chance, Jimmy Bartlett, who had played for the Rangers, was in the Coliseum watching us and was beside himself with laughter.

Shore noticed Bartlett and summoned one of our forwards, Harry Pidhirny. "Mister Pidhirny," he asked, "who is that young gentleman with the smart remarks?"

"That's Jimmy Bartlett."

"Fine. Thank you very much."

A week later Jimmy Bartlett was a member of the Springfield Indians. Jimmy led the team in goals and assists throughout the playoffs, but when we went into the finals against Rochester, Shore had Egan bench him. He never played another shift and, actually, his career was ruined. Bartlett didn't make it back to the NHL after that. You couldn't beat The Old Man.

Those of us who played for Shore always wondered whether there was anybody in this world capable of trimming The Old Man's sails. We got our answer in the fall of 1957. The Bruins, who had operated Hershey as their American League farm team, decided to link up with Springfield. Shore would still own the club but the Bruins would operate it and a little, bald guy named George (Punch) Imlach was named the manager of the Indians, and later the coach.

If you didn't know better you wouldn't figure that Imlach could handle The Old Man, but Punch had been around a long time and owned an inner toughness that comes from working the minors for many years. Right from the start I liked Punch. He had a very positive attitude about life in general and hockey in particular. He knew that I had just about given up on making the NHL but he encouraged me nonetheless. "You should still try for the big league," he said. "Mark my words—someday I'll be in the National Hockey League." I laughed to myself when he said that. Punch Imlach in the NHL. What a joke! But, by gosh, he did it, in spades.

What he couldn't do was take enough wind out of Shore's sails to last very long in Springfield. The problem with Punch was that he'd come to the Indians from Quebec, where he had had a free hand running the Aces. Even though the Bruins ran the Indians, Imlach still had to deal with Shore at the arena and that meant trouble.

Before the season was even half over Shore had tried to get the Bruins to fire Imlach at least three times. But the Bruins—who were still operated by Lynn Patrick—would have none of that. By the middle of November, Imlach and Shore weren't even talking to each other, and they both occupied offices in the same building.

A major cause of the friction was the dual operation of the team. Shore owned some of the players on the team and the Bruins owned the rest. Naturally, Shore wanted his skaters played a certain way and when Imlach disobeyed there was hell to pay.

The actual split between the two occurred over the issue of goaltenders. The Indians carried two goalies, Claude Evans, a pudgy goaltender who rarely left his feet, and Al Millar, who was less fat and less orthodox. Shore owned Evans and the Bruins owned Millar.

Imlach was partial to Millar. Al had played for him in Quebec and the Aces had won the Edinburgh Trophy, emblematic of the senior championship of Canada. He was also the best goalie in the Quebec Senior Hockey League. Millar's credentials were a hell of a lot better than Evans'. But Evans had one thing in his favour—Shore liked him, in his way.

We usually played our home games on Saturday night at the Eastern States Coliseum in West Springfield and normally made our goaltending plans a day or two in advance. Since Imlach was both g.m. and coach of the team it was Punch's job to decide which goaltender to use.

Shore didn't buy that kind of thinking. The Old Man summoned Punch into his office and demanded to know who would be in the nets on Saturday. Imlach told him it would be Millar.

The Old Man said nix to that. He would play Evans and that was all there was to it. Imlach started to give him an argument but Shore wouldn't budge. "Are you giving me an ultimatum?" Punch asked.

Shore didn't answer. He just stared at Punch, hoping that, sooner or later, Imlach would crack, agree to play Evans and the dispute would be ended, then and there. But Imlach returned Shore's stare. Finally, after what seemed like an eternity. The Old Man said, "Yes, it is an ultimatum." With that, Punch thanked him and left the room.

On Saturday night Al Millar, Punch's man, was in the net. He had told Shore that *he*, Imlach, was running the show, and if Eddie didn't like it, he knew what he could do.

The rest of us were horrified because we had been around Shore long enough to know that even if you win a battle with The Old Man, as Punch had done, you're apt to lose the war in the long run. Imlach knew that as well as anyone, including Millar.

Sure enough, Shore sought retribution—and got it. In no time at all Millar was traded; not once but four times that season and, I'm sure, it was because he was Imlach's man in the battle of the wills. So, while Millar was bouncing around from Chicoutimi, Buffalo, Boston, (he even played a couple of games for the Bruins) and Quebec City, Evans was our goalie and, the damnedest thing was, he turned out to be good enough to get us into the finals.

Imlach didn't hurt either. He turned out to be one hell of a good leader; we respected him for his inspirational qualities as well as his knowledge of the game. I think even Shore would acknowledge that. In fact, after we had been eliminated in the Calder Cup finals Punch ran into Eddie in the corridor at Eastern States Coliseum.

The Old Man looked at his upstart manager. "I guess you had yourself a pretty good year, son," Shore said.

"I guess so," said Punch. Then, each went his separate way. Imlach got a job with the Toronto Maple Leafs the following season and turned a terrible club into a contender almost overnight. Within a few years he had won four Stanley Cup championships and was the toast of the hockey world.

Punch got to be a pretty big man but he never forgot the little guys with whom he had once worked. I remember him visiting Springfield long afterward and I happened to be standing in the corner of the rink. Shore had suspended me, and I was feeling mighty low. Punch was with his entourage, led by King Clancy, and he very easily could have ignored me in the crowd. But he stopped, walked over, shook my hand and immediately asked about Rose and the family. I was so touched, tears came to my eyes. To think that a man with four Stanley Cup Championships would walk out of his way to come and talk to me: Everyone was watching him, with his fuzzy cream-coloured fedora, and as he talked to me, my heart swelled with pride. The whole episode picked me up when I was at another low point in my career. I was having a hard time even practising with the Black Aces. The little episode had a profound impact on me.

When Punch left the club, Shore cancelled his agreement with the Bruins and took over complete control of the Indians. Needless to say the zanyness never ceased, only the characters were different. We had a tall, skinny goalie named Jacques Caron who didn't follow The Old Man's directions very carefully. One day they got into an argument that led to one of the most bizarre scenes imaginable; right out of Laurel and Hardy. First, they shouted at each other, then they started swinging and then the two grown men stood there, kicking each other in the shins!

Another time Caron complained of a stiff neck within earshot of Shore. When Jacques realized that The Old Man had heard him, he quickly said, "No, Eddie, it's all right."

Too late. Shore moved Jacques into a chair right in the middle of the dressing room and grabbed him around the head. "Relax," he shouted.

The trouble was, every time Shore shouted "Relax!" you'd get more tense. With his big hands, he began twisting Caron's head. There was no way the poor goalie could relax. Well, the tighter Jacques got, the harder Eddie twisted his head and neck. We all sat there silently watching, not daring to say a word as the ritual went on and on.

Shore kept twisting and pulling until he finally gave Caron one especially empathic swing of the head. At that moment Dennis Olson couldn't contain himself any longer. "Eddie," he inquired, "did you ever have one of those things come off in your hands?" Even Eddie smiled at that one.

Stiff necks and sore backs were not the only ailments to avoid if Shore was around. He also had cures for the common cold. Jimmy Anderson, poor fellow, one of our leading scorers, also led in the cold-catching department. For some reason, Anderson was also the target of many practical jokes and Eddie's whipping boy. Once, in the middle of winter, some of the guys sneaked into the dressing room while Jimmy was out on the ice practising. They got a big pair of scissors and cut the pants from his suit at the knees. Since Jimmy didn't have any other pants he put on the newly-trimmed pair and walked out to his car in the parking lot. Who should come walking in the other direction but The Old Man. "You idiot," he yelled at Anderson. "No wonder you have the flu; walking around in the middle of winter wearing Bermuda shorts!" Jimmy, as usual, paid later.

My medical encounters with Shore were no less comfortable. He learned that I had broken a toe during a game and insisted that I try his cure. He had two tubs, one with boiling hot water and the other with ice water, sitting next to each other. He insisted that I stick my leg into the boiling water, right up to my knee. "Eddie," I pleaded, "can't I just stick my toe in the water. Isn't that sufficient?"

But, sadist that he was, Shore would have none of that. I inserted my leg in the cauldron as tears rolled down my cheeks. But it taught me a valuable lesson; don't let The Old Man learn about an injury because the cure always was worse than the wound.

Only a precious few escaped Shore's black list. Lorne (Gump) Worsley, the goalie, was one of them. He had been a star with the New York Rangers but had run into difficulties with the Rangers' management and had been sent down to Springfield as a disciplinary move. The Gump had heard all the horror stories about Shore, how we had to sweep out the rink, blow up balloons for ice shows, pop the popcorn for the concessionaires and all the rest. But Shore was more than civil with Worsley.

Gump was called back to the NHL within weeks, but not before he had scared my wife, Rose, almost half to death. It happened this way: Gump had left his family in New York and had no place to stay in Springfield. He asked if he could stay at our house. I said, sure, it was okay, but I hadn't cleared it with Rose.

Gump and I got back to the house at about three in the morning after a few. Rose had our baby, Cindy, in our big bed leaving Cindy's crib empty. Now, don't ask me why, but The Gump, who was called "The Beer-belly goalie," *climbed into my daughter's crib* and fell asleep.

Snoring to beat the band, Gumper slept through the night and into the morning. When Rose awakened, she instinctively made her way to the crib where she noticed a hand draped over the side. She quietly tip-toed to me and shook me awake saying, "Don, Don, there's a little boy sleeping in Cindy's crib." I said, with my head pounding from a hangover, "Aw that's just the Gumper, go back to sleep." Hockey wives sure have to be understanding.

The Rangers also shipped us another funny man named Larry Cahan, who needed to be punished, so he had to serve some time in Siberia (Springfield). He was a huge defenseman who had legs as big as tree stumps.

Larry is probably the funniest man I've ever met and always seemed to be in trouble with The Old Man. For instance, we played Buffalo one Sunday night, and Larry wanted to go out with his buddies in Buffalo. So he told our coach, Glen Sonmor, that he wanted to miss practice Monday in Stamford, Ontario, to visit his sick mother in Toronto (who happens to live in Vancouver).

Glen said, "All right," but told Larry to be at practice for sure Tuesday at 8 a.m. I said to Larry, "Be careful. The Old Man would love to catch you at something so that he can suspend you."

Larry proceeded to go out on a two-day binge. But he had told his buddies that no matter what, he had to be at the Stamford rink at 8 a.m. Tuesday.

Well, Tuesday morning at 2 a.m. they are all going home and Larry had passed out. One guy said, "What are we going to do with Larry? He has to be at the rink by 8 a.m." A second friend said, "Let's break into the

Stamford rink and leave him there." A third friend said, "Cripes, he'll freeze in that hatbox." And a fourth friend added, "No he won't. He's got enough antifreeze in his system to keep him going."

So they all laughed, broke into the arena, took him to one of the dressing rooms and left him there. They thought it was a great joke. When we arrived at the rink we went looking for Cahan and seeing no Larry, we walked to the pitch dark dressing room. Somebody flicked on the light and I walked into a corner where I heard some strange noises. There was Larry stretched precariously on a bench, wearing his hat, coat, and gloves. His arms were folded as if he were in a coffin. I thought he was dead; he was half-frozen.

Sure enough, he was still breathing, so we shook him a few hundred times and got him to open his eyes. Eventually, he was sober enough to tell us the story. Having Cahan around made life worth living.

Another fellow who got stuck out in the cold was my old buddy, Floyd Smith. This was another mid-winter scene in another cold spot, Buffalo. We were in the team bus, ready to take off when Smitty decided to get a large bottle of Coca-Cola, leaving with the words: "Don't forget me, guys." We were all in our shirt sleeves—Floyd as well—waiting to get a card game going.

Somebody opened a new deck and we got right into the game, forgetting about good buddy Floyd. Meanwhile, he had bought his Coca-Cola (the store had been more crowded than he had figured) and dashed back into the cold in his shirtsleeves to rejoin us on the bus.

Sorry, Floyd, but there was no bus. Nobody had done a head count and we were so involved in the cards that nobody noticed we had taken off without Smitty. There he was standing on a Buffalo street corner in below-zero weather in his shirtsleeves. The bus was about 50 miles out of Buffalo when it suddenly dawned on me that Smitty wasn't in the card game. I called down the aisle of the bus: "Hey, Smitty, don't ya wanna play cards?" There was no reply, so I got up and went looking for him. No Smitty. Then, it dawned on me that we had left him behind in Buffalo with a large Coke. I suggested that we go back for him but the answer was an unequivocal "No way!"

Smitty had to catch a plane to meet us at our next destination. Our bus driver, Paul Le May ("All the way with Paul Le May") was not one to wait for anyone. He could move that bus, all right, but once, enroute to Rochester, he was barrelling along so fast that he ran into a huge partridge that couldn't fly out of the way of the windshield. The front windows shattered and glass went flying all over Pat Egan, who was coaching at the time. Nobody was terribly hurt; except the partridge. Egan got hold of it and when we got to the hotel that night he had it cooked for dinner. We never wasted much in the minors.

As far as I was concerned it was one of the few good moves Egan made while coaching the Indians. My relationship with him was bad from the beginning and deteriorated after that. The relationship reached the point of white hot hatred by the 1959-60 season. My playing had nothing to do with it; it was a question of an irretrievable personality conflict and, at the time, Egan had the upper hand. He knew that if I really busted his chops he could send me to the farm club in Three-Rivers, Quebec. If Springfield was the Siberia of hockey, Three-Rivers was Devil's Island (or so we were led to believe).

For some reason, I felt pretty secure about staying in Springfield. We had just moved to another apartment, had finished putting the stereo, the fish tank and the television in place, and then I left for a game with Providence. After the game I went out with the boys for the usual beers and got home at about two in the morning.

I couldn't find Rose. She wasn't in the living room and she wasn't in the kitchen, so I walked upstairs to the bedroom and there she was, fully dressed, standing on the bed. "What in hell are you doin' up there?" I asked.

"You're a nice guy! I've been here for two hours," she said. "There are mice all over the place. Take a look."

Sure enough, the mice were acting as if it was *their* apartment. I set up a mouse trap and we got into bed. *Snap!* The trap went off. I got out of bed, emptied the trap and put another piece of cheese in it. Got back into bed and began dozing when—*Snap!* It went off again. Within an hour there were ten more *Snaps!*

The next morning I went to see the landlady and she promised to bring the fumigator over in a day or two. But that was all academic, as it turned out. That day I showed up for practice and Egan walked into the dressing room and handed me a letter. "Here's a little present for you," he said with a smile on his face.

I opened the letter. "Please report by tomorrow afternoon to Three-Rivers, Quebec." Egan must have thought that I would haul off and belt him. Nothing of the kind. I looked up, smiled and said: "Thanks a lot, Pat old boy, toodle-oo!"

Now it was time to say good-bye to The Old Man. I shook his hand and said, "By the way, Eddie, how *do* I get to Three-Rivers from here?"

"Nothing to it, Madagascar. You go up through New Hampshire, then over to Vermont and when you hit the Canadian border, turn right."

"Thanks a lot, Eddie. I'll see ya around someday."

As I drove home I thought, "Poor Rose. Wait til she hears where we're going now! Oh well, she'll be rid of the mice, anyway!"

CHAPTER TEN

Three-Rivers Or Bust

As soon as I learned that I was destined for Three-Rivers in the beautiful province of Quebec, I was reminded of the advice Rose's mother had given her before her first visit to Kingston: "When you reach the Canadian border, make sure you put on your sweater."

I figured I would need more than a sweater in Three-Rivers. A French-English dictionary would be a basic requirement along with a road map and a nice warm coat, although I never did find the coat that was cozy enough for 30 degree below zero cold.

In one hour we packed all our belongings in the big Oldsmobile 98 (with bald tires) and headed north like a trio of gypsies. I drove while Rose and Cindy occupied the back seat. The rest of the car was packed with every bit of belonging we could squeeze into the fuselage including a week's supply of groceries. (We couldn't afford to throw them away.)

Scrupulously following Shore's directions, I made a right turn at the Canadian border and pulled up in front of a coffee shop. By now it was pitch-dark and we had absolutely no idea where we were, other than the fact that it wasn't Tahiti. On top of everything, the engine conked out.

I went inside and asked a guy for help but his French and my English didn't get along. He shrugged his shoulders and it was then that yours truly realized that he really *was* lost. There was only one thing to do, bring Rose and Cindy into the coffee shop, warm up, say a prayer, and then try the car again.

Meanwhile, Rose was worried about her future home life in her new faraway land. "Do they have TV in Three-Rivers?" she asked. "Oh, yeah," I said. "Do they speak English?" she wondered. "Oh, yeah," I said. I really, "Oh, yeahed" her this time but the truth was I had no idea what Three-Rivers would be like.

Having warmed up in the coffee shop, we decided to give our gas guzzler another try. Our prayers were answered. The motor turned over and we plunged into the darkness of the Quebec countryside in search of Three-Rivers.

Sure enough, we missed it and wound up on the wrong side of the St. Lawrence River. We had to catch a ferry back to the other side and while we were aboard I walked over to the captain's cabin, and soon heard a familiar sound: cheers from a hockey rink. The Montreal Canadiens game was on the air with Danny Gallivan. I felt a tingling sensation, listening to the ebb and flow of the crowd roar, but then I began getting depressed. I should have been there, I felt, and here I was stranded on a ferry boat somewhere in the St. Lawrence heading for a town I had never heard of before. I looked up at the black, Canadian sky and said, "God, what have I done to deserve this?"

I knew the answer. I had stood up to Pat Egan. I had stood up to Eddie Shore and I was arrogant, so *this* was the price I paid. It was as simple as that. Nothing could help, I knew that, so the trick was to make the best of Three-Rivers. The only problem was, Rose and Cindy were paying right along with me. As my father used to say, "You reap what you sow." One day I'm going to have to change.

We finally found the town, moved in to a motel and, since it was so late, decided to leave all our belongings, the groceries and what not, in the car until the next morning. It was not one of my smarter moves.

I got up the next morning and said to Rose, "Look, I have to go to the rink for an early game. You and Cindy catch breakfast at the motel restaurant and I'll see you later." I got in my car to go to the rink and noticed that all the groceries were frozen, all the jars broken. I can still see the broken ketchup bottle and that red substance all over everything.

My welcome to the Three-Rivers hockey club was warm and pleasant. We won the game, I played well and the boys liked me enough to invite me out for a beer before dinner. My conscience said I should get back to Rose and Cindy but my new teammates were so friendly and hospitable that I decided it would be an affront to them if I refused. Besides, I figured that Rose would be watching TV and all would be well at home. So I began drinking and drinking until, finally, at about ten p.m. I couldn't persuade my conscience that there was any more reason to stay at the bar.

I walked into the room and there was Rose with tears in her eyes.

"What happened?" I asked. "I'm starving," said Rose. The motel restaurant was closed on Sundays and I had been out with the car, having a good time with the boys. Poor Rose and Cindy hadn't eaten for thirty-five hours! There was only one thing to do; I bundled her and Cindy up and took them back to the bar where I had been drinking with the boys. I got Rose a sandwich to tide her over until our next CARE package arrived.

It didn't take Rose very long to discover that Three-Rivers was not the paradise Springfield had been. All she had to do was flick on the television set to make that discovery. Every show was in French and my poor wife couldn't *parlez-vous* a word of it. The only English-language TV available was on Tuesday nights at eleven. And it always seemed to be a horror movie. Watching English television was the highlight of the week for us.

Rose did her best to learn the new language but it wasn't easy. One day she went to the local hairdresser to have her hair cut. When the owner, a French-Canadian lady, asked Rose how she wanted her hair cut, Rose put up her hands as if to say "Just take a little bit off." Ah, but the French lady thought she meant "Just leave a little bit on." Rose came home wearing a brush cut.

Both of us thought we had seen a lot of snow in Springfield but Three-Rivers proved us wrong. The North Pole couldn't have outdone the snowbanks we saw. One night a teammate of mine named Toughie Hall walked out of one of our parties when the snow was piled up two feet from the top of the telephone poles. Toughie was walking along with a bottle of beer in each hand, fell, and was buried in the snow. Just then a snowplow came along and just missed shovelling up Toughie by two feet. I could just see the headline: DRUNKEN HOCKEY PLAYER KILLED BY SNOW PLOW.

Hard as it may be to believe, Three-Rivers began to grow on us. The French people were hospitable to a fault. My teammates were regular guys and the entire experience proved how easy it was to have a good time on $4,500 dollars a year.

At the time, the Three-Rivers team and the Springfield Indians were affiliated with the New York Rangers. The fall after I arrived in Three-Rivers, I was invited to the combined camp only to discover that the Rangers had added another team to their system, this one in Kitchener, Ontario.

A lot of my old buddies showed up at the camp including Springfield guys like Bill Sweeney, Bruce Cline, Jimmy Anderson, and Parker MacDonald. As friendly as they were, there was also the every-man-for-himself jungle law that everybody accepted. Your best friend could be demoted to the Yukon and you wouldn't bat an eyelash. Everyone was concerned about himself, his own self-preservation. We all wanted to be survivors. The feeling was similar to that in the trenches. When a soldier sees his buddy killed he feels awful about it but the first thing that comes to his mind is, "Geez, I'm glad it wasn't me!"

When I got the word I was being sent to the Kitchener team I considered it another demotion. This was a team in the Eastern Professional Hockey League which, at the time, was considered beneath the American League. (Three-Rivers was also in the Eastern Pro League.) I had still hoped to make it to the top, dreamer that I am.

As I was preparing to leave, I ran into my old buddy Floyd Smith from Springfield. He knew I was heading for Kitchener but he didn't give a crap. Not even a word of sympathy. As I walked out of the hotel, he yelled over to me, "Hey, Grapes, you owe me two-fifty from our euchre game."

I couldn't believe it. Here I was, as low as I could get, and all he could think of was his lousy two-fifty from a card game. "Okay, Floyd," I said, "tell you what I'll do, I'll flip you—double or nothing."

I flipped. He won. On to Kitchener. (Funny how little things like that stick in your mind.)

Well, all my fears about the new team were foolish. We had some dandy hockey players like Jean Ratelle, Rod Gilbert, Dave Balon, Jack McCartan, Red Bownass and Dennis Olson.

Rose and I enjoyed Kitchener, but the team didn't get any farther in the playoffs than we had in Three-Rivers. After Hull-Ottawa eliminated us, we headed back to Kitchener on a charter flight. Even though we had lost, the guys had bottles of champagne and were drinking away until two of my buddies, Mel Pearson and Sandy MacGregor became good and crocked.

It wasn't too bad until they decided to invade the cockpit, unannounced. The plane was descending on an instrument landing and the cockpit was supposed to be closed and dark so the pilot and co-pilot could study the instruments. Without notice, Pearson and MacGregor threw open the door and blinded the pilot and co-pilot. They momentarily lost control of the plane but righted it just in time to avert what could have been a crash.

When the plane came to a stop an announcement was made: "Will the members of the Kitchener hockey club please remain on the plane."

A few minutes later four members of the Royal Canadian Mounted Police, resplendent in their uniforms and wide brimmed hats, walked down the aisle. They escorted Pearson and MacGregor out of the plane, then the rest of us were allowed to leave and wait in the team bus while our two pals were interrogated behind closed doors. About half an hour passed when Pearson emerged from a torrential downpour. He was still furious but we managed to contain him, pushing him to the rear of the bus while a group of Mounties waited in the rain outside the bus. Eventually, MacGregor was released and we returned home, ending another hockey season.

From a guy who once thought he would be a National Leaguer, I had now become an Eastern Pro Leaguer. Granted it was a drop of a couple of rungs on the hockey ladder but at least I was playing, making a few bucks, and having fun. After Kitchener, I wound up playing for Sudbury after being traded to the Detroit Red Wings organization.

Sudbury is a mining town in Northern Ontario which is, if you can imagine it, colder than Three-Rivers. "Where is Sudbury?" asked Rose when I came home with the news. "North of Toronto," I said. "Don't worry, you'll love it." To that Rose offered the deathless line: "Don, it seems to me I've heard that one before."

True to form, Sudbury was as cold inside as it was outside. We rented a three-room apartment with the bathroom in the basement. It was so cold down there that you had to take a blanket with you whenever you went to the toilet.

It was while playing for Sudbury that I became embroiled in one of the meanest fights of my life. We were playing Hull-Ottawa, a team with a working agreement with the Montreal Canadiens. Like the parent club, Hull-Ottawa had a good, fast club.

Suddenly, a brawl erupted on the ice. I was sitting on the bench at the time when I noticed that Bob Armstrong, their player-coach, had grabbed our goalie, Carl Wetzel, from behind and was punching him. I was sitting next to Eddie Stankiewicz and said, "If he hits Carl once more, I'm going over."

Armstrong hit him, all right, and over the boards I went. I dashed to the scene and wound up, as I approached Armstrong, as if I was throwing a baseball. My punch caught Armstrong right in the eye. Down he went with me right on top of him. Then, Stankiewicz, who was as mad at him as I was, gave him a couple of shots, too, while blood was running down his face.

To our amazement none of the Hull-Ottawa players moved in to help their coach. (I later discovered they weren't very fond of him.) We were eventually pulled off and felt we had done our duty to our goalkeeper.

After the game I got a tip from one of the Hull-Ottawa players. "Tell Grapes to watch it because Armstrong says he's gonna get him with the stick."

We played them again the next night but I didn't believe that Armstrong would want to make any more trouble. I made the mistake of falling down in the Hull-Ottawa zone while Armstrong was on the ice. He took his stick and jammed it at the back of my head, just above the neck. He probably thought the blow would knock me out, but it didn't. I got up and hit him right over the head with my stick, knocked him down and then jumped on him again, just as I had done the night before.

The linesmen finally pulled me off although I let go reluctantly. As I got up (with the linesman's arms around me) Armstrong kicked me right in the chest with his skates. When would I learn that when you get a guy down, you don't let him up?

In the middle of that season, I received a phone call in Sudbury that my father was gravely ill. I returned home and found him in extremely poor condition. He had been operated on for lung cancer and there was little hope for recovery. I saw my father just before he passed away.

"Donald," he said, "I was never worried about your brother, Richard, because he is getting an education and he'll always get ahead. But, I am worried about you. I'm worried about your future."

I guess Dad had a right to worry. No education, no trade. At this time I must have been a disappointment to my Dad. If there was the slightest line about me in the papers—and I'm afraid there wasn't too much—Dad would cut it out. What a kick Dad would have had seeing me coach the Bruins, or watching me on *Hockey Night in Canada*. (Maybe he is watching.) At any rate, Dad died of lung cancer at age 62.

Although we didn't expect him to come up for my father's funeral, Rose's dad, Paul Martini, drove to Kingston from Hershey to pay his respects. Paul was in his early 40's at the time, in perfect health and a wonderful man to boot. He stayed with us for two days and then drove back.

Paul and his nephew Jimmy were on their way back to Hershey when their car hit a patch of ice and crashed. Paul was killed instantly.

It was a tough time for Rose and me, both our fathers gone in the space of a week.

The following fall I returned to the Detroit Red Wings camp. There was no doubt that I was a minor leaguer for life now, but I was a good one. Still, the stigma of being a busher never left you, especially at a training camp with guys who were in the NHL. The big-leaguers, with precious few exceptions, treated us like dirt. There was one key exception: Gordie Howe. He was just like any other guy. He would practise with us, even *talk* to us. When you're a minor leaguer and a man like Gordie Howe says hello to you, it's like the thrill of a lifetime, especially since most of the others treated us so badly.

Don't get me wrong. Most of us never really minded because we felt okay about ourselves. We knew that a lot of us were in the minor leagues because we didn't have the talent. But, some of us were there because we wouldn't play politics or kiss ass.

I didn't stay with the Red Wings very long. Sammy Pollock, the very wise general manager of the Montreal Canadiens, decided that he wanted an enforcer to protect some of his younger, less belligerent skaters. He made a deal with the Red Wings and I became a Canadien for two rolls of tape and a jock strap.

Don Cherry, a member of the Montreal Canadiens, had not been one of my expectations but, then again, I was willing to give it a whirl. I reported to The Forum and found myself sitting in the dressing room next to Jean Beliveau and Boom Boom Geoffrion, two of the greatest players ever to lace on skates. Next thing I knew, one of the Canadiens' trainers handed me a brand new pair of gloves. It was the first time in my hockey career that any club had given me a new pair of hockey gloves. I was stunned.

Through the hockey grapevine we had heard over the years that the Canadiens ran a first-class outfit. Now I was seeing it first-hand. Everyone, from the lowest farmhand to people like Beliveau and Geoffrion, was given the royal treatment. If Beliveau got $15 for taxi fare, so did I. Everyone was treated like a human being and I'm convinced that is why Montreal always turned out such good hockey clubs.

Toe Blake, who had been the left wing on Montreal's fabulous Punch Line with Rocket Richard and Elmer Lach, was coach of the Canadiens and he ran a tight ship and a terrific training camp. Toe didn't do much yelling and screaming; if a player made a mistake he would just glare at him with a stare like a laser beam. Everybody was very serious at Blake's camp, including goalie Jacques Plante. He was so dedicated to keeping the puck out of the net that when someone did score he would break his stick over the net.

For me, the best part of the Canadiens experience was the fact that I would be playing for Kenny Reardon's team. Reardon had been a very rambunctious Montreal defenseman when I was a kid and he had become my idol. Now Reardon was Vice President of the Canadiens and I was dying to meet him. I had already met his brother, Terry, who was the manager of the Providence Reds of the American League.

The trouble was that Kenny and Terry Reardon were look alikes and I had never met Kenny before. Well, on this day, Kenny came down to the dressing room to chat with some of the boys and he walked over to me. He was smoking a pipe, same as Terry always did. "Don," he said "I'm glad to have you here."

"Thank you very much, Terry," I said.

I didn't realize my mistake until Gary Bergman, a young defenseman like myself, turned to me when Kenny walked away and said: "I wouldn't call him Terry any more if I were you!"

My one big chance with my hero and I blew it—the story of my life.

Naively, I thought I had a shot at making the big team with the Canadiens but it was not to be. One night I went out with Claude Dufour, a goalie in the Canadiens' organization. We had a few beers before knocking off and the next morning Sammy Pollock, the big boss, called me into his office.

"You know, Don, I have plans for you in this organization," Pollock said. "But I understand that last night you had a couple of beers."

"Yes, Sam," I said, "I did have a couple of beers. There's no use lying about it."

He went on: "If we decide to promote you in our organization, you will have to observe our rules; and one of them is that we will not stand for any drinking. I'd like you to promise me that you will observe that rule."

I knew I was going to blow what could have been a good job but I wasn't going to snow Pollock.

"Sam," I continued, "I've always had a couple of beers here and there and I'll probably continue to have them. I could lie to you but I won't. Much as I like the job, I also like my beer so I'd rather not make any promises to you."

Pollock thanked me and told me to come back the next morning for my ticket. I had no idea where he planned to send me. When I returned he surprised me. "How would you like to go to Washington?"

Hmmm. The last I had heard Washington had a team in the American League. The idea of playing in the capital of the United States intrigued me, especially since it was so close to Rose's home in Hershey. I told Pollock that it sounded good to me.

He pulled out a contract which called for a $750 raise over my previous salary. I would now be earning $5,250 for the year which, to me, sounded like a lot.

"Here are your plane tickets," he said, handing me the envelope. I shook Pollock's hand and left, impatient to tour the Washington Monument and Lincoln Memorial.

When I got outside and opened up the envelope I nearly fainted. The "Washington" Pollock had in mind was Spokane, Washington, 3,000 miles away. "Rose," I insisted, when I phoned her with the news, "you'll love it."

"Don," she replied, "it seems to me I've heard that song before."

Packed into our 1960 Pontiac and loaded down with groceries, we headed west for another new and enriching experience. I'll say this for Spokane: it wasn't as cold as Three-Rivers or Sudbury, nor as tough as Springfield, but it sure was far from home.

The common denominator, as always, was the hockey players. The players with the Spokane Comets had a special toughness about them that gave this team more of a frontier spirit than any of the other clubs on which I've played.

The defensive corps was right out of the movie *Slapshot*. My partner turned out to be a mean cuss named Cornelius Patrick Madigan; alias the Mad Dog. It was an appropriate nickname, as time would tell. Another defenseman was Fred (Sandy) Hucul, a fellow who had had a cup of coffee in the NHL with the Chicago Black Hawks but who, now, was a confirmed minor leaguer. We called Hucul "Stoneface" because he considered a smile obsolete. The fourth defenseman was Bill Shvetz whose nickname was The Destroyer. 'Nuff said.

I was supposed to be the new tough guy on the club but the veterans were wary of me, especially Madigan. Sooner or later they were going to test me and the showdown finally happened when we were in San Francisco for a game with the Seals. A group of us, including Madigan, were sitting in a tavern called the Jack Tarr having a couple of beers when Madigan and I got into an argument. One word led to another until he finally said the fateful words, "Let's settle this outside." (Only later did I learn that Madigan was one of the best street fighters in hockey. He used to beat up his own teammates before the team picture!)

So here we were walking out to the parking lot in a pouring rain and wondering what each guy had in him. He pushed me and I pushed him. (One of the guys had warned me not to go down or Madigan would kick me in the head.) I said, "Go ahead. I'll give ya the first shot. Take the first shot!"

I was bluffing but, under the circumstances, I had no choice. Somehow, Madigan liked the way I put it. He wouldn't take the first shot. We shook hands and became the best of friends. Just like that. Only later did I discover what it was like to get into a street fight with Madigan and it was scary. The confrontation took place in a bar where Connie and I were innocently having a few beers. Connie went to the john. Meanwhile, a military policeman came in, sat down beside me, and started talking hockey.

Connie, who was always looking for trouble, returned and noticed that the MP was sitting on his stool. That shouldn't have been a problem since there was an empty stool on the other side of me but Connie wanted his stool back. "Hey," he snapped at the MP, "that's my seat you're sitting on."

The MP was unimpressed. "Sit over there," he said, pointing to the empty stool, "I just wanna talk to Don for a little while."

"Move!" shouted Madigan.

The MP once again suggested that Connie take another seat but before the soldier could finish his sentence Madigan had suckered him with a punch in the face. Well, no self-respecting MP was going to take that. The soldier swung back at Connie and what ensued was a brawl that could just as well have been staged at the MGM studios in Hollywood. The two of them bounced from the bar, across the room, back to the bar, breaking chairs and glasses in the process.

Meanwhile, I just sat there at the bar, sipping my beer; I didn't miss a drop. Finally, the big soldier managed to get Connie down on the floor but he was scared. He didn't know what to do because Connie had a wild look in his eyes and he was crying (which we knew was a bad sign for anyone tangling with Mad Dog). The MP turned to me. "Help me, please," he implored.

"Lemme get up," Connie demanded. "Lemme up."

So, the stupid MP released Madigan and Mad Dog thanked him by kicking the soldier in the groin so hard I thought his leg was going to come out the other side. The soldier went down and I realized that if Mad Dog followed through again he might kill the guy, so I nailed Connie against the wall and just held him there. Normally, I wouldn't have been able to do that, but Madigan was tired from all the brawling and could hardly move. Meanwhile, I motioned to the MP to get the hell out of there while the getting was good. He picked himself up and ran like hell.

When Connie saw that the soldier was getting away he kneed me in the groin and tried to bite me but he was smart enough to realize that he wasn't going to catch the soldier. He finally cooled down. He didn't say another word to me until practice the next day. He showed me the black-and-blue marks on his arm where I had been holding him in a death grip and said, "If you ever grab me again in a fight, Grapes, you're a dead man."

I have no doubt that he meant every word of it. Mad Dog had earned his nickname. One of our teammates, Jim Holdaway, will attest to that. Jim found out about Madigan's disposition during Christmas week. Connie, who was single, made a ritual of taking bottles of good cheer to the married folk on Christmas Eve. They would invite him in for a drink, they'd chat for a while, and then he would be on his merry way.

Well, on this night Madigan, who was always lonely on the night before Christmas, stopped at Holdaway's apartment. He knocked on the door and Jim opened it, but not all the way. Holdaway kept the chain on while Connie said, "Merry Christmas, Jim." Instead of inviting Madigan inside, Holdaway took the bottle, thanked Connie and then closed the door in his face.

Our place was next on Mad Dog's itinerary. We welcomed him in, let him stay for the night and had a hell of a good time, chatting and boozing. Except for one thing: Connie told me what had happened at the Holdaways and, in a typically sinister way, added: "I'm gonna get that guy." There were tears in his eyes when he said it so I should have known what was in store for poor Holdaway. The day after Christmas I found out at practice.

During the intra-squad workout Holdaway skated in on Madigan. Mad Dog reacted the way he had to the MP only this time he took his stick and just caved in the front of Jim's mouth, knocking most of the teeth out of his skull.

We were sitting in a bar that night when the evening news came on. Connie yelled, "Hey guys, look at this!" The news was showing Holdaway being carried out of the dressing room on a stretcher. Connie thought it was great. He had only one comment. "I bet when I knock on that guy's door again, I get invited in."

Compared with Madigan, I was a lover, but I did have my share of scraps. My most memorable "triumph" was recorded against a fellow named Larry McNab, a big tough guy who played for the San Francisco Seals. At The Cow Palace, where the Seals played, there was a huge banner proclaiming: "Heavyweight Champion of Hockey—Larry McNab."

McNab knew that I was the new resident policeman on the Comets and, as was the custom in those days, he decided to test me. Unfortunately for me, the night we met I was wearing a new pair of gloves. The moment McNab and I clashed, he instantly dropped his gloves but I couldn't get mine off; they were so stiff. While I was struggling to get the damn gauntlets off my hands, McNab slugged me ten times on the head. (He hit me so hard I couldn't comb my hair for a week.) But I taught McNab a lesson. He couldn't play again for six weeks after the fight.... He had broken his hand on my head!

There must have been something good about Spokane, fights or no fights, because the following May, Rose gave birth to Timothy Patrick Cherry. And that summer, while living in Hershey, I helped build the Reese's Peanut Butter Cup factory. I was wheeling cement buggies to the construction site, keeping in very good shape and wondering what my next hockey destination might be. Little did I realize that my next stop would be Rochester, New York, and a semi-permanent one at that.

CHAPTER ELEVEN

The Crow And I

A man named Joe Crozier, otherwise known as The Crow, entered my life after my Spokane experience. Crozier, who had once played defense with my old buddy Punch Imlach, was now a coach in the Toronto Maple Leafs' system. When the Maple Leafs purchased the Spokane hockey club our paths crossed.

In the fall of 1963, I was invited to the Maple Leafs' training camp in Peterborough, Ontario. Here I discovered none of the equality that had existed with Jean Beliveau and Boom Boom Geoffrion at the Canadiens' camp.

Once again I was exposed to hockey's caste system—to the extreme. At the Maple Leafs' camp there were two dressing rooms, one for the big team and another for all the serfs like myself who would be assigned to their minor league affiliates. The Maple Leafs had a room the size of a football field. The NHL players were given fresh new socks, new underwear, new everything every day. Royalty couldn't have been given better treatment.

The room we minor leaguers shared was so small that we could only use it in shifts. And because guys were always going in and out the room was always steaming. Instead of getting fresh uniforms we had to wear wet underwear, wet socks, and use wet equipment.

That was tolerable because I was used to it but what was even worse was a new system of exercising that Imlach introduced—land training. He imported two instructors from The Royal Military College to get us in shape. They had us doing all sorts of nonsensical indoor workouts. Once, they had us on stage and one of the guys was so tired he fell off the stage and broke an arm. After the land training Brian Kilrea's back was never the same. I survived, although those three mile walks to the rink didn't make practice any easier.

Needless to say the land training made it imperative for us to have a nip or two later in the day. Regulations forbade us from drinking in public but we found a way around that. The guys discovered a Royal Canadian Air Force Club that welcomed players. Once again we were segregated: the minor leaguers sat in the kitchen while the big leaguers had the use of the lounge and living room.

One of my old teammates, defenseman Larry Hillman, was lucky enough to make the transition from the minor leaguers to the majors. He had been promoted by Imlach to the big club and, literally, went from the kitchen to the stuffed leather chairs of the lounge.

Larry was a good guy and we wished him well but he made a social gaffe we didn't let him forget. One night we were camped in the kitchen when Hillman, who was now a big shot in the living room, decided that he would make points with his new NHL buddies. He went to buy a dozen hard-boiled eggs for them but to do so he had to walk past us poor slobs in the kitchen. You would have thought we were a collection of lepers, the way Larry ignored us.

Hillman bought the eggs and walked past us back to the lounge where he handed the eggs to the NHL guys. This infuriated me so I got up, walked out to the NHL gang and pulled up a chair near Hillman. Mocking a butler, and making sure that Larry heard me, I said: "Does anyone want more eggs? Larry will get you some more eggs, if you like. Do you want some toast? Larry will get it for you."

They didn't appreciate my humour but I didn't care because this much I knew: the NHL guys might have been better skaters and better scorers but they weren't tougher. Nobody said a word.

For the rest of the season Les Duff made sure that everywhere that Larry went, there was an egg waiting for him. In his gloves, his skates, his bed, his car, everywhere. When Larry was sent down to Rochester from Toronto, Les made sure there was an egg in his locker waiting for him.

One fellow who apparently liked my style of play was Crozier, who was coaching the Maple Leafs' affiliate in the American League, the Rochester Americans. He wanted an enforcer for his club and arranged my transfer, much to my dismay. The Spokane club had moved en masse to Denver and all my friends had gone with it. I wanted to stay with them and also wanted the opportunity to play in Denver because I had heard what a great city it was.

But once I arrived in Rochester I changed my mind. For one thing it was an attractive city and for another I was with an extremely strong hockey team. We were so powerful that even the NHL clubs tried to avoid playing us in exhibition games because we'd hammer them. Once we played the Maple Leafs, who had been the Stanley Cup champions, at Maple Leaf Gardens in Toronto and beat them 9-1.

Near the end of the game, I looked over at Imlach behind the bench and shouted so that all his "champions" could hear: "Hey, Punch, how long are we gonna play this game, until your guys get a couple of goals?" For some reason the brand, new gloves worn by the Maple Leafs players had caught my attention. I looked down at them and then down at the old, torn gloves the Americans had given me. Then I glanced at the scoreboard and laughed uproariously. (How to win friends and influence people!)

One of the best players on our club was Bronco Horvath, a center who had been a big star with the Boston Bruins for awhile but now was a bit over the hill. He still had a sharp shot and a very sharp tongue. Bronco liked to sit up at the front of the bus, on the far right side, and bug the driver constantly. Usually, the driver would ignore Horvath but, occasionally, Bronco would overdo it. Once, Bronco was chattering away while the driver minded his own business, keeping his eye and, seemingly, his mind on the road. Eventually, Horvath dozed off with his legs propped up on the exit bar in front of him with his right leg rubbing against the exit door, in his stocking feet.

According to law, a bus is supposed to come to a complete stop at railroad tracks so that the driver can open the door and be sure there are no trains coming. Sure enough, we came upon some tracks and the driver brought the bus to a halt. He opened the door and Bronco's foot, which still was leaning against it, actually went out the opening, toes first.

Les Duff, who had the quickest sense of humour of anyone I ever met, was watching the scene.

(One time, we were all waiting for the team bus, and a rookie asked Les, "Duffy, how long is the bus going to be?" Duffy said, "About sixty feet.")

Well anyway, Duffy realized what was about to happen and whispered to all the guys. "Don't make a sound." The driver made sure that Bronco's toe was in place and then slammed the door shut on Horvath's foot. Bronco literally hit the roof of the bus screaming and, as far as I know, it was the last time he ever bugged a bus driver.

Horvath took a lot of his chatter to the rink and was regarded as something of a joker but he also was a superb shooter and a player with more confidence in his ability than anyone I've ever met. You could see it on the rare occasions when he would take a penalty shot. Other players in that situation would be nervous, fidgety, and looking for advice. Not Bronco.

I remember one penalty shot. Bronco casually skated over to me at the bench. "Grapes," he said, "this is what I'm goin' to do. I'm gonna fake to the left then come back to the backhand on the right and put it in the top corner."

Sure, sure, I said to myself, that'll be the day. But, damn, if he didn't do it just as he had laid out for me. While all the guys were patting him on the back he gave me an "I told you so" wave of his hand.

Crow also had a very talented right winger named Jimmy Pappin. Jimmy had the most cutting tongue of any person I have ever met, cruel and to the point.

One time, when I had a fight with Dennis Hextall, who played for Buffalo, I was cut for about twenty stitches. Rose said she didn't think a fist could do so much damage. Anyway, we had Dennis' brother Bryan playing for us. As I was getting stitched Pappin yelled, "Hey Grapes. Why don't you get even with Hextall? Punch Bryan!" Even the doctor stitching me laughed.

One day Pappin was assigning horse racing dollar values to all the team members. Mike Walton was worth $150,000, Peter Stemkowski was worth $100,000, Al Arbour $20,000 and he went through the whole team without mentioning me. So I said, "Jimmy, what about me?" He thought for a minute and then said, "You know those Clydesdale horses that pull the starting gate out before the race, Grapes? Well, that's you."

Crozier recognized Pappin as a problem but also realized that Jimmy, like Bronco, was a terrific asset to the team, when his offensive abilities were properly harnessed. The problem was with Pappin's head. He was moody. He marched to his own drummer and you could never tell when he was going to be up for a game. Just before the playoffs Crozier took me aside and said he wanted me to room with Jimmy. "We gotta get Pappin goin' for the playoffs," said Crozier.

Fine. It was okay with me, but the trick was finding a way to goad Pappin without him knowing it. But Pappin was sharp. As soon as Jimmy realized that I was rooming with him he knew what was going on. Once he realized that Crozier had placed someone there to get him going he laughed and laughed. I planned my strategy accordingly.

One afternoon Jimmy and I were in our hotel room, getting ready for the afternoon nap when I casually remarked to him. "Y'know, Jim, Crozier had me room with you to get you goin'. That really makes me laugh."

He asked why and I could tell I had piqued his curiosity. "I'll tell you why," I went on. "We don't need you in the playoffs. We've got a good enough team without you. Besides, what would you do in the playoffs? You've done nothing for us so far."

At a glance, I could tell Pappin was getting good and angry. "Is that so?" he shot back. "I tell ya what. I'm gonna score a few goals tonight."

I interrupted. "Don't make me laugh. I'll betcha twenty bucks you don't get anything tonight and you don't get five goals all through the playoffs."

"It's a bet!" he said.

That night he went and got a hat trick, and he was dynamite in the playoffs. So, who was the genius, The Crow or me? (It cost me twenty, so it must have been The Crow!)

Another beaut was my good friend, goalie Gary Smith, also known as Suitcase because he had played for more teams than just about anyone in the business. He was also called the Axe for an interesting reason. Gary was walking down the street one day when he spotted a fellow carrying an axe in his hand, chasing a woman. Gary sped across the street and downed the guy with a flying tackle. In the process he removed the axe from the guy's determined grip. He made TV and all the papers, so naturally, it was "Axe" from then on.

One day, while we were awaiting a flight at an airport, Gary sat next to me and very offhandedly remarked that he had something personal to discuss with me. "Go ahead," I said. "Don," he went on, "you're such a good friend that I have to tell you that you have one fault that we all wish you would correct."

I began to wonder; are they getting exasperated with my yelling, my fighting or my drinking? "Don," said Gary, still deadpan, "you have too much hair in your nose!" and he meant it! (Only a good friend would tell you something like that!)

Our captain and fellow defenseman was Al Arbour, who was one of the few defensemen in professional hockey to wear ordinary glasses during a game. His nickname, for obvious reasons, was "Radar." There were times I figured that Al actually did use radar to get around because his glasses would get terribly fogged up during the heat of a game.

Al would be on the bench, resting between shifts, when it was time for Darryl Sly to come off. Darryl would be at the gate yelling at Al, "Come on Al, Hurry up, Al." Al would sit there cleaning his glasses while some guy had a breakaway. Darryl would go nuts.

Off the ice Al was very conservative although he had the odd beer with us every once in a while. His wife, Claire, was a lovely lady and we enjoyed their company very much. One night, though, Arbour went completely out of character and, in the process, lost himself a baby sitter.

Baby sitters were not easy to come by in those days, but Claire had managed to find a young girl who had agreed to sit for them. She was a teenager who had never sat for a hockey player before and, admittedly, was a trifle frightened by the thought. Claire had assured her that there was nothing to worry about and that they would be home by one o'clock. The sitter still wasn't sure. She had heard too many stories about hockey players being animals. Still, she decided to give it a try. "My husband," Claire said while leaving, "is a very nice, quiet person."

We had a team party that night, and it was a lulu, especially for Al.

He really tied one on at the party. As promised, the Arbours returned to the house at one a.m. Claire went in through the front door while Al went down to the basement to unleash their little black poodle.

Claire got into the house all right but Al tripped and fell head first down the cellar stairs and opened a terrific gash on his forehead. Blood began gushing down his face and all over his suit as he made his way to the stairway that led to the kitchen. Meanwhile, Claire had gone to the bedroom to get some money to pay the sitter who was waiting in the kitchen. All of a sudden, the cellar door opened and Al climbed out, blood dripping off his glasses, blood all over his pants. He looked like a fugitive from a Frankenstein movie. All of the sitter's fears were confirmed. She let out a banshee yell, ran out of the house, dashed down the street, and was never seen by the mild-mannered, conservative Arbour family again.

The Rochester club played some games in Toronto. One night we all stayed out after curfew. The next morning Al came up to me and asked, "How many people do you think there are in Toronto?" I said, "About two million, I guess. Why?" Al said, "I'm driving back to the hotel at 1 a.m. after our party, and guess who's sitting in his car, parked at a red light, right next to me? Stafford Smythe (the owner). What's the odds?" Only to Radar would these things happen.

My defense partner, Darryl Sly, was also my best friend while I played in Rochester. He was an interesting fellow. As hockey players went, he was one of the best, but he had so much money that he never seemed to have the incentive to work as hard as he should have in order to make the bigs. We were great pals and I roomed with him for six years. We had the same habits, waking up at the same time and going to bed at the same time.

Darryl was a little smarter and a bit more creative than most hockey players. He was the first guy I knew to wrap a plastic raincoat around himself during practice, tape it, and then skate around to sweat more and take off weight. His strength and ability to absorb punishment were awesome. He liked to dare anyone to punch him in the stomach as hard as they liked. Many guys did but nobody ever hurt him.

Darryl could be a problem for The Crow. Like other coaches, Crozier loved to make speeches. And like other coaches, Crow often picked the wrong time to give them, usually early in the morning. Personally, I never had trouble with speeches. When a coach started talking, I would stare right at him throughout his harangue. By contrast, Sly would sit with his hands over his head, leaning on his knees, looking down at the floor. It was an efficient way of listening to the coach while sleeping.

This particular day, Crozier went on longer than usual and certainly longer than necessary. He paced back and forth, up and down the room and his talk began to sound like the drone of bagpipes. I kept staring at him but when Crow reached the end of the room and began to turn again, Darryl simulated a snore, as if to say to me, "Isn't this boring?" But Darryl had his head down so that Crow couldn't see or hear him. But I could and I couldn't stop laughing. It was like lunch at school. The more I tried to stop, the more I laughed. I knew I was in trouble, but I just couldn't stop and Darryl showed no mercy. He just kept letting on—only to me—that he was snoring. Tears were rolling down my cheeks when Crow angrily left the room.

A few minutes later a note was delivered to me: "Cherry, I want to see you in my office."

He benched me for three games. But that wasn't the only punishment. He had Darryl and me do an endless, torturous skating exercise around the net. Around and around we went until we got dizzy. While we did it the two of us memorized all the words to the poem *In Flanders' Fields*.

Sly's trademark was an ankle he had hurt as a kid. It hadn't healed properly and when he walked it would crack. Whenever Darryl came into the hotel late, I could hear him the minute he got off the elevator.

He had a habit that would drive the wives crazy when we went out drinking. He would order a beer, remove his false teeth and then drop them into his brew and go on drinking.

With all his strength and courage, Sly had one weakness—frogs. He was deathly afraid of the amphibians and would go absolutely insane if he saw one. I guess with him it was legitimate *frogophobia*. It didn't take long for the guys to find out about it and that meant only one thing—a prank had to be pulled on Darryl.

As it happened, Darryl was rooming by himself at this training camp, setting himself up for the grand ploy. One night, several players went out and got drunk and then headed for some farmland outside of town. They were armed with flashlights and a couple of bags in which to store the captured frogs.

The boys found the swamp they were looking for and began catching frogs by the dozens. The only trouble was that they were on private property and the farmer who owned the land didn't cotton to the idea of six strangers splashing around in his swamp. He called the police and half an hour later sirens were wailing and lights flashing as the cops descended on the frog-hunting hockey players.

Two big cops, their flashlights probing the darkness, came upon the players. "What'n hell are ya doin' here?" they demanded.

When the boys explained, the cops couldn't control their laughter. They doubled up and, of course, let the players finish their hunt, all the while explaining to the farmer that the players meant no harm.

With a huge catch of frogs, the guys headed back to the hotel, stashed them in a bathtub and then laid a plan for getting them into Sly's room. They decided to wait until Darryl went out drinking the next night, get his room key, and plant the frogs all over his suite.

Sure enough, Sly went out the next night and the boys got hold of his key. They had about fifty frogs and let them loose before conducting an orderly retreat. When Darryl returned he wasn't exactly sober and he just opened the door and plopped himself on the bed without even turning on the light. He was out before he realized that he had fifty new roommates.

Eventually, Darryl came to and was startled to hear a strange sound—a sort of *plop-plop-plop*—in the room. He reached over and turned on the light. For a moment he thought he was having a nightmare because the room was filled with frogs, jumping off tables, jumping on the window sill and, worst of all, jumping on Darryl.

Once he realized it was not a nightmare and that his heart was still beating, Darryl ran out of the room and down the hall. Frantically he banged on the door of my room. "Don, Grapes, help, my room is full of frogs!"

I was fast asleep at the time and it isn't often that I'm awakened to hear that there are frogs in my buddy's room. I thought he had the DTs or something. I put on a bathrobe and ran out to calm him down. Then, I walked down the hall to his room and, sure enough, the place was crawling with frogs.

I went into the bathroom and found a big pail and began filling it with frogs. "Hey, Darryl," I said, "I've got all the frogs. I'm gonna take them down to my room. You can go back to sleep."

Darryl was reassured and thanked me for my trouble. He went back to his own room, turned on the light, looked around, just to be sure there were no Kermits left in the place, saw none, and went back to sleep again. (Little did Darryl realize that when he turned on the light the frogs had hidden under the dresser and behind the sink.) A minute after the light went out, he heard the frightening *plop-plop-plop* again. On went the light and when Darryl saw the frogs again, he grabbed his pillow, ran down the hall and banged on my door again. He begged me to let him sleep on the floor of my room providing I kept the other frogs locked in the bathroom till morning.

I agreed and Darryl finally fell asleep again. In the morning, I went to his room and rounded up all the stray frogs, put them in the back seat of the car, and deposited them on the bank of a nearby river. Poor Darryl never got over that one.

Another interesting character was our goalie, Gerry Cheevers. He was a thoroughbred. (Gerry also liked the horses and later became the owner of a stable of racers.) Talk about courage, Cheevers (we called him Cheesie) was right up there at the top.

Red Berenson, who had one of the best backhand shots in pro hockey, once went around me and let go a devastating backhander that caught Cheesie flatfooted. Before he could duck, the hunk of rubber slammed right into his mouth, knocking out all his front teeth. If ever a

Jack Butterfield, President of the American Hockey League, presenting me with the Calder Cup which the Rochester Americans won in 1966-67.

Me as a Rochester American, 1967-68 when we won the Calder Cup again.

man was a mess it was Cheesie. Yet, the next day Gerry showed up at practice with stitches in his mouth, his teeth gone and his gums a mess.

"Crow," I asked, "does Cheesie actually have to practice with us?"

The coach looked at me as if I had asked the dumbest question in the world. "Of course he does," Crozier replied. "What do you think this is, a circus?"

We had a game two nights later and Cheesie was back in the nets, but not for long. He sprawled on the ice to make a save and while his arms were stretched out, Pit Martin skated right over Gerry's hand cutting all his tendons.

A couple of nights later he had to represent the club at a Hickok Award dinner. Gerry was a sight: His hand was swathed in bandages; his arm was in a sling and he hardly had any teeth left in his mouth.

I could sympathize with Cheesie because I had been through a lot of that misery myself. Once, we were playing an exhibition game in Victoriaville, Quebec. I was hit between the eyes with a stick and was bleeding badly. It was a guaranteed stitch job but there wasn't a doctor at the rink. With my uniform on, I was taken to a Volkswagen and driven five miles to a dark house. My driver led me to the door, still holding the bloody towel to my face. We walked up a flight of stairs and into a dimly-lit room.

While we waited for the doctor, the nurse asked me "for my records" my name, weight, marital status, names of my children, my father's name, and my mother's maiden name. The nurse had a hell of a time with Palamountain.

I was told to lie down on the table. How could I refuse? A little, old guy came out, looked at my wound and, in nothing flat, stitched it up like a master. I thanked him, walked down the stairs and back into the VW. My chauffeur drove me back to the rink and I skated right back onto the ice as if I hadn't missed a shift. In fact, *I hadn't missed a shift.* A big fight had erupted after I'd been hurt. It took a hell of a long time to resolve it. While they were battling, I had been repaired and hadn't missed a thing.

By now The Crow understood that I was a glutton for punishment and, from time to time, he would take advantage of me on that count. A good example was the time we were playing the Quebec Aces in the finals. Quebec had a hell of a team that year; Doug Harvey was on defense and Gump Worsley was in the net. (Both are in the Hockey Hall of Fame.) For the purposes of disturbing the peace, the Aces had a rambunctious young defenseman named Bryan Watson.

It was a rough game and with about a minute-and-a-half remaining, we were down 5-2. There was no way we were going to win but The Crow decided that he wanted me on the ice. He benched Arbour and sent me out. He didn't expect me to score any goals but he did expect me to settle a score; preferably with Watson who had spent a good deal of the evening running at our smaller players.

In no time at all I moved into the Quebec zone and camped in front of the Aces net. Sure enough, Watson came up from behind and blasted me with a crosscheck. I dropped my stick and gloves and began throwing lefts and rights at him. He wasn't doing badly himself. The fight went on and on until the linesmen finally separated us and led Watson to the penalty box.

The officials appreciated the intensity of the battle and sensed that the two of us would surely go at it again if we weren't separated. A cop came to stand between us but I managed to reach over the cop and nail Bryan right between the eyes. Two cops grabbed me, only this time they held on even harder. While I was tied up, Guy Gendron of the Aces skated up behind me and hit me over the head with his stick. It was a dandy.

Believe it or not, all of this was taking place on Christmas Day. I still wasn't through with Watson. I managed to get back at him again in the penalty box. I picked him up and threw him out of the box but, unfortunately, he grabbed my head and we both tumbled out together onto the ice.

The odd part of the riot was that Jack Riley, who was then president of the American League, had been in the stands watching the game but decided to leave with two minutes left in the game so that he could go to Christmas Mass. Riley was in his car listening to the game when the riot erupted. The next day the headline in the paper read: RIOT IN COLISEUM WHILE PRESIDENT ON WAY TO CHURCH. (Poor Jack!)

On top of that my wife and Claire Arbour were having Christmas dinner at our house with the kids and watching the game on television. They were just about to start eating when the blood began to spill. Claire hollered to Rose, "Rose, come quick! There's a big fight." Rose just went on basting the turkey and yelled back, "What's Don into now?" There was little peace on the ice and good will toward men on that Christmas Day.

Riley fined me $175 for my efforts but Crozier had a deal whereby he would reward a player $25 for having a good fight. So I came out $150 short. With the $25 I bought my son, Timothy, a nice suit for $15 and took the rest and bought the boys a few beers.

Crozier liked the fact that I had fought but he had strange ways of showing his appreciation. Soon after the Quebec uproar I wound up riding the bench. He kept me off the ice for two-and-a-half periods—my legs began to feel like lead—and then gave me some ice time. When I did get on the ice, I couldn't move, and Red Berenson waltzed around me and scored.

This infuriated me but that was exactly what Crow wanted, he would do it again and again. Another time my mother, grandmother, and brother came to see me play. We beat Quebec, 10-1, that night but Crozier didn't even put me on the ice for one shift. When I walked into the dressing room after that embarrassment, I broke my stick over a steel garbage pail, threw my equipment all over the place, and Crozier loved every minute of it. He wanted guys who would get good and mad if they were benched.

He did it another time and, after the game, we had to get out of the dressing room in a hurry to catch a bus for an out-of-town game. I was furious again and, before we got on the bus, I started complaining about it to Rose. Well, she was fed up listening to me so she said, "Hey, don't give me the lip! There's Crozier standing by the bus. Why don't *you* go over and tell *him*?"

With my overnight bag in hand, I walked directly to Crozier who was standing alongside the team bus. "I can play on this team," I shouted and, at the same time, hit him with my bag. "I want to play tomorrow night in Hershey!"

The Crow didn't get angry. He let me have my fit and then replied: "Do you think you're good enough to play against Hershey?"

"Yeah," I insisted.

"Okay," said Crozier, "you'll play."

I dressed for the game the next night against Hershey—but I didn't get on the ice. Call it The Crow's revenge.

Actually, Crozier was less of a problem to me than some physical ailments that had been plaguing me for years. The worst, by far, was bronchial asthma, which had afflicted me on and off for many years. I knew some players whose careers had been ruined because of asthma. Gilles Tremblay, a terrific winger with the Montreal Canadiens, had to quit in the prime of his hockey life because of it.

Only someone who has actually suffered asthma can appreciate the torture it inflicts upon an individual. To me, the feeling is akin to drowning: you gasp for air but can't fill your lungs with it. I would get the feeling at training camp when the exercises began. The Crow would have us do wind sprints and I would lose my breath and my head would spin. I reached a point where I couldn't take it any longer and finally went to see Crozier about it. As far as I was concerned my career was *kaput* and I didn't expect any sympathy from The Crow.

What a surprise. First of all, Joe talked me out of quitting. Then, he suggested that I see his doctor for an examination. "But, Joe," I said, "I've seen nine million doctors and all they give me is pills and mists." But Joe insisted that I try his man and I did.

Doctor MacVeigh informed me that I had the lungs of a 90-year-old man. However, he suggested a treatment—cortisone and antibiotics—and built me up for ten days. Well, at the end of fifteen days my lungs were as clear as a bell and I was back playing as if nothing had happened. To me, that doctor was a saint and I never forgot him for what he did for me. In fact, during the playoff finals that year against Quebec, I was on the ice for the last three minutes of the game and when the buzzer sounded, I had the puck frozen along the boards. I saved the puck and gave it to the doctor when we returned to Rochester.

Of course, I wouldn't have had the good fortune of finding the doctor if it hadn't been for The Crow. In a sense, he helped prolong my career—and maybe even saved my life—at a time when I was ready to pack it in.

The Crow and I became close in other ways, too, mostly because of his superstitions. Lots of sports people have their rabbits' feet and other tokens of good luck, but few could match Crozier. Once, after a particularly bad loss, he was so angry that he punted a huge steel garbage can across the dressing room and broke his toe in the process.

After the doctor fixed him up, Crozier had to wear a special plaid slipper over the injured foot. What do you think happened? We started winning. Well, after we had won about three in a row, Crozier's toe was healed and he was able to wear regular shoes again. But Joe would have none of that; not while we were winning. The plaid slipper became his good luck charm, and we continued winning. Crow simply would not remove his sock or his slipper; and we won something like 20 games in a row. We eventually lost and off came the magic slipper.

It was Crow who adopted my son, Timothy, as another good luck charm. On the morning of a game Rose got very sick and was in no shape to take care of the lad so I decided to bring him along to the dressing room with me. Crozier understood the circumstances and allowed Tim to sit in with the guys while we had our team meeting. He maintained decorum, didn't make a sound and all went well. In fact, we won big that night.

By the time we had our next home game Rose had recovered enough to be able to handle Tim so I left him with her the morning of the game. We lost that night and Crow put two and two together; we won with Timothy and lost without him. He summoned me to his office. "Why didn't you bring Timothy this morning?" he demanded. "It's *your* fault that we lost the game." (He was serious.)

Crow demanded that I bring Timothy to the morning skate of every game. Rose wasn't happy about the result of this exchange, but went along with it anyway.

At age three, Timothy Cherry became a fixture in the Rochester Americans' dressing room. He would toddle around the dressing room, picking up the tape and cotton that the players had used for their shin pads and then thrown away. There was only one problem and that was the salty lauguage that is as much a part of the dressing room as is the smell of liniment and tape. In fact, cursing was so much a part of our lives that I didn't even think twice about it having an effect on my son.

I learned my lesson a few weeks later. Telling Tim a story every night before he went to bed was a family ritual. One night, I came home about 8 p.m. with a pretty good glow on because I had had a few with the boys. I lay down beside Tim and started telling him about how the Three

Little Pigs were going to build a trap to catch the wolf. I was rambling and making up the story as I went along, and I wasn't paying much attention to what I was saying because I was falling asleep myself.

"Well, Timothy," I related, "the wolf was walking along the trail in the woods, heading for the big trap that was covered with sticks and leaves. Now, guess what the wolf did?"

Timothy thought for a moment. "What did he do?"

"He jumped over the trap."

Hearing this, Timothy replied: "Aw F---!" and used the favourite four letter word of hockey players and most athletes!

I knew I wasn't feeling any pain, but I said to myself, "I couldn't have heard what I think I heard. How could a three-year-old kid say this? I must be dreaming." Finally, I said, "Timothy, what did you say?"

He looked at me as if I was crazy and then, with a touch of anger in his voice, added: "The f---ing wolf jumped over the trap!"

I staggered out of the room, shaking my head. Not only was he uttering x-rated words, but he was putting them in at the right time and with perfect inflection. I sent Rose in to talk to him and the little guy looked up at his mother and said: "I guess Dad's mad at me." Then he told Rose the story and she was in a state of shock too!

After I had calmed down sufficiently to deal with the issue, I had a long talk with the boy. "Timothy," I said, "about this swearing. It's a bad habit. You've got to promise me that for the rest of your life you won't swear; otherwise I won't take you to the dressing room."

More than fifteen years have passed since that moment and I have never heard Timothy utter a cuss word since. As promised, I allowed him to continue visiting the dressing room but, in retrospect, I wonder if it was very wise. There were many heavy episodes that might not have been appropriate for a young boy, particularly when a player named Red Armstrong was involved.

Red was a hard-living, hard-drinking character who, like myself, wasn't happy when Crozier kept him on the bench. I remember one incident after we had won the championship and were celebrating at a local hotel when Armstrong was still seething about being kept off the ice. (I was just as angry because I hadn't gotten much ice time either.) Instead of enjoying the festivities, Red was fuming about being benched. When The Crow walked into the room, Red cornered him, pushed him, and said that he should have been played. This was going on in the mezzanine while I was downstairs on the main floor. Armstrong was beginning to get violent so the team doctor came running down to get me to protect Crozier. (I didn't know whether to side with Red or Crow.) I could see that Armstrong was really going to lay him out so I grabbed Red by the shirt, ripping all the buttons off, and hustled him out of the hotel, and into his car. As he left the joint, Red kept shouting: "I'm gonna get you later, Crozier; I'm not finished with you." I finally sent Red on his way.

Crow, who hadn't been feeling well for other reasons, was in tears by now and the doctor was concerned about Joe and also worried about what Armstrong might do to him.

The doctor asked me if I would drive over to Crozier's place and protect Crow in case Red followed through with his threat to "get" Joe. I asked Darryl Sly if he thought we should go. Darryl said: "We might as well. You never know what Red will do. But, let's take a few beers along."

So, we left our wives at the party and drove over to Crow's and sat in front of his house for an hour, sipping a few. Finally, I said to Darryl, "Are we nuts or something? Red's not coming here. Let's get out of here."

I was right. Red had gone to a bar to party with his friends, and was having a good time. But that isn't the topper to the story.

After the season, my nice guy friend Crow said he didn't think I could make the club next season. He gave Sly a raise and inserted a note in the envelope, thanking him for all he had done on the night Armstrong had threatened to kill him. As for Armstrong, he too got a raise. So much for loyalty. When would I learn?

I did get invited back, and obviously there was nothing more in my future than minor league hockey. Frankly, I didn't mind. The money was little, but the times were good and the buses always got us to our destinations.

In the dead of winter, travelling by bus was tough. You'd drive all night, the inside of the windows would frost up, and the wind would come whistling through the bus. We had to tape the inside of the windows to keep them from freezing. The floor was always wet from snow and spilt beer, and your feet were always cold. It sure was great to travel for eight or ten hours on a bus when you had a charley horse. Many was the time I would sit in the bus in my shorts, an ice bag taped to my leg to relieve a charley horse, sipping a cool one, and playing poker.

I know it sounds crazy, but trips were fun. The team had a special camaraderie, closeness. And trips built character and an inner toughness that was important in later life. Just check how many coaches in the last ten years paid their dues in the minors.

The few times we actually flew, it was in an ancient DC-3 that must have been on loan from The Smithsonian Institute. On one trip, the crate caught fire so many times we hardly worried about it. I recall our goalie, Bobby Perreault, hollering up to me, "Grapes, tell the pilot the plane's on fire again!" There was smoke coming out of the tailpipe but nobody was particulary concerned; we were used to it.

My marketability as a hockey player was fast approaching the zero point. If there was one thing that worried me it was being put in the same position as other fringe players who would be left hanging in the wind, uncertain if they had a future left in the game. I was always reminded of a time I was sitting in Crozier's office as he was planning a new season with the Americans. Players would call him and he would tell his secretary to take their number that he would call them back. As each player phoned, he would turn to me and say, "Can you believe that guy? Well, I'll leave him hangin' for a while."

I thought to myself; "Crow, you'll never get the chance to do that to me."

Ah, but he did. It was the summer before the 1969-70 season. I wanted to find out what plans Crozier had for me so I phoned the office. They said he wasn't in and took my number. No return call. I phoned his hotel and left a message. No call. I called and called and never heard back from him. Finally, I told Rose, "I'm gonna phone him once more. If he doesn't answer my call, Rose, we're gone. *I'm retiring.*"

I placed the call. I was told he wasn't in so I left word, and waited. As usual, I didn't hear from him. "That's it," I told Rose, "I'm retired."

I reported for my construction job at Kodak where I had been working for years during the off-season and prepared for a life without hockey. A month went by and it was almost time for training camp. One night the phone rang. It was Crow. "Okay, Don," he said, "which camp do you want to go to? Vancouver or Rochester?"

"Sorry, Joe," I said, "but I'm through."

He didn't believe me. "C'mon, Don," he said, "don't be silly. We've been on four championship teams in four years. You can't quit now. Where do you want to go?"

"Crow, thanks for everything, no hard feelings, but this is it. See ya later. Toodle-oo!"

CHAPTER TWELVE

Comeback

As the 1970-71 season began there were two things farthest from my mind: one was becoming a hockey player again and the other was becoming a professional hockey coach.

Hockey was rapidly moving out of my orbit. I was 36 years old and felt comfortable about retirement. I never had delusions of grandeur. I was quite happy with my construction job at Kodak and after sixteen years of pushing a puck for a living I figured that I could go sixteen years pushing a jackhammer for my bread and butter; a tough job, but an honest one.

I'm sure some folks would regard it as a comedown, but not me. For one thing my supervisor, Whitey Smith, was a sweetheart. Here was a guy who was not only my boss but also my best friend. How many workers can say their boss picks them up in the morning and drives them home from work in the evening? Well, that's what Whitey did for me. Life was beautiful—too beautiful.

One day I was called into the office and told that I was no longer needed. Business was slow, the boss said, and he read off a list of names of guys without seniority. I was one of them. It's hard to duplicate the nauseous feeling when you're told you're being laid off. I had it then, and hoped to heaven I would never have it again. What surprised me was that Whitey and some of my fellow workers took it harder than I did. Whitey was literally in tears. The others seemed to be in shock. It took me about a minute to pull myself together.

Then, I remembered one of our fellow workers, a Scotsman named MacGregor who collected twenty-five cents a week from all the guys. We called it a flower fund and the money was saved for anyone who got really sick. As I was leaving I told the men that I'd like to discuss something serious with Mr. MacGregor. The guys, who were still sober, couldn't figure out what I had in mind. I looked at each of the fellows, deadpan, and then said, "Well, now that I'm laid off, does this mean that I get my twenty-five cents back from the flower fund?" That ended the mourning; now it was time to find a job.

Very simple, yes? No, it was awful. So bad, in fact, that I began to think about something that had never entered my mind before—collecting unemployment insurance. Nobody in my family had ever done that, and there was a certain feeling of humiliation involved, but I decided to investigate it nonetheless. Some fun. Getting the third degree for homicide has to be a lot easier than the grilling they give you at the unemployment office. About half-way through the questioning I thought, "What if Dad could see me now?" and I said to the lady, "Thank you very much." I turned around and walked out of the place.

It was a grand gesture, I'll have to admit, but I still had no money in my pocket and I did have a family to support. I was alone; had nobody to joke with and, at this moment, I hit the lowest point in my life. I began questioning my friends' loyalty to me, started to think that the world was against me. Paranoid was the word. Unless you've been unemployed, you don't know that feeling of helplessness you can't shake. You feel so empty, and you question your ability. You see everyone else going off to work and your heart aches. That's why when I hear that a person is unemployed, I can really empathize. But again, the experience builds an inner toughness and a will to survive at all costs.

God forbid anyone should ask, "How's it goin' today?" I'd immediately figure that the guy was poking fun at me. Never had the words "Nobody knows when you're down and out" had more meaning for me than during my period of unemployment. But through it all my buddy Whitey stayed by me, a true friend. Then I got a break; if you can call it that.

I got a job as an automobile salesman. Cadillacs, no less. At least Rose liked it. The company gave me a new Cadillac to drive, which was nice for starters. The job was something else. Whitey had warned me that I wasn't cut out to be a car salesman and that, maybe, I shouldn't have even bothered to try it.

But, when one is hard-up, one does anything. I was hard-up. I wanted to work, so I took the job and hated every living minute of it. The clue was the morning. I'd wake up and want to go back to sleep, and I wasn't tired. I knew that I had to get up, so the next thing I would do was pray for rain, hoping that nobody would come to the showroom.

The Lord did not intend for me to sell cars. First of all, I was used to hard, physical work, and all I did as a salesman was stand around all day. Secondly, to be truthful, if you want to sell cars, you have to have a bit of larceny in your heart. Thirdly, I hated going up to people and practically beg them to do me a favour and buy a car. I didn't really believe in the product and I didn't enjoy the act of conning people. Most potential customers were decent enough, but one day a fellow walked in and I engaged him in conversation. Nothing personal, nothing unusual. I just wanted to show him our line of cars. (Better I should have dealt with Harry Sinden.) This guy was ornery and that's giving him the benefit of the doubt.

I tried very hard to be reasonable with him—until he said "All you car salesmen are alike."

That did it. I nailed him against the wall and would have pushed him through, but I managed to control myself a little and loosened my grip.

Somebody upstairs must have been giving me a message. Later I found myself alone in my bedroom. I got down on my hands and knees and looked up to the ceiling. "Lord," I said, "is this a life for me? I can't stand myself anymore. What am I going to do? I've worked hard. I've tried to be honest."

I know you've read many times about the Lord taking a liking to someone and that person being touched and helped. But I swear, it was as if someone put a new feeling into me. I suddenly knew exactly what I was doing, I got the old bounce back and I was ready to go. I will never forget that two minutes for as long as I live. It changed my life.

When I got off my knees, I knew exactly what I had to do. I went down to the sales manager's office to give him the word. But before I could get a sentence out of my mouth, the guy said, "Don, do you think you're cut out to be a car salesman?"

It seemed as if the Lord had talked to him, too. I thanked him for his patience, shook his hand and walked out into the sunshine. It was one of the happiest moments of my life, a heavy weight had been lifted from my shoulders.

What to do? What could I do? Here I was, 36 years old without even a high school diploma. I was a hockey player, period. So, what else could I do—I decided to make a comeback. (Desperate times make desperate people.)

My only hope was Doug Adam, general manager and coach of the Americans. I made an appointment to see him in the middle of July with training camp a good two months away. When I walked into his office he looked me over. It was embarrasing; I was 30 pounds overweight but Adam wasn't fazed. "Sure, we'll give you a chance," he said. And true to his word, he did.

Getting back into shape was almost as hard for me as selling Cadillacs. I bought myself a plastic sweat suit and a stationary bicycle. I put the bike in the back yard, donned the suit and pedaled like a mad man. When it rained I carried the bike into the attic and pedaled some more. Then it was off to the YMCA for more exercise and back home again. The most torturous aspect of the regimen was the fact that I was off beer. But counterbalancing that was the great motivator—fear of hunger. I was determined to earn another paycheck as a hockey player, not as a car salesman, and certainly not in an unemployment insurance line. I hoped my heart would hold out.

Soon word got around that I was trying for a comeback. My buddies at Kodak couldn't believe it; and wouldn't believe that I could make it. My pal, Whitey, was on my side and put fifty bucks on it. Every time I felt like quitting—or grabbing a beer—I thought of Whitey and the faith he had in me. That spurred me on even harder, and in five weeks I had cut my weight from 220 pounds down to 190. I had won fifty bucks for Whitey and was ready for another training camp.

Was it worth it? At first I suffered serious doubts. At 36, I was being treated like a fourth-string Junior. They gave me old gloves, shabby shoulder pads, the kind of equipment I wouldn't give to my kid playing shinny on a pond. But at least I wasn't selling cars. With that in mind, I went out and started scrimmaging.

At first I figured the rookies would give me a lot of grief. After all, we were battling for jobs, but they were more than friendly. In fact, what fooled me was that they were nice and seemed to want me to make the club. (I never could figure that out.) The bottom line would be the exhibition games. It was like 1954 all over again; I was auditioning for a job.

The first game was against my old club, the Hershey Bears. Unfortunately for me, the Bears had been practising for three weeks, while we only had a week under our belts. I played like I was a one-legged defenseman with a hernia. If someone had reviewed my act as "terrible," it would have been kind. Guys were walking around me left and right and moving in to score. After the game I phoned Rose and told her I had doubts about making the club. Thank heaven, she didn't quit on me. "Keep trying for another week or so," she said, "and see how it goes."

I skated out for the second exhibition game extremely doubtful about myself but willing to follow Rose's advice. For the first ten minutes I was absolutely nothing again. Then—bang!—it all came together and everything was beautiful again. It was as if I had turned the clock back a decade. I moved the puck confidently, bodychecked without fear and saw the ice clearly and as a whole. I played well enough for the Americans to offer me a contract—$11,000 for the season. It was the most money I had ever made for playing hockey.

Now it was time for the start of the season; the real stuff. Our opponents were the Cincinnati Swords. I couldn't wait. But before the opener Doug Adam announced that I wasn't to suit up. It turned out that the AHL was considered a development league for the NHL and the rule stipulated that each team could only play six guys over 26 years old. Don Cherry was the odd man out.

I was in a state of shock when Adam gave me the news. All that hard work for nothing. There wasn't much I could do, but watch and hope—that the Americans would get killed. They obliged, losing 8-1 to Cincy. Next time, Adam had me in the lineup.

The good vibrations I had from training camp carried over. I took a regular shift and came off with a plus-two. In the game after that—even though we lost—I got a goal and an assist and was named *the* star of the game. Overnight, I was leading the team in scoring, leading the team in plus-minus figures and was picked the star in two out of the three games. I *had* pulled off the comeback. Life was beautiful. Or, was it?

At the time Rochester was linked with Vancouver of the NHL and the Canucks didn't have me in their plans. But they were interested in seeing some of the kids develop. So, when we left for a road trip again Adam gave me the word—stay home! Not that I blame him; he had orders from the Canucks and there was nothing he could do about it.

There was no way I could keep my game sharply honed by just scrimmaging or playing the odd game and pretty soon I started to slip. Still, Adam would throw me in the odd game and I played as hard as I could. Most of all, I was determined, just as I had been in my younger days, that nobody would push me around. I didn't care how young, strong, or big the enemy might be; they would hear from me, if they began taking liberties.

The presiding policeman of the league at the time was a young, muscular left wing named Dave (The Hammer) Schultz. He played for the Richmond Robins, a Philadelphia Flyers farm team and he had set all kinds of penalty records in the Eastern League and also the AHL. When we went down to Richmond to play the Robins, the rink was packed. Not surprisingly, a lot of fans had come out to see Schultz beat up on somebody. I was ready for him.

Early in the game, Schultz got hold of the puck at our blue line and dumped it into the corner. I went in to get it and so did another Richmond player. We froze the puck, causing a whistle. Just then, Schultz gave me a shove. This was one of his favourite ploys; start with a push and then come back with the punches. Or, quickly move out of danger. With me, he moved out of danger. Somehow he must have sensed that I wasn't intimidated by him the way other players had been. I had seen him fight and I knew if I got the first one in I could hold my own, but if things started to go bad, there was still the stick. I still had some of the old fire left. I thought to myself, "What a great act he's got going. He's filling the rink and he's got all these guys buffaloed. He must be doing something right."

My teammates appreciated what I was doing and even though I wasn't playing all that often they looked upon me as the bull elephant of the squad. On one hand this was a compliment but on the other, it began to make me increasingly uneasy.

The players, for a number of reasons, had grown disrespectful of Doug Adam's coaching. They didn't fancy his autocratic attitude, his insensitivity, and his apparent aloofness about hockey in general. When Doug would lecture the club on a matter of strategy, the players almost routinely would turn to me as if awaiting my affirmation. After a while even Adam began looking over at me for approval. This was ridiculous. I didn't need any of the hassle and I didn't want it. All I wanted to do was finish the season and earn my $11,000. No more, no less. I just wanted to put some food in my family's mouths. But the kids kept mimicking everything I did. If I had a bad morning and didn't feel like working hard, they would take it easy, too. If I had the blahs, they had the blahs. Finally I took some of the guys aside and said, "Look, you gotta cut out this nonsense, or I'm going to be gone."

But the club had gone too far beyond Adam's grasp. Once there was a fight on the bus and *I* had to break it up because the coach couldn't do a thing. I realized this was burning up Adam, but also that it wasn't good for me. "You guys are gonna get me fired," I told them. When I told them that, they said, "Nah, Don, *you're* gonna be our next coach." All I could say was what I felt: "Will you guys shut up!"

Adam's problem was that he did nothing to indicate that he gave a damn about coaching. One night, we were beaten 10-1 by Richmond and he got on board the bus as if we had just routinely won another game. He sat in front reading a golf magazine. In fact, all he ever seemed to do was read golf books or magazines. But in spite of his nonchalance about losing, he did have his rules and they proved to be his undoing. Mostly, the rules had to do with clothes. Doug, himself, was the neatest man I have ever met. He was as immaculate when he got off the bus as when he got on, and he had the good looks to go with his clothes.

One of Doug's rules was that the players had to wear shirts and ties on the bus, no matter how long the trips. Sometimes, the bus rides ran as long as eight hours, but still, he insisted that shirt-and-tie were mandatory. Well, one day we were ready to take-off when a player walked on without a tie.

Adam: "Where's your tie?"
Player: "I don't have one."
Adam: "Go home and get one!"
The player said, "But I live over a half hour away from here."
Doug: "Go get it."
Can you believe he was going to make us wait an hour on the bus while this kid went home? I said, "I have an extra tie in the dressing room." So we all got off the bus and went into the dressing room. I gave the guy my tie and cut a strip off a towel for a tie for myself. I put that on, we climbed back on the bus and away we went.

Another rule had to do with hair length. At a time when everyone, including the Prime Minister of Canada, was wearing his hair down to his shoulders, Adam decreed that the Rochester Americans *had* to have short hair.

And finally, there was the no-beer-on-the-bus rule. That one just about did Doug in. We would get on the bus, the motor would start, we would be off and rolling when you could hear the cans opening and the boys guzzling. There was nothing Doug could do about it by this time, any more than he could do anything about the drinking of soda pop in the morning, which he also hated. Usually, the kids would want pop early in the day because they had been drinking the night before and were dry and thirsty. One time we were in Baltimore, waiting on the bus, when a pushcart came along. The vendor had pop and hot dogs. Nineteen guys went out and bought pop, right in front of Adam. It irritated Doug no end, but there was nothing he could do about it. I mean, he couldn't suspend the whole team.

Doug was living in 1950 and there was no way he could turn the calendar ahead. We had a practice one afternoon before a road trip and after the workout one of the guys who loathed Adam got really drunk. When we loaded up, he sat in the back of the bus with me.

Doug had spotted him when he got on and had bawled him out for drinking. The guy sat down beside me and, as the driver revved up the motor, he pulled out a knife. I nearly dropped dead when I saw it because I knew what he planned to do. I quietly put the arm on him—trying very carefully not to make a scene—and sat with him the whole trip.

Our leading scorer was Jim Wiste who had played for the Chicago Black Hawks and Vancouver Canucks before winding up in Rochester. He was a good guy with few faults, but one idiosyncracy: he liked to have his skates sharpened just right. If they weren't sharpened to his feel, he'd moan. But, he *was* our leading scorer. Well, one day he went into Adam's office to beef about the skates. "I don't think you like it here," said Adam.

"No, no," Wiste insisted, "I do like it here. It's just that I don't like the way the skates are being sharpened."

Next thing we knew, Wiste had been traded. Adam got rid of our best player, just because he complained about his skates.

Meanwhile the "discipline" got worse and worse. He forbade players to use anything but straight sticks, and the seeds of the rebellion began to sprout. A couple of players began growing longer hair. On the bus, some of the kids would sing songs from *Hair* and other pop musicals and Adam would get livid. The mutiny was out in the open.

Our fans also were getting mutinous. When we were hammered, 9-1 at home the shit really hit the fan. After the game some of our own Rochester rooters went after Adam and actually attacked him in the arena. He escaped pretty much unscathed but, by this time, everyone seemed to realize that the inmates were running the asylum. Me, all I wanted to do was have a few drinks and forget it. An old defenseman pal of mine, Bob Blackburn, and myself went out and started to have a few, well into the morning.

It was two o'clock when I walked in and there was Rose waiting up for me, obviously furious. "Do you realize," she said, "that the club has been phoning you since 11 o'clock? And they've been phoning every half hour on the hour! They want to see you."

"Well, it's too late to call now," I replied.

"No, it isn't," she insisted. "They want to hear from you, no matter what the hour."

I got on the blower and, sure enough, they wanted me to come right down to a local luncheonette for an emergency meeting. My wife was still angry but I calmed her; or so I thought. "Rose, old girl, don't you worry. When I get home I'm gonna be coach of the Rochester Americans."

She couldn't understand that. Her husband coaching a professional hockey team. No way! But I had it all figured out before I left the house: if they had wanted to fire me, they would have waited until the next morning before giving me the news. They certainly wouldn't have phoned me every half hour.

Besides, Adam, who was still the general manager, must have figured that by having me coach he would bail himself out. I could imagine him telling the directors: "Look, we're payin' this guy $11,000. The fans love him. The players love him. The media love him. Let's see what he can do; and if he can't do it, let him die."

Sure enough, when we sat down over coffee at 3 a.m. the offer was made. I could become coach of the Rochester Americans *at no raise in pay*.

Did that bother me? Not on your life. I laughed at it. What mattered was that I suddenly felt supremely confident that I could be a leader of hockey players and do something positive for this team. "I'll take it," I said.

Returning home the conquering hero, I expected Rose to be tickled to hear the news. She wasn't. In fact, she still wouldn't talk to me. That drinking bout had been a little too long to suit her and, to tell you the truth, to suit me. I greeted my first day as a professional hockey coach with a profound hangover. But I was coach and I was ready to go.

As for Adam, he acted as if I was there to coach for a day, two if I was lucky. At the press conference announcing my new position, a reporter asked Doug about my future. "Yeah" he said, "Don has the job now but you know how it is—coaches are hired to be fired!" (Great stuff. Here I am starting off my first day on the job and the g.m. says I'm hired to be fired.)

Now, the test would come. Could I handle eighteen hockey players—each with different personalities, different hang-ups, different playing styles, and all much younger than I was? I felt exceptionally confident about it, as if I had been born to the job. I felt like the newly-appointed captain of a ship; except that this ship had several leaks.

We had one guy, Bobby Lalonde; a little fellow, very fast, who belonged to Vancouver. I knew that the Canucks wanted him to play, but I also knew that he didn't give a damn and I had chapter and verse to back that up.

Lalonde knew that Vancouver wanted him to play as much as possible, but he was not my type of player and, as far as I was concerned, not helping us win games. When I didn't play him, Lalonde would phone his father, his agent, and the Canucks front office, in that order, to bitch about me. I didn't care, because he had lost my respect by his actions. Once, we were in Providence for a game and it was a big one for us. Providence was the team we were trying to catch in the playoff race.

So, what do you think Lalonde did? He brought his girlfriend to Providence for a visit and told me he didn't want to play; claimed that *he had come up with a sore groin*. Why, he didn't even go to the game. He sat with his girlfriend in the car while the rest of the guys were playing their hearts out on the ice, while decimated with injuries. Some guy.

Buffalo was playing Vancouver the next night, in Buffalo, so I wanted to see how badly his groin was really hurt. I said to Bobby, "Vancouver needs a player in Buffalo tonight. How are you? Is your groin all right?" Lalonde said, "Oh yeah, Great!" He had found a twenty-four hour cure. So, when he walked into the Vancouver dressing room that night with his skates and said, "I'm ready to go, coach," they all had a big laugh.

Two weeks later, Vancouver really did ask for Lalonde, for a game in Toronto. So I told him, and he thought I was kidding again and he didn't go. When they called and asked where Lalonde was I said I didn't know, but that he had been told. There are always ways of getting even.

We were sixteen points out of a playoff berth and, slowly but surely, we began to close the gap. Oddly enough, this did not make any impression on Doug Adam. He resented the way I was going with *my* players and my theories about motivation. His biggest knock against me was that I was thinking too much as a player and not enough as management. But the game of hockey had changed, just as the people who were playing it had changed. The old authoritarian methods of the 1930s were no longer workable. Now you had to make the players *want* to play for you. *Motivation* had become the most important word in the game.

My theory on motivation is that if you work hard for your players, they'll work hard for you. I did everything I could for them right down to making demands of the public relations department so that the players could benefit. (The p.r. man and his secretary didn't like me, because they felt I was a tyrant.) The players knew I was sacrificing my job for them, so they gave me everything they had.

One guy who busted his gut for me was a goalie named Lynn

Zimmerman. Management didn't like him because he had long hair and they said I shouldn't play him. Our other goalie, Serge Aubry, had the strangest contract of all. The deal was that if he didn't play in so many games the Canucks had to give him a bonus of $5,000, if you can believe that one. But that's the way it was. Aubry was an all right guy, but he was having a tough time and Zimmerman, who was considered a journeyman minor leaguer, was not. I played Lynn but every time I did I'd get heat from the Canucks. They wanted to save money; what did they care whether or not we made the playoffs?

Adam was a company man and whenever I did something to benefit the Americans, but which was counter to the Canucks' philosophy, he would get upset. The Zimmerman affair was one running problem but that wasn't all. We were getting closer and closer to reaching a playoff berth when we lost a tough game one night. After the game I got a call from Adam. "Well, Don, what are ya gonna do?"

Naturally, I assumed he was talking strategy or player changes or some such significant matter related to getting the team into the playoffs. I then explained what I had in mind for the next couple of games.

"No, no," said Adam, "not that. I mean Garth Rizzuto. What are we gonna do about him? *He's growing a mustache!*"

That's not the capper. We were in the last part of the homestretch and everyone was keyed up because we were just a couple of points out of a playoff berth. At this point, Adam demanded that all the players break in a new pair of skates. Now anyone connected with hockey realizes that it sometimes takes weeks to break in a pair of new skates. In the process, the players often feel terribly uncomfortable with the new blades on. So, I had to fight Adam on still another front.

Still, we remained in contention and got a break when the Canucks sent us Bobby Schmautz, a hard-nosed, hard-shooting forward. Schmautzie and I hit it off immediately. I played him more and more until, finally, in one game he was on the ice for a good 50 minutes of 60. Meantime, I benched Bobby Lalonde.

Schmautz was averaging about two points a game and I was sure he would spearhead us into the playoffs in spite of Adam. When Schmautzie first arrived in Doug's office he was wearing a turtle-neck sweater. Neat, mind you, but not a shirt and tie. Adam stared at him momentarily and said, "On this club we *all* wear shirts and ties." Schmautzie looked at me as if he had just been cast for *Alice in Wonderland*. That night he went out and got so drunk he could hardly make practice. Unfortunately, Schmautzie played so well for me that the Canucks, who were going nowhere, recalled him just when we needed his goals for the final playoff push.

Now we were down to the last couple of games and it looked as if we might make it. On the one hand I was hoping to keep the guys concentrating on the race, and on the other I was hoping desperately that Adam, who continued to butt in, wouldn't make the players so crazy that they would be distracted enough to blow the whole thing at the very end.

We had a game in Springfield—another big one—but it was on the same day I had a commitment to coach the Pittsford High School team in a Saturday morning championship game. I decided to meet the guys in Springfield. They would go on the team bus—tragically, with Adam—and I would hook up with them at the arena.

My friend Hans Tanner who also covered the Americans for the *Rochester Democrat-Chronicle* and I were chatting a day before the game and I mentioned that I would meet him in Springfield. "You're making a mistake," he said. "You'd better not let them travel alone with Adam. There might be a mutiny."

I should have known better. I should have realized the intensity of the players' hatred for Adam and that it was like mixing fire and gasoline allowing them in the bus together, without me.

From all reports the bus drive was chaos on wheels. The sight of Adam sitting in the front seat seemed to kindle all the fury that had built up over the season—the long hair edicts, the tie-on-the-bus code, everything.

As soon as the bus took off, Adam tried to doze off. Knowing that he detested the pop music of the day, the guys began a chorus of "(I Can't Get No) Satisfaction" to the stamping of their feet and several guys did imitations of The Rolling Stones. Other players would shoot water pistols, and the din was such that Adam couldn't have fallen asleep if he had taken an overdose of ether. But even that wasn't enough. Some other guys got the bright idea of starting a bonfire in the aisle. In a matter of a minute the flames were reaching the ceiling, forcing the bus driver to pull over to the side of the road.

They managed to extinguish the fire and the ringleaders finally simmered down and at least momentarily put aside any further thoughts about an uprising. The amazing thing about it all was Adam's attitude when I finally met him in Springfield. He wasn't upset about the fire in the bus and he wasn't angry about being awakened by the raucous singing. What bugged him was the fact that two of our best players, Lynn Zimmerman and Bob Walton, still had long hair. To Adam, *that* was the most outrageous act of defiance and demanded immediate reprisal. "Are you gonna back me up on the hair issue?" he asked.

Here I was, trying to get the guys psyched up so that we could sneak into a playoff berth and Adam was making a federal case about hair styles. "Look, look," I pleaded, "I'll have them get a trim, but not now. Lemme get ready for the game."

He persisted. "Don, you have to decide which side you're on. Now, are you or are you not going to become a company man?"

There was really no need to reply but I did: "I do what I think is right. I'm not a company man." Having said that, I knew I was finished, as long as Adam was in charge. That would come later. Now for the game. The way I figured it, if we could handle Springfield, we could gather the momentum we needed for the last big thrust into the playoffs. I was very high for this one, in spite of all the problems; in spite of Doug Adam.

Every so often Adam would find someone he wanted pushed into the lineup; usually a player I wanted benched. There was a right wing by the name of Dave Westin he was foisting on me. I said we didn't need him. He said we did, because we were shorthanded. No, I insisted, we don't need him. "Well," snapped Adam, "dress him anyway. And play him."

I was so disgusted I decided not to press the issue. Once the game began I would make sure that Westin didn't get any ice. The sad part was that I let him dress for the warm-up. I had a very strict team rule, especially at this time of the season, that during the pre-game practice nobody was to shoot high at the goaltenders. "Keep your shots low," I warned them as they went out for the warm-up.

My goalie for the night was to be Zimmerman. Long hair and all, he was the better of the two and he was on a roll. Zimmy looked good in practice. Then Westin skated in and rifled the puck at Zimmy's head. To save his life, Zimmy put his hand up in front of his face. The shot broke his hand. Zimmy was finished, which meant I had to put Aubry into the nets and Serge hadn't played for a long time. Still, we built up a 3-0 lead in the first period and were looking good. But Aubry couldn't hold them. They came back with three. Then, we rallied and won by a big score.

The 16 point deficit that had faced us earlier was nearly wiped out. We had won something like 18 out of 26 games and were down to our last game. Our opponent was Cincinnati. If we beat them we were in; otherwise it was fun while it lasted.

My old buddy, Floyd Smith, was coaching the Swords, who had first place locked up, and he started a goalie who didn't figure to be a problem for us. But the son-of-a-gun played the game of his life. Still, our guys persisted and we went into the third period leading, 3-2. From then on, we got even better and outshot them 17-1. Can you believe that, we outshot them 17-1 and on that one shot they scored and on our 17 shots, we got zip!

We missed the playoff berth by a hair. We were tied in the standings with Providence, but they had one more win. After the game I wasn't down, I was subterranean. Still, I kept my cool, explaining to my young son that you must have grace and act like a gentleman, and not be a sore loser. No ranting, no raving. We did our best and lost. And I was cool and collected, until the statistician brought me the scoresheet and I saw the shots-on-goal for the third period. I grabbed a stick from the rack and smashed it on the floor, breaking it clean in half. Then I took another stick and broke that one too. Then, another and another until I had wasted ten sticks in a row. So much for self-control, grace, etc. Timothy was wide-eyed—a fine example!

The only sure thing ahead was that either Doug Adam or I was going to get fired, and I've never known a situation where a coach fired his general manager. Obviously, if the fans had had their way Adam would have gone bye-bye a long time ago. At the last game of the season the fans gave me a "night" and when Adam was introduced the fans booed for over five minutes as he tried to talk.

The bottom line was the Vancouver Canucks. They had put Adam in charge and as long as the Americans were connected with the Canucks, there would be no way that Adam would be relieved of his job. A couple of days after the season ended I read the handwriting on the wall. Rick Sayers, a reporter for the *Rochester Times-Union*, asked Adam about my future. His reply would have a familiar ring for me in the future.

He admitted that I "did a good job on the ice," but it was my off-ice activity that displeased him. Was I a thief? No. Did I cheat on my wife? No. Was I a drug abuser? No. So, how did I hurt the club with my off-ice activities?

"Sure all the guys loved him," said Adam. "He'd do anything for them. But until he learns to be management, he'll never be a coach."

I couldn't leave bad enough alone, so I answered Adam in print. I told the newspaper guy exactly what I thought of the situation and it wasn't good. "My aim is to win at any cost," I said. "I feel that telling a player to do this and not to do that—as Adam did—is like living in 1945. The way to coach in sports today is to motivate the players. That's what I tried to do."

Knowing that I was a goner, I figured that I'd shop around for work. The experience behind the Americans' bench convinced me that coaching *was* for me, but where? I had gotten one tip that the Charlotte Checkers of the Eastern League were looking for somebody, so I decided to check that out and, meanwhile, wait for Adam to drop the guillotine. It fell two weeks later. He phoned and asked me to meet him in his office. I didn't expect to get a five-year contract.

As I walked into Adam's office, I had to pass both the club secretary and the public relations man, neither of whom ranked on my all-time favourite list. Both of them were wearing big grins on their faces as if they already knew that I had been canned. I made a mental note of their smirks for future use.

Adam was sitting behind his desk, pompously smoking a little, black cigar. He puffed, blew a plume of smoke and said, "Don, we're making a change in your department."

I thought to myself, "Who's in my department?" Then I remembered: I was the only one in my department. I said good-bye and walked out. The public relations man and the secretary were laughing now. I couldn't resist the temptation. "You shouldn't chuckle at me that way. I'm like a bad penny. You never know when I'm going to turn up. Toodle-oo!"

Well, here I was again, no job, bad-mouthed by management and loved by the fans, players and media, who couldn't hire me anyway. When I got home Rose asked me if I was planning to go to the hockey meetings in Montreal where everyone with a job offer would show up. "I'm not going to go begging," I said.

That really grated one of Rose's nerves. "Oh," she said, "you're not going to beg for a job. You're too proud. You never think of your family. You never think of your son and daughter going to college. We never have any money. Just you, that's all you can think of."

When I stopped to think about it, she was right. Rose was exasperated by my behaviour. No money, no job and no intentions of looking for one. I had to make a move of some kind. Out of desperation I phoned Bud Poile, the general manager of the Canucks, just for a couple of leads.

"To tell you the truth, Don," Poile said, "if you were *your brother* I would hire you. Sorry." *Click!*.

Shortly thereafter, I received a call from a man who identified himself as Al Manch. He owned the Charlotte Checkers, the club I had checked out earlier. He was interested in me coaching the team and wondered if I'd come down for an interview. Under the circumstances, who could say no?

Manch was a nice man who picked me up at the airport and drove me to a meeting with the group of Southern gentlemen who helped run the team. For a minute I thought this club was directed by the cast from *Gone With The Wind*. You could cut their drawls with a knife and still have a "y'all" left over.

It took about half a second to realize that these guys wouldn't know which end of a hockey stick was up. But they did have the money and they did operate the team. So, when all was said and done, they owned the puck.

Finally, we sat down, very cordially, and the men began grilling me. They wanted to know my "philosophy of hockey." They asked me about the rudiments of coaching and the most far-out questions imaginable, from the relativity of pucks to transmeditation. When I was released from the meeting, I excused myself and took a long walk to think about what had transpired. It *was* a bummer, that was for sure, but it also was a hockey job and that was nothing to knock.

As I walked through town in the rain, several thoughts coursed through my brain, and for a change I was filled with self-doubt. Here I was, 37 years old, and unemployed—again! Why did I always have to prove myself in a fight? All I had to do was cooperate with Doug Adam and I still would be sitting pretty in Rochester.

I questioned my stubborn streak; the phone call from Joe Crozier— granted it was late—offering me another chance to play; Doug Adam asking me to be sure the guys cut their hair and my challenging him. "When," I asked myself, "am I going to learn?"

Soaked to the skin, I returned to my hotel room for more contemplation. I got into bed and cracked open a book. All of a sudden I felt something strange, something foreign, on my body. I put the book aside momentarily and there, as big as my thumb, was a cockroach running across my chest.

That did it. I picked myself up, packed my clothes, checked out of the hotel and returned home. My decision did not sit well with Rose, but I had decided to stick to my guns. I might starve—and my wife and kids might starve, too—but that Charlotte hotel cockroach did me in.

Through the whole mess, I knew there was one factor in my favour—things could not get worse, they *had* to get better.

Little did I know how prophetic that was.

CHAPTER THIRTEEN

Comeback

II

Here I was, without a job again, with nothing on the horizon. I should have been worried, but I had that gut feeling that the Lord would help to turn things around. Boy, did he turn things around with a vengeance.

Bob Clarke (the friend who had got me started coaching at Pittsford High School) phoned and said:

"Don, seven businessmen and I have bought the Rochester Americans and we'd like you to coach."

"Great Bob! I'm ready."

"Don't you want to know the salary?"

"Who cares?"

"It's $15,000."

I hung up and excitedly told Rose.

She asked: "Why not g.m. too?"

I called Bob back, and we agreed that I'd be g.m. for the same salary.

There was one problem. The season was six weeks away and the team had no players. The NHL had expanded again and the World Hockey Association had just come along. I didn't care; at last I had found a general manager with whom I could get along—me! If nothing else, I marvelled at my progress. In three days I had been transformed from a down-and-out, unemployed, old hockey player with a roach running across his chest to a coach and general manager of an American League team.

I could not forget the looks of joy that covered the faces of the public relations man and his secretary the day I had been fired. I wondered how they would react when they learned that I was now their boss, and what I would do about them. (I wasn't thinking kind thoughts.) I didn't want to fire them immediately. I decided that I would let them suffer a bit, for maybe a month or two.

But I had more important things on my mind than revenge. I still had to put a team together. I got hold of my friend Hans Tanner, the hockey writer with the *Democrat-Chronicle*, and asked him to sit down with me and help lay out a team. Hans agreed and the first question he asked was who my first choice—assuming I *had* a choice—would be for the Don Cherry-run Rochester Americans. I said Bob (Battleship) Kelly. He was a tall, tough forward with a quick temper and could he ever handle his dukes.

"Where did he play last year?" Tanner asked. I couldn't for the life of me remember, so we looked it up and it turned out that Kelly had been at Omaha but he also had been suspended for punching out his coach. Just the kind of guy I wanted. We decided to try to get Kelly. That left eighteen more places to fill, so I laid out an itinerary for scouting the NHL training camps in hope of wangling a few players cut from the big teams' rosters.

My first stop was going to be London, Ontario, where the Bruins were training, but as luck would have it, Prime Minister Trudeau was starting his political campaign in the town and I couldn't get a hotel or motel room. So, I went back to the car and drove ninety miles to Kitchener where the Rangers were training. Emile (The Cat) Francis was running the team at the time and I knew that he was an early bird. I made a point of being at the rink at 7 a.m., when the other bird dogs were still asleep. But as I approached the front door of the rink I noticed a big sign saying "PLAYERS ONLY!"

What to do? I went back to my car and then got a brainstorm. I was once a player; why not become a "player" again? I took off my tie and sports coat and then I went limping back to the front door. I hobbled to the entrance to the rink and pretended that my back was out of whack. The guard sized me up for a moment and then said, "Tough practice session yesterday?"

I put on my most serious look and replied: "It sure was." And then kept on walking. Then, I got lucky; my old teammate Bronco Horvath was there and he introduced me to Denis Ball, one of the top Rangers' brass. I sat across the aisle from him all morning watching the big club practice and looking for players who might be possibilities for the Americans.

I didn't know who they would give me. The Rangers' top farm team was Providence in the American League. The leftovers from Providence would be sent to Cape Cod of the Eastern League. Denis gave me a list of a dozen players who *might* be available to me and rated them. Then, I drove to London and talked with Milt Schmidt of the Bruins. At one point, I felt I was spending most of my time driving the ninety miles from Kitchener to London. I knew that the Rangers and Bruins were the clubs I had to get help from and the Rangers, at least, came through.

Denis phoned one night and said, "I've got some players for you. Do you want Battleship Kelly?" Was he kidding? If it meant carrying Kelly a hundred miles on my back to training camp I would have been willing to do it. They sold us Kelly for $7,500, and sent us seven more skaters, I didn't figure to get scorers, so I wanted guys with size who could batter people around. I wanted to play the game physically.

With a little scrounging here and a little there, I managed to put together a team, but the proof would be on the ice when we held our first scrimmage. It was late September and the NHL clubs still hadn't made their final cuts so, whatever happened, we weren't facing a catastrophe quite yet. Still, the first workout scared the pants off me. Talk about a ragtag team, this bunch didn't even look like a good amateur club. Unfortunately, the new owners were there watching and, like me, they were absolutely sick, and I knew it.

"Hold tight!" I said. "We'll get better; don't worry about it. Don't panic." They weren't particularly convinced but, luckily, the NHL clubs began making their final cuts and a few more mean fellows, who were willing to try hard, joined our club. Gradually, with my assistant general manager and public relations man John Denhamer working night and day, our prospects began to improve and the owners were relieved.

Best of all, we had Battleship Kelly who lived up to my fondest expectations. There were no ifs, ands, or buts about Battleship; he was a great fighter and a solid hockey player. We played that image to the hilt. Kelly would bandage his hands—just like the professional boxers—before a game. As the teams lined up for the National Anthem, the house lights would dim and one spotlight would focus on Battleship. He would hold up his long arms with all the tape on his hands and the crowd would go wild.

Brother, could he ever fight. One night we were in New Haven and Kelly got into a scrap with Kevin Morrison, who had to be one of the best fighters in professional hockey. Fights on the ice usually are nothing to write home about but the Kelly-Morrison bout was right out of the *Gunfight at the OK Corral*. Morrison's reputation as a good man with his dukes had spread around the American League and so had Kelly's, but the pair had never met before and a lot of people had been wondering what would happen if they ever did clash.

The prelude to the main event was a couple of small skirmishes that enabled Battleship and Kevin to pair off. But once everyone realized just who the two sluggers were, all other action froze. The referee, the linesmen and the players stopped everything they were doing and formed a circle around Kelly and Morrison. A strange quiet came over the building as if the thousands of fans realized that they were about to witness a very special collision of strongmen.

The battlers approached each other cautiously; each waiting for the other to strike the first blow. Suddenly, Kevin lashed out and caught Kelly with a quick jab and then all hell broke loose. Morrison was clearly the aggressor at the beginning and did a great job of putting Battleship on the defensive for the first few seconds, but I could tell that Kelly was hanging tough with a purpose. He finally got his long arms untangled and then began to pummel Morrison with a series of lefts and rights that first drove Kevin to the boards and then, after an awesome wallop, draped him over the boards.

That was the only thing we won. New Haven beat us on the scoreboard, but I remained undaunted and, at game's end, I stood on the boards with Kelly and held his arm aloft, as if I was saluting the heavyweight champion of the American League. Battleship then skated around the rink three times with his arms triumphantly upraised. Needless to say, the New Haven fans went wild, throwing things at my man. No matter. We were hot stuff; the people were coming out to see Don Cherry's Rochester Americans. Hockey is but another form of entertainment and we *were* entertaining.

Most important, we had developed an image; we were, first and foremost, a tough team. Reporters liked to ask me what I wanted in a hockey player. The answer was simple: to play on my team he *had* to have guts, otherwise there was no room for him on the Americans.

A lot of coaches will take players as long as they can score goals, even if they are gutless. If you have one guy who is willing to go into the corners and get his brains bashed in, why shouldn't some other guy go into the corner as well? That was my philosophy in putting together a successful team. Once the guts requirement was fulfilled, I then looked for skating ability, and hockey sense. A lot of players can shoot well, skate and stickhandle but they don't have hockey sense, which is essentially intuition on the ice.

Our play-'em-tough credo soon had reverberations around the league. Battleship Kelly, our chief enforcer, became the scourge of the AHL. Some players on the opposition simply did not want to come out on the ice against us. Prior to a game against the Americans these players would develop what we came to call "The Rochester Flu." This "flu" was of very short duration. As soon as the game against the Americans was over, it would disappear and the player would be ready for action again.

There were a lot of Nervous Nellies around who didn't appreciate our robust approach to the game. Some coaches and managers complained about our tactics and, of course, the referees would often give us a hard time. I remember a game we had with Hershey. The place was packed to capacity, a standing room only crowd, and we brutalized the Bears. We took a lot of penalties but they beat us, 6-1. After the game the Hershey coach, Frank Mathers, actually shook the hands of the referee for a job well done. I was infuriated. I told the newspaper guys that the score was deceptive; it really was a tie because we put *five* of their players out of action.

Hershey wasn't the only one of my old "home towns" where I suffered grief on my return. Barrie, Ontario, was another. That, you may recall, was where I played my junior hockey with the Barrie Flyers. I always felt a special affection for the town and decided one year that it would be nice to return there and play an exhibition game against the local senior team now being coached by my old pal, Darryl Sly.

This game was a good lesson in how quickly the fans forget. I returned to Barrie not as a home town-hero-made-good but as coach of the enemy team, an *American* enemy team at that. It didn't matter to them that we had come to Barrie to help raise money for the local club. We gave them about $1,400 worth of equipment and it cost us $2,000 just to get there. Well, anyhow, the game began and, as always, we started hitting and the fans immediately got upset. The tension grew more intense as the game got more violent. As it happened, I was in an unfortunate position. Because we were carrying a surplus of players there was no room for me on or in front of the bench so I was cramped into a two-by-three foot space behind our bench, right in front of the regular seats.

Midway through the third period a big fight broke out on the ice and the fans were really going crazy. Two of them walked down from the upper reaches of the arena and sat down directly behind my position at the bench. Their feet were just about at the level of my head. These guys started abusing the players, trainers and me and kept telling us how rotten America was. Granted, with Watergate going on at the time they had a good target, but they finally went beyond the bounds of acceptable fan abuse. The language was awful so I politely asked them to let up. Well, all that did was encourage them into even more profanity. As I walked back and forth in my tiny coaching space they began harassing me in particular and even started to touch me.

I had invited a few friends from Rochester to come over and watch the game that night and I was particularly embarrassed for them. Once more, I tried to quiet the abusing fans but, this time, they turned on me and offered the challenge, "Why don't you come over here and make us shut up?"

Before I could make a move, I felt a sharp whack on the top of the head. Since there were no police or ushers around to maintain decorum, I decided that I had to take matters into my own hands. I dashed from my cramped position, over the boards, and toward my two antagonists. One of them fled, screaming, but I nabbed the other guy and after a bit of a tussle threw him back into the crowd. More fans invaded our bench area and pandemonium reigned. I was knocked down and landed on my back, breaking a bench in the process. At that moment I was stunned, and didn't know what was happening although I was later told that fans were trying to hit me and players, who by now were themselves being attacked, were stepping on me.

In the next moment the wife of one of the two guys who had originally been bugging us, jumped on my chest and began kicking me in the face. (Fortunately, the sharp-pointed women's shoes were not in vogue at the time.) That woke me up. After taking a few more blows, I decided that I would invoke an amendment to the Men's Liberation Act, so I kicked her where the sun don't shine until she retreated, shouting "I wish I had killed you, ya bum!"

The police arrived after the fight had ended but that was just the start of my troubles. I was arrested and charged with assault causing bodily harm. Me, a guy who had never even had a speeding ticket in his life, never been in jail, never been in court. Next thing I knew I was in the police station being fingerprinted and having my picture taken, like a common criminal. I hired a lawyer and he laid the cards on the table.

"One of the guys claims you damaged his suit and it's worth eighty-two bucks. If you pay for the suit and apologize to him and his wife, he'll drop the charges."

To begin with, his clothes weren't worth eighty-two bucks. For another thing, what was I supposed to apologize for? My clothes had been ripped, my adopted country had been insulted, and I had to stay in Barrie for an extra two days while Rose was in a Rochester hospital being treated for a kidney stone. No way was I going to apologize. Which meant only one thing—we would have to go to trial.

Maybe if I had had an idea of the torture I would have to endure at the trial I would have been more restrained to begin with, although I doubt it; the provocation was too severe. In any event, I had to make five trips to Barrie before the actual trial got underway.

The trial opened with my enemy—the guy who started it in the first place—telling the court that I was the rottenest, worst guy in the world. Listening to him, you would have thought snakes looked good by comparison. For the whole day I had to listen to him give it to me. How I had beaten him up and kicked his wife, the whole bit. I couldn't say a word of rebuttal.

My turn came the next day. I stood before the judge and began answering his questions. The more I talked, the more my opponent would chuckle and generally make disparaging asides about me. The more he turned and laughed with his friends the more I became exasperated. I thought to myself, "If I'm going to jail, I'm going out on my shield, because this weasel is not going to laugh at everything I say."

I finally said: "Your Honour, I sat here all day yesterday with my mouth shut, listening to the charges and the answers to your questions. Now that I'm up here, he's making a mockery out of everything I say. Do I have to take this?"

The judge looked down at me and I thought, "Uh oh, he looks mad. I'll bet he says 'control your temper, Mr. Cherry, because that's what got you here in the first place.'" But, the judge cleared his throat. "No, you don't, Mr. Cherry." Then he turned to my accuser and snapped: "One more word or action from you and you'll be put out of this court room."

The questions came fast and furious and I did my best to answer them as did my players, who sought to defend me. Some of my players went wild trying to defend me. For instance, my goalie, Bob Sneddon, said he saw the whole thing and that I never laid a finger on the man. Well, how in the world could Bob have seen it; he was in the net, one hundred feet away, wearing his goalie mask, I found out later.

I tried to be as truthful as possible in answering the questions, but I had no idea how the judge was leaning. Finally, after hearing me for several hours, he said, "Mr. Cherry, you remind me of a person who momentarily lost his cool."

"You're absolutely right, Your Honour." With that, he ended the trial and invited us back for the verdict the next day. I wasn't convinced that I would be handed a "not guilty" verdict, but I wasn't feeling too depressed either because a lot of people had rallied behind me, including Darryl Sly and Bep Guidolin, the former NHL player who preceded me as coach of the Bruins. Somebody asked Bep why he had come and he joked, "If Don is going to get sixty days I wanted to assure him I'd be sending fresh macaroni and chicken to the jailhouse."

Now it was time for the verdict. Preceding me on the stand was the fellow who had originally preceded me at the station house when I had been brought in. This fellow had thrown hot water at his wife in a dispute and the judge sentenced him to ninety days in jail. He was up for assault causing bodily harm, the same charge I had. Was I going to get hit for ninety days, too? I had started to visualize myself in prison stripes behind bars when the judge began addressing me:

"Mr. Cherry, I don't believe a word of what your players said here on the stand. Your players would lie their way to hell for you, so I don't believe them and I'm going to have to convict you!"

My head began to spin and my knees got weak, but the judge went on, turning to my enemy: "On the other hand, I find the actions of the plaintiff disgusting." He then ripped into the guy for defaming the United States and instigating the riot. Finally, "I find Mr. Cherry an honourable gentleman who just happened to lose his cool in the moment of battle. Sentence suspended!"

Instead of keeping my big mouth shut, I immediately got to my feet. My lawyer was afraid I was going to louse up the whole thing and grabbed my arm, but it was too late. "Your Honour," I proclaimed. "Someday I'm going to be coaching in the National Hockey League and I want you to know that I will never allow myself to become involved with people like this again. That is a promise."

"That's all I want to hear, Mr. Cherry," said the judge who then cleared the courtroom.

The question was, could I keep my word? The test came during a game in Richmond, Virginia. We had gotten into an extremely physical match-up with the local club, the Robins, and I was in rare form, standing on the bench, yapping away at the referee. As I stepped down to my normal position, an older man leaned over and corked me dead center and stunned me momentarily, shouting, "How do you like that—you no good sonofabitch!"

Instinctively, I reached up and grabbed him by the collar, pulled my arm back and began the inevitable follow-through to his jaw (which probably would have killed the old guy) when a vision of the judge in Barrie came to mind and activated my arm emergency brake. I merely pushed the guy out of the way and resumed coaching.

That act of contrition probably saved my career, because I would have been drawn and quartered in Richmond for hitting one of their Southern "gentlemen."

The notoriety of the Rochester Americans did not hurt us at home or on the road. During the 1972-73 season our leader was Battleship Kelly. He played in 70 games, scored 27 goals and 35 assists for 62 points and wound up with 206 minutes in penalties. I loved Battleship like a son and I would have liked to have him remain in Rochester as long as I was the coach and general manager, but I also had an obligation to the kid; he belonged in the NHL and I made it my business to try to arrange that he move into the bigs. I made a deal with the St. Louis Blues for $50,000, which was a big profit, because we had originally obtained Battleship for a song.

A week after the deal had been completed a huge box arrived at the house. I opened it up and there was a colour television set with a note from Battleship Kelly (and his agent Charles Abrahams), thanking me for what I had done for his career. That says something for Kelly's class.

With Battleship gone, I needed another enforcer for the 1973-74 campaign. There was only one thing to do; scrounge around the training camps in September, 1973 to see what the big-league clubs had at the bottom of their barrels. Since I had had success in finding Kelly, I figured I might come up with another diamond-in-the-rough. And I did, at the training base of the St. Louis Blues.

The player in question didn't look like a hockey player when I first cast eyes on him. Standing six feet tall and weighing 200 pounds, John Wensink was wearing a hairdo that looked like a willow tree, embellished by a frightening Fu Manchu mustache.

His skating was so atrocious I had half a mind to buy him a pair of double-runners. Yet there was something about him that I liked; call it an animal instinct, a ferocity that went far beyond anything that Battleship had betrayed. The Blues had him ticketed for Port Huron, a team in the International League, which was below the AHL. I made a deal with the Blues and within four days, Wensink was a Rochester American. In my heart I knew that the fans would like him as much as they had enjoyed Kelly.

The Blues g.m., Chuck Catto, and their chief scout came down to see John play his first game. They came to me after the game and said, "Don, we're sorry. We didn't mean to stick you with a player as bad as Wensink. You can let him go." I said, "I thought he played great." They looked at me as if I was nuts, because John had played terribly, but I could tell there was something there.

Besides beef, I needed some scoring punch. Buffalo had a winger called Murray Kuntz. I bought him for the Americans and he made me look like a genius, scoring a league-leading 51 goals that year. Then again, there were some guys who made me look like a bum. The classic example was a moon-faced defenseman, Jean Gauthier, who played for the Montreal Canadiens and about a dozen other teams both in the minors and the NHL. When I spotted him, Gauthier was still Canadiens' property, so I approached Sammy Pollock, general manager of the Montreal club and a fellow regarded as a genius for knowing and manipulating players. "Sam," I said, "I'd like to sign Gauthier."

Pollock agreed, but offered me a bit of advice. "You can have him; but if you're smart you'll only sign him until Christmas." That seemed ridiculous and I told Pollock so. "Sam, I'm gonna sign him the whole way."

So, what happened? Half way through the season Gauthier came up with a sore back *and didn't play a game after Christmas*. I learned then and there that I wasn't so smart after all.

Much as I was personally embarrassed by the Gauthier episode, I really couldn't complain about the season. Wensink became my pet project and he proved to be a winner. We had another big, tough team of mean hard workers who wanted to show everyone that they belonged in professional hockey, and the result was crowds like they never had before in Rochester.

The rink's capacity was about 7,000 but one night we had 8,200 jammed into the place. We even had the fire marshall on our side and I had given him a special spot to stand and view the game near rinkside. (One night a club owner, not realizing who the fire marshall was, ordered him to move from his spot. That cost us a thousand customers a game.)

Although we had a number of quality players, the essence of our club was Wensink. He intimidated the opposition and was loved by his teammates. He didn't have the same offensive skills of Kelly but I worked with him all the time, even after all the other players had finished practice.

One day when we were practising at an out-of-town rink—just Wensink and I—everybody else had left the arena and it was dark. I was trying to teach him how to stand, keeping his position in front of the net while the enemy defensemen try to clear him away. I took the part of the enemy defenseman and John was to try and keep me from upsetting him. So, there were the pair of us high sticking, punching and generally knocking each other all over the place. We were so intent on this personal battle that we did not even notice that the home team had arrived at the sidelines and were watching us intently, completely incredulous. You see, by this time Wensink was punching me and I was counterpunching him until, finally, I looked over to the sidelines and there was this collection of players, all standing there with their mouths agape. Needless to say, that team was a little bit more afraid of us the next night. The special relationship I had enjoyed with Wensink endured throughout his stay in Rochester, but don't imagine that I enjoyed all my players on the Americans or that the vice was versa.

We had a goalie named Gaye Cooley who shared the goaltending chores with Lynn Zimmerman. Although Zimmy was our property, Cooley belonged to the Boston Bruins and was "on loan" to us.

Superficially, you might get the impression that Cooley was a reasonable guy. He attended Michigan State University and had been a star in the National Collegiate Athletic Association tournament in 1966. But college doesn't always guarantee knowledge nor does it invariably produce level-headed hockey players.

Once, we were enroute to Jacksonville, Florida (which then had an AHL franchise, believe it or not,) and had to make a special stop at the airport in Atlanta. While we were waiting, Cooley had a few drinks, and then a few drinks too many. By the time we got back on the plane he was feeling no pain, which I wouldn't mind except that there were a few dozen passengers on the plane who took a dim view of him. As we moved to the back of the plane, Cooley patted one of the stewardesses. I quickly moved in on him and thrust him into a back seat, then I took the seat immediately ahead of him.

I had had my fill of Cooley from other incidents and I was hoping that we could settle down for a peaceful ride on to Jacksonville when I heard the goalie grunt, "You son of a bitch."

He had grated the nerve. I flew out of my chair, grabbed him by the throat and sunk my fingernails into his Adam's apple. Cooley tried to get up but I had him well-pinned and my fingernails were now digging his flesh. Some of the guys got scared and started to get up. "Don't anybody move!" I insisted. "This guy has had it coming to him for a long time." Cooley's eyeballs were tilting up to his head.

I slammed his head against the tray that was hanging from the chair in front and then let him go. Cooley knew, instinctively, that he should not attempt an act of retaliation. I knew that the lesson had been well-administered. I returned to my seat secure in the knowledge that my goalie would no longer be a problem to me.

Wensink, on the other hand, *was* a problem although for different reasons. He had taken his enforcer role very seriously; maybe too seriously and for that I have only Don Cherry to blame. On the other hand, you have to remember that this was the 1973-74 season when the Philadelphia Flyers were rampaging through the National Hockey League making goonism the key to victory. Wensink, whom everyone called Wire, because of his hair, desperately wanted to make it to the NHL and he figured that the shortest route was via the upper cut.

Well, he very nearly got thrown out following a game against the Nova Scotia Voyageurs at our rink in Rochester. Wensink's opponent on this night was a big winger named Len Cunning. He and John weighed about the same but Cunning had three inches on John. That hardly mattered once the punches began to fly. Wensink flattened him and once Cunning was down, wouldn't let him up. By the time the officials separated them, Cunning was in such bad shape that he had to be taken to the hospital.

Normally, I don't get unnerved over a hockey fight, but this one put the fear of God in me. Meanwhile, the police had been summoned and they questioned Wensink who really didn't seem very bothered.

After talking to reporters, I made my way to my office, where eight owners had gathered. They didn't look happy but I was pleased with the 2-2 tie so I couldn't figure out their problem. Finally, one owner said "I have a high reputation in this city and I'm not going to see it go down the drain connected with a player like Wensink. That animal goes!"

I knew John and I were in trouble. John was only doing what I had encouraged him to do, although he had gone too far this time, but I couldn't let him down. I said, "If he goes, so do I."

I won my point and, ironically enough, a month later, when Wensink had been sidelined with a knee injury, our attendance dropped about a thousand per game, and the same owner who had wanted to can Wensink kept bugging me about him coming back because our gate was slipping. Strange people in this world we live in, yes?

The sudden peace-in-our-time bleats of a few of the media made absolutely no impression on me or my players. Wensink knew that I wanted him to play rough and we continued on our merry way. Mind you, we did not barrel through the AHL with impunity. There were some teams who gave us a hard time and some who could be almost as tough. We learned that lesson one evening in Providence during a game against the Reds. Their version of Wensink was a husky left wing named Bertwin Hillard Wilson, Bert for short. On this night Wilson began doing a number on Doug Ferguson, a little guy out of Cornell University who was playing center for us. You could hear the drumbeat on Ferguson's head all over the Providence rink.

One of Wensink's jobs—and any "policeman's" for that matter—was to protect the little men from being stomped on by the bullies. As soon as I saw what was happening to little Ferguson I leaned over Wensink's shoulder and calmly intoned: "John, would you like to go out on the ice for a spin?"

John tilted his head upward and replied: "I'd love to go out on the ice for a spin, Grapes."

"Well," I suggested, "be my guest."

You would have thought World War III had just begun. François Ouimet, one of our defensemen, and Andy Peloffy of the Reds went at it and then there was a wild battle between our goalie, Lynn Zimmerman, and Ron Fogal, a huge Providence defenseman. (Zimmy ultimately received a $200 fine as well as other automatic fines totalling $150 "for malicious use of a stick in an attempt to injure an opponent." Fogal's fines totalled $500. Zimmerman also was suspended for three games for his stick attack. Fogal was sidelined two months with torn knee ligaments suffered in the fracas.) Meanwhile, Wensink was out there getting Wilson off Ferguson and bodies were flying in all directions. John Muckler, coach of the Reds, left his bench with a stick in his hand, trying to attack me. By now the melee had gotten so out of hand that the State Troopers had been summoned, but they couldn't get there soon enough. Blood was being spilled all over the place (including on the glass partitions) and the Reds were still trying to destroy Wensink. But he kept knocking them down as fast as they came at him. For once, I used my head and stayed cool. I would not be suckered out there and I'm glad I stayed put. I knew I was in enough trouble already.

For being such a nice guy I was hit with a $500 fine. Naturally, it bugged me but I still maintained my cool. When a reporter asked me about it I said, "If that's the penalty I'll take my punishment—I only wish I hadn't bought my wife a fur coat for Christmas. Maybe I'll have to take it back now."

The fellow I was worried about was Wensink. He received a ten-game suspension because *I* had sent him out on the ice. I was tormented by my action and by the thought that I might have ruined the kid's career. Only time would tell. Meanwhile, Wensink, under suspension, returned to his home in Maxville, Ontario, and we went on with our business of playing hockey, and trying to duck criticism. The worst of it emanated from Providence where John Muckler and the Reds' owners tried to play saints while portraying me as the devil incarnate. (I liked it.)

The schedule called for us to return to Providence eleven games later, which was precisely when Wensink's suspension was to end. Needless to say, all those Providence hypocrites who had been criticizing us weeks earlier now were trumpeting the return engagement as the greatest game of all time: Wensink returns to the scene of his crime. Unknown to the Providence promoters, Wensink had been called up to the National Hockey League for a three-game trial with the St. Louis Blues. (He wound up with no goals, no assists, no points, no penalties.) I decided to rub it in a little, and phoned the Providence papers: "Seeing that you and your city figure John Wensink for an animal, I'm not going to bring him to Providence!"

Of course, the owner of the Reds went berserk because Wensink's absence figured to cost him 5,000 fans at the gate—and it did. But we still managed to have some fun. You see there was a little Italian guy in Providence who was a wild hockey nut.

More than anything in the world, this guy wanted to get on the ice in uniform and skate with a professional hockey team. Naturally, he wanted to do it with the home team, so he asked Muckler about it and Muckler said nothing doing. That's when he got in touch with me. "If you let me skate in the warm-up with the Americans," he said, "I'll give you 500 bucks."

I thought to myself: 500 bucks isn't bad. With that money we could throw a team party. Why the heck not? Besides, the guy looked like a hockey player. He was 26, and solidly built. I said, okay, he was on. So, the guy got dressed with us, put on the skates and walked out on to the ice with the rest of the Rochester Americans.

As soon as he stepped on the ice a group of about 300 fans went crazy. You see, the guy had made a $500 bet with his friends that he would skate with the Americans and there he was!

Of course, I use the term "skate" loosely in this case. He could hardly stand on his pins and as he laboured around the rink I could hardly look. But he was undaunted; he waved to his friends like a conquering hero and also waved to the crowd. Unfortunately, one of the spectators happened to be Jack Butterfield, the president of the American Hockey League.

My Italian hockey player completed the warm-up without mishap and returned to the dressing room where, as promised, he peeled off five one hundred dollar bills and shook my hand. (I also received a stern letter from Butterfield cautioning me against further indiscretions, and saying that I was ridiculing the game, etc. He was right—what a dumb thing to do.) I gave the money to the team captain, Rod Graham, and what a party we had.

The departure of Wensink to the St. Louis Blues gave me cause for concern because I feared they would use him exclusively for goon purposes when, actually, he was developing into an efficient, if not high-scoring, forward. The Blues, somehow, managed to mis-use Battleship Kelly and ultimately traded him to the Pittsburgh Penguins. As luck would have it, the Penguins and the Blues were scheduled to meet on the night that Wensink was to make his NHL debut.

This bothered me a great deal. I had babied John along and I realized that there were still some fighters around it would not be good for him to meet, at least not just yet. Kelly was among them. The prospect of Wensink fighting Kelly disturbed me because it would be like two of my sons going at each other. I had to do something about it, so I took Rose, Cindy, and Timothy to Pittsburgh and checked into the same hotel as the Blues. I phoned Battleship and invited him over for lunch after his morning skate.

Wensink was already at the table. I introduced them and the three of us chatted and ate and then John excused himself. He had to attend a team meeting. Once Wensink was out of earshot, I leaned over the table and levelled with Battleship. "You know, Bob, I've never asked you for anything but today I'm going to ask you a favour. I know why St. Louis brought John up. They're going to throw him out there near the end of the game to fight with you but John isn't ready to fight you. I'm asking you as a favour not to fight with John tonight." I said good-bye to Battleship and wondered what would happen.

Sure enough, Wensink was kept on the Blues' bench until the final five minutes of the game. At last, out he came and he plied his wing as best he could. Not surprisingly, he was matched up with Battleship. Once, twice, three times, Wensink checked Kelly. (In those days if anyone hit Bob that hard his gloves would fly off and he would start swinging while the Pittsburgh organist played *Anchors Aweigh*.) But this time Battleship minded his business. He didn't fight; he didn't even *look* at John. I'll always respect Battleship for his class that night.

After his three-game trial with the Blues, Wensink returned to the Americans and continued to play his robust game. Then, he injured his knee and was out for a few games, so we let him go home and rest up until he was ready. Meanwhile, we had taken off for Jacksonville where we were to play a game that would determine first place. Suddenly, I got a brainstorm. Wensink has been such a great help to the club, why not bring him down so that he could enjoy some sun and relaxation.

We got the message through to him and he said, fine, he would love to meet us in Jacksonville. Our game was scheduled for the next night but Wensink had not yet arrived. About an hour before game time I began making up our lineup which had to be turned in to the referee prior to the opening face-off. As I scrawled in the names I realized that we were two men short so just for the sake of filling up space I wrote Wensink's name on the roster. I just liked to see John's name on our lineup even though I knew that he wasn't going to play, let alone show up in Jacksonville. Who knows, maybe I figured that the sight of John Wensink on our card would scare the other coach. In any event the game began and Jacksonville really took it to us. Knowing that John wasn't on the ice, they began pushing our club around.

With about five minutes remaining in the first period, I casually looked over my shoulder at someone standing about ten feet from the bench. It was John! He had quietly arrived during the first period and was minding his own business, watching the game. I walked over to him, shook his hand and said, "John, go get your equipment on."

He thought I was kidding. "John," I insisted, "go get your equipment on." Now he knew I wasn't kidding.

When the second period began the Rochester Americans had one more player in the lineup than they had had when the game began. Once the Jacksonville players saw him they went bananas. The coach yelled, "You can't do that. You can't put him in the game. He's not in the lineup."

I called the referee over and requested that he produce the lineup. There it was, John Wensink's name in the lineup. I had no intention of playing him; all John did was stand at the end of the bench, growling at every Jacksonville player who skated by. From that point on the home team became infinitely tamer and, from our viewpoint, more manageable. We won the game and clinched first place over-all. After that we went out and partied well into the night, almost forgetting that we had chartered a fishing boat to take us out in the Atlantic the next day. We made it to the boat a half hour late on a beautiful, sunny morning. But we were so hung over from the partying that not one single guy from the team had the energy to drop a fishing line into the water. The captain just cruised around while we slept in the sun, getting a burn. Eventually, one of the fellows dropped a line into the water but all he caught was a turtle!

For all intents and purposes I could have remained in Rochester for the rest of my life. As general manager, I could do exactly what I wanted with the team. I was given a free car. I was making $25,000 a year. I was doing commercials and banquets. I had my own players. If I didn't like a player, I could get rid of him without a hassle. There was no pressure.

But, there also was no big-time. The entertainer in me demanded that I make it to the top. Rochester was beautiful but, no matter how you say it, it wasn't *numero uno*. When the Boston Bruins called I had to answer.

CHAPTER FOURTEEN

Remembering Bobby Orr, Phil Esposito, Brad Park, And Other Friends

Looking back, the second best thing about being hired by the Boston Bruins was the fact that, at long last, I had made it as a coach in the National Hockey League.

The first best thing was that I was coach of the team for which Bobby Orr was a player. Mind you, I didn't say that I *coached* Bobby Orr because that would be the most presumptuous thing any coach could ever say. *Nobody* coached Bobby Orr. He was the greatest hockey player I have ever seen, Gordie Howe and Wayne Gretzky included. I felt that there was very little I could do to improve on Orr's perfection. From time to time, though, I would drop little hints here and there.

Actually, it was not easy to deal with Bobby on any level—player or friend—because he was such an unusual person; and I don't mean that in a negative way. It was simply that with all the pressures on him, socially, physically, and otherwise, he became a significantly detached individual; one who was conspicuously wary of others.

A case in point: I was brand new at the job in Boston and really hadn't had a chance to sit down with Bobby. One day I noticed him sitting alone in a hotel coffee shop in Chicago. I walked over, sat next to him and tried to make conversation. At first, he seemed friendly so I began thinking about what subjects might interest him. I knew he was from Parry Sound, Ontario, a town on Georgian Bay, so I figured it would be a

162

good idea to talk fishing. "Whaddya catch?" I asked him and immediately we swung into a chat about hooks, lines, and sinkers.

At first he seemed very enthused about the chat but then, like a smart defenseman divining an attacking play, he quite obviously sensed that the only reason I was talking about fishing was to make conversation with him—and he clammed up. I didn't lose him forever with that incident, but it did take me a while to get to know him.

Unfortunately, Orr didn't have a press agent who could trumpet the good works he did very quietly. Bobby would visit a Boston-area hospital three times a week just to cheer up the sick kids. He didn't tell anybody, not even his close friends on the team and certainly not me. But one day I had to take my son, Timothy, to the childrens' division of Massachusetts General Hospital and I began chatting with some of the nurses. They told me that my all-star defenseman was a regular visitor.

Orr wouldn't tell anyone because, despite his widespread appeal, he loathed the limelight. Game after game, win or lose, whether he was the hero or insignificant, the reporters would chase after him. If we won a game, 3-0, the newspaper guys wouldn't seek out the goalie who got the shutout or the guy who scored the hat trick, they'd want to see Bobby. This bothered him to the extent that he began to hide in the trainer's room just so that some of his teammates could get some of the limelight.

Demands upon him were relentless wherever he played. Once, we had an exhibition game in Moncton, New Brunswick, and we left Bobby home to rest. The fans were furious when they learned that Orr had not come. They even threw cans and pop bottles at us when we took to the ice. Another time we were in Springfield, Massachusetts, and the arena was packed in anticipation of Orr. Bobby played that night, but he got into a fight early in the game and referee Dave Newell threw him out.

As Orr trooped off to the dressing room the owner of the Springfield hockey club realized that he'd have a riot on his hands if Orr only played a couple of minutes and then was finished for the night. He grabbed Newell. "Are you crazy? Do you want a riot? You gotta get Orr back in the game!"

I give Newell credit. Instead of going through the red tape rigamarole that some others might have, he simply sized up the situation and ordered Orr back on to the bench. And Bobby obliged.

It was but another example of Bobby's unselfishness; a trait I got to know and respect as I coached the Bruins. There was one time when Orr and Phil Esposito were running neck-and-neck for the scoring championship. Time and again Bobby would find himself in excellent scoring position, but instead of firing the puck he would look around for someone to pass to and often it was Phil. So, finally, I asked my defenseman Carol Vadnais what was going on with Bobby and why he was squandering potential points. "Don't you know?" he said. "He's trying not to get too far ahead of Phil for the scoring title." He risked the Art Ross Trophy in order to make the team play better.

Orr was so intense about winning that he would react in curious ways to success; like the time we were playing the Canadiens in an exhibition game and Bobby let one of the Montreal forwards walk right around him. He felt a sense of personal insult about being beaten and on the very next play he grabbed the puck and went through the entire Canadiens team to score. When he returned to the bench, I leaned over and said, "Nice goal, Bobby!" But he was still hot under the collar over being beaten. In a very derogatory tone, he shot back at me: "Oh, thanks, coach. Thanks a lot." What he was really telling me was, "Are you kidding—just shut up and coach." I learned early just to let him play his game; you don't pull the reins on Secretariat.

Those who had the good fortune to watch Orr in action have special manoeuvers they treasure, I have fond recollections of a trick he pulled one day while all alone after a practice. I was there having a relaxed skate with Vadnais while Orr was standing alone with a puck at the far corner of the rink parallel to the net. Bobby hit the puck so that it flew about four feet in the air, then he took the stick and batted the puck again high in the air about ten feet over his head. As the rubber came down, and without even looking at it, he batted the puck forty feet into the top corner of the net—on a backhander no less.

Well, I couldn't believe what I had seen and, privately, Vadnais couldn't believe it either. After about a minute Vad and I looked at each other and, finally, Vad said: "Did you see what I just saw?"

I said, "Yes, and I'm glad you mentioned it because I thought my eyes had failed me."

Of course that wasn't the only time I felt that Orr had caused me to see strange things. Another time we were playing the Flames and I had Bobby out on the ice killing a penalty. He had a habit of going behind the net, coming out to the east and then doing figure-eights back behind his net again. On this occasion Bobby got the puck behind our net and slowly moved up along the right boards. None of the Atlanta players dared run at him at the time because they knew they would be deked and caught out of position, so they all sat back as he moved up the side. He crossed our blue line, the center red line, the Flames' blue line and then moved into the corner near the Atlanta net. Now the Flames figured that they had him trapped—literally in a corner, so the whole team ran at him, including the goaltender. Suddenly, Bobby accelerated, went behind the net, came out the other side and put the puck into the twine on his backhand while the entire Atlanta team was flat on the ice!

Most players would jump around or hot-dog it after scoring a goal like that, but not Bobby. As soon as the red light flashed he put his head down because he knew he had embarrassed the entire Flames team; he hated embarrassing people.

While all these amazing accomplishments were taking place Bobby was suffering constant pain in his ailing knees, especially his left knee. If it had been up to me I would have spotted him as a regular rather than subject him to all the pain he was enduring, but there was no way he'd allow me to bench him. He *had* to play. From time to time I would pretend to ignore him and select other players to take the ice when it would have been Orr's turn but he made sure that I knew he was there, reminding me that he *expected* to take the next shift. I simply could not ignore him.

One of Bobby's idiosyncracies was the manner in which he laced his skates. He would lace them so loosely that they were almost falling off his feet. Interestingly, the only other guy I ever saw lace his skates like that was Eddie Shore who, with Orr, was one of the two greatest defensemen of all time, and one of the two greatest skaters.

Another strange thing about Orr was that he disdained new equipment. He liked to wear beat-up old shin pads that weren't fit for a neighbourhood rink. Once Bobby had the shin pads in place he would insert a thick layer of cotton to build up the cushion between his knee and the pads. That five inches of cotton meant a lot to Orr. Once, our trainer, Frosty Forristall, thought he had lost the cotton and you would have thought, judging by Bobby's reaction, that the plans for the atomic bomb had been lost. Fortunately, Frosty found the cotton.

Unlike most players, Orr didn't wear socks when he played; just skated in his bare feet. He felt it gave him a better feel for the skates. Then, there were his gloves, which were really unusual. Instead of thick padding, he had a thin lining sewn in that gave him a special *rapport* with his stick.

To Bobby, his stick was a finely-tuned instrument. In between periods, no matter how tired he was, he'd get up and shave his stick. I once asked him why he didn't have one of the equipment men or trainers do it for him, but he just shrugged and kept on shaving.

It was pretty clear to Orr that I made it a practice not to tell him how to play his game but one day he approached me and said, "Grapes, give me a little crap, too, won't you please? Include me in when you're givin' it to the rest of the guys."

I decided to take him up on his generous offer and began looking for an aspect of his play to criticize. I finally hit on something. In one-on-one situations, where an opposing forward would skate in on Orr, Bobby had a habit of training his eye on the puck rather than on the man. I told him I thought he could improve on his defensive work if he concentrated on the man and not the rubber. Right after that we had a game against the Los Angeles Kings. In the second period one of the Kings bore down on Orr and Bobby made a textbook play, right in front of our bench, taking the man out as perfectly as a coach could expect. But while he was doing it, Bobby looked over at me and laughed, waving and pointing to be sure I saw what he was doing. The players broke up.

Another time we were playing the Washington Caps and Bobby was out for a face-off. The Caps center was lining up his players around the face-off circle and motioned to a young rookie defenseman to stand over to the right. At that moment the rookie looked at Bobby and Bobby shook his head and told him to go back over to his left—and the guy did it. I couldn't believe it: the kid thought so much of Bobby that he knew Bobby wouldn't lie to him. (P.S. The puck went to the kid.)

Considering his knees, Orr probably absorbed more abuse than any other hockey player. Once he was playing in an All-Star game when Bobby Hull was playing left wing for the Chicago Black Hawks. When Hull was in form he could fire the puck at a speed of 120 m.p.h.

On this occasion Hull wound up for his big slapshot and the puck rammed Bobby right in the groin. Orr crawled off the ice in frightful pain and crawled down the hallway. Five minutes later he was right back on the ice again—in an All-Star Game!

Another time he was crosschecked in the back of the neck by a Washington player and suffered whiplash. The blow was so severe that Orr couldn't hold his head up and when he came off the ice at the end of the second period, he had to lie down. When the buzzer signalled the players back onto the ice, a couple of guys had to lift up Bobby's head and body at the same time. He insisted on taking the ice for the next period. "Bobby," I said, "we've got the game won. Take it easy; there's no problem at all with these guys." But he wouldn't take it easy. He went out and played; how, I don't know. But to this day, if you see Bobby Orr in the street and you're behind him and call his name, he won't just twist his neck around, he'll have to turn his whole body—all because of the whiplash suffered that night against the Caps. (I know, by now you are thinking, "Can this guy really be this great? And is this guy Cherry in love with Orr?" My answer to the former question is yes and my answer to the latter question is . . . yes.)

As difficult as the physical aspect of Orr's life had been, the social part left him little pleasure, simply because the fans were always after him. Solitude was virtually impossible, what with the demands of the media and fans. I remember once after we had played an afternoon game at Boston Garden, we then had to catch a plane for an out-of-town game. Rose, Timothy, Bobby, Phil Esposito, Carol Vadnais and I were all driving out to the airport together from Boston Garden. The car was parked in the Garden and from there we would drive down a ramp and out the Garden's back exit. The problem, as it usually was in Orr's case, was that the fans always seemed to figure out where the players were and how they were making their exit.

Sure enough there were a hundred kids waiting for us as we headed out of the building. It was frightening and Bobby, who had had enough trouble with fans already, sensed that there would be trouble if we stopped. "Grapes," he implored me, "don't stop! We'll never get to the plane."

But Phil wanted me to stop. "Hey," he said, "we'll sign a few autographs. What's the difference?" And with that, Rose rolled down the window.

Well, I'd never seen anything like it. The kids, seeing Bobby, began storming the car, climbing through the window, ripping his tie, his clothes, throwing books at him to autograph; it was unbelievable. We finally escaped with our lives, but there never was peace for Bobby. I remember when he and his wife, Peg, went shopping for a toy to give to their baby son. It was the first time he had ever bought anything for the baby and was in a toy shop when somebody recognized him. The people pushed him against a wall and he couldn't escape for an hour.

Even his own players would bug him. Before a game other players would send him sticks to be autographed for their fans or their uncles or cousins. Bobby would take all the sticks into the showers and sit down and autograph them just so the other guys wouldn't see him. He felt embarrassed about the whole business.

Working with Orr, for me, was like being a museum curator watching an extremely valuable piece of art disintegrate before your eyes. It was evident to me—as, I'm sure, it was to Bobby—that the relentless pressure he applied to his body would ultimately take its toll on his ailing knees. Doctors had made it clear that there was a limit to the abuse he could absorb and, likewise, a limit to the number of times they could employ surgical techniques to repair the damage.

I would try to find ways and means to lessen the punishment doled out to Bobby, but it was virtually impossible to curb his reckless—and great—play. He would not take it easy during a game when we had it won, no matter whether the foe was a humpty-dumpty team or champions like the Montreal Canadiens. It all was rooted in Orr's pride in his workmanship. He felt that he had to play to the hilt, even in an exhibition game. When we lost Bobby felt it was his fault.

I'm glad he never went into coaching, because he had the curious notion that everyone on the team thought and would act the way he did and thus would expend as much energy. As a result he was ruthless with teammates he felt did not try as hard as he did.

Opponents had so much respect for Orr that few would ever deliver a cheap shot at him. There was one exception and that was Hilliard Graves, a journeyman forward who had bounced around the league and was playing for Atlanta at the time. Graves had one thing going for him; a somewhat sly method of skating up low against an opponent from the side, and nailing him around knee level. The element of surprise combined with Graves' lower center of gravity enabled him to disable a few players around the league. We knew he was after Bobby and did our best to ensure that he didn't hurt him.

One time in Atlanta Graves took a run at Bobby. He missed, and Orr just laughed. But it drove me nuts! I grabbed a player named Hank

Nowak and threw him on the ice, yelling, "Get him', Hank!" Hank skated into the play, but then came back to the bench almost immediately. "Get who?" he asked seriously. The bench broke up. (Hank once told me he only needed six games for a full pension, but couldn't find anyone who'd give him a break. Life is cruel . . .)

I'll never forget the very last game Bobby Orr played for the Boston Bruins. We were at Madison Square Garden and big John Davidson was in the nets for the Rangers. Playing great at the time, Davidson had the biggest, heaviest catching glove I had ever seen in my life.

On this night John was really hot, and he robbed Bobby twice of sure goals. The score was tied in the second period when Orr glided over the red line, moved up to the Ranger blue line, and uncorked a real beauty of a slapshot. As he wound up, I could almost hear Bobby saying to himself: "Davidson, this puck's goin' by you . . . or it's goin' through you!" Bobby's shot was so hard it knocked the glove off Davidson's hand, and actually drove Davidson back into the net—no mean feat.

An hour after the game I noticed Bobby limping onto the bus. Asking him what happened, he replied, "Geez, Grapes, I don't know. I was standing and talking to Rod Gilbert at the top of the tunnel, and when I turned to go, something popped. My knee seems to be locking." Little did I know at that moment that he was saying to me, "Goodbye, Stanley Cup."

The Jacobs brothers had bought the team. Since they were from Buffalo, I don't think they really knew what Bobby Orr meant to the people of Boston. The Jacobs seemed like nice enough guys; but I could see that the team was going to be run like a business and nothing else. They left the hockey to Harry Sinden, including signing Orr. Meanwhile, Alan Eagleson was Orr's agent and I could see fireworks ahead.

When the Jacobs folks realized how troubled Bobby's wheels were, their attitude toward Bobby turned negative, just as he was up for a new contract. Naturally Orr wanted a multi-year deal, but he also wanted the deal guaranteed.

The Jacobs weren't interested in any of that and the rumours immediately began to swirl that Bobby Orr, a Boston institution, would soon become a Chicago Black Hawk. Although the contract was none of my business, I asked Bobby about it. "Grapes," he said, "they're treating me like I'm a horse ready to be shot."

Cripes! he was still the best in the league—even on one leg!

The kid who once was in love with life and hockey was now turned off and bitter about the game he still was playing. In a sense he was still naive. He couldn't quite understand the all-business attitude of the Jacobs family, nor could he fathom why Harry Sinden wasn't helping him; especially in view of the fact that Bobby had done so much to help put Harry on the hockey map.

Once the negotiations between Orr, his attorney, Al Eagleson, and the Bruins began to make print, the stilettos came out and it seemed that everyone was at everyone else's throat. I must admit that I acted like a dummy. I kept telling the press that, oh, yeah, Bobby will be back with the Bruins and, the fact of the matter is, he almost *was* going to return to the team rather than move on to Chicago.

The turning point occurred—and nobody really knew this until now—over an article Bobby read in the local paper. Orr had become disgusted with all the bickering. He finally decided—based on what he told me—to hell with the negotiations, to hell with the contract guarantee; he wanted to stay with the Bruins, no matter what.

Bobby had become a Boston institution just like Bunker Hill. It was unthinkable, even to him, to go elsewhere to finish out his playing career.

He was returning to Boston and had just flown into Logan Airport. In his mind, he was prepared to wear the Bruins' black-and-gold until they told him he couldn't lace on the skates anymore. As he left the airport he picked up a paper and turned to the sports pages. When he got into a cab he began reading a hockey story. He was appalled by what he read.

There in black and white was Sinden's mouthpiece, Tom Johnson, saying that he thought Bobby Orr had had it. Orr told the cab driver to turn the taxi around and take him right back to the airport. He booked himself a flight and flew home. He was through as a Bruin because he didn't want to play with these people anymore.

Management played it cagey and even as we approached the June draft meetings there was some hope held out that Orr would remain a Bruin. But when I met with Harry and Tom at the Montreal meetings, I knew it was game over for Bobby. I was absolutely heartbroken because not only was I losing the greatest hockey player who ever lived, but I was losing a good friend. After a while, though, I began thinking as a coach, mulling over the compensation—in terms of players—we would receive if Orr wound up in a Chicago Black Hawks uniform.

I already had about four solid Chicago players picked out and from my standpoint, it looked like we'd have a Stanley Cup contender just based on the compensation alone. What I didn't realize was that there would be *no* compensation for the Bruins in this particular deal. The greatest hockey player who ever lived would simply go from the Bruins to the Black Hawks, and all Boston would get in return were newspaper stories about the deal. That was it.

Then, of course, there was Phil Esposito. Esposito, to me, was one of the most colourful persons ever in the NHL. I have to laugh when people would say he scored "garbage goals." Phil would laugh, too, and say, "Who cares what they call them—they all look like slap shots in next morning's papers. Who cares how they go in, as long as they count?"

The thing I will always remember most about Phil was the 1972 Canada Cup. He had the courage to go on TV between periods and say that the team and players didn't deserve the abuse Vancouver fans and fans across Canada were heaping on them. He said that the players were truly doing their best and that, instead of booing and ridiculing, they should all get behind the team. It's the first time a hockey player rallied a country. Phil Esposito turned around the fans, the media—and most of all, he turned around the players. I think Phil Esposito won the Canada Cup that hot night in Vancouver.

There were some who charged that Phil was more interested in his own point total than the welfare of the team. I never felt this way. I honestly think that Phil figured he was doing the best for the club by playing three and four-minute shifts instead of coming off the ice sooner. Maybe he was right. He won a lot of scoring championships and he also played on two Stanley Cup winners.

Unfortunately, Phil's demand for ice time did have an adverse effect on others, particularly Andre Savard, a young French-Canadian center for whom the Bruins had high hopes. Andy's line would generally follow Phil's onto the ice, except that Phil always stayed on extra long. I can still see poor Andy's face as Phil would go through two or three extra shifts. Andy would sit astride the boards waiting and waiting and waiting for Phil to get off. We all said that Andy sat astride the boards so long waiting to get ice that by the time he got married he'd be sterile!

Among Phil's high priority sensitivities, his hair ranked right at the top. He loved his hair and would treat it accordingly. After a game he would sit in his brown-and-white kimono, apply a white solution to his hair and then sit with the conditioner settling in to make it even more beautiful. I remember one night, we were playing a crucial game at Boston Garden and as I patrolled the area behind the bench I noticed the back of Phil's neck. A dark substance was running down his neck. "Phil," I said, "you look like you're oozing dark blood." He felt the back of his neck, looked at his palm and said: "Grapes, I'm gonna kill that hairdresser!"

Phil was superstitious, but not nearly as much as some people thought. The one thing he insisted upon was that his sticks and gloves be laid out in front of him in the dressing room before each game. Heaven help the trainer or player who would accidentally kick those sticks or move those gloves.

Esposito's natural talent for scoring once prompted me to ask him how he had learned to become such an efficient goal machine. "Grapes," he said, "when I'm goin' good I just get the puck and fire it at the net and I just figure the net hasn't moved in fifty years so I'm bound to be on target. The rest will take care of itself. It's like being a baseball pitcher; he should never aim the ball, just rear back and throw it. I never aim the puck because I know that when I aim it I'm not goin' good."

Phil could score from any angle. I once saw him split the enemy defense, fall to his knees and, while still on his knees sliding toward the net, put the puck in the top corner of the cage.

We had gotten off to a terrible start. We had been hammered badly in Philadelphia by the Flyers and then in Buffalo by the Sabres. After the Buffalo disaster Harry huddled with me. "What do you think of us sending Phil and Vadnais to the Rangers for Brad Park and Jean Ratelle?"

It was a dynamite package but I had to think for a moment. We had lost in the first round of the playoffs the previous year. Now we were playing terribly. One of two things was about to happen—either we changed players or we changed coaches. Needless to say, I preferred the former option.

Harry insisted to me that, yes, the deal was very much alive and that he was heading for Buffalo to discuss it with Emile Francis, his counterpart with the Rangers. I had mixed feelings about the deal even though my survival instinct told me that I had to choose between me and Phil. Still, there were signs that Phil was trying to adapt to my grinding style of hockey and that he was at least willing to make adjustments in his own offensive behaviour. While Sinden and Francis were conferring at the Buffalo airport Phil approached me and revealed that he had been thinking about his playing and was willing to listen to me. "Grapes," he said, "I'm gonna try it your way from now on."

I thought to myself, how ironic. The wheels of the trade were turning and, even if I had wanted to stop them, there was nothing I could do about the Sinden-Francis negotiations. As I headed with the team to Vancouver, I couldn't help thinking about what would happen if the deal did take place. I wondered about Phil and how he'd take it and also Vadnais, who was one of my best friends. Vad sat next to me on the jet heading west. It was one of the most uncomfortable flights of my life; I felt as if I was going to a guy's execution but I couldn't say a word about it. I kept thinking how cruel this business of sport can be.

When we arrived at our hotel in Vancouver I did something I rarely do when on the road, I stayed in my own room glued to the telephone. Sooner or later, Harry *had* to call, either to tell me that the deal had fallen through (then maybe it meant that *my* goose had been cooked) or to give me the final details of the trade. Finally, at 11:30 p.m. the phone rang.

Harry: "Don, they went for it."

Me: "I can't believe it."

Harry: "Believe it. And now the crap's gonna hit the fan. You watch, tomorrow."

Me: "Whaddya mean?"

Harry: "You're out there with them; I'm here. You're gonna have to tell 'em. It's Phil and Vad to the Rangers for Jean Ratelle, Brad Park and Joe Zanussi."

Me: "I still can't believe it."

Harry: "Don't tell 'em tonight. Wait til tomorrow morning. There's no sense telling them tonight. They might as well get a good night's sleep since they're going to Oakland tomorrow. Besides, you never know what they're gonna do when they hear this. I'll be in touch."

Harry hung up and I sat there for a moment, numb from the neck up. Finally, I picked myself up and went down to the hotel bar where I had a few beers by myself and thought about what was going on. I had mixed emotions. On one hand, I was losing two friends. On the other hand, I had to think of the club and I also had to think about *my* future. Besides, I was elated to be getting two quality hockey players like Park and Ratelle.

Bobby Orr was still with the team at the time and the prospect of having *both* Orr and Park on the points for the power play was just too good to be true. Then, I realized that *I* had to deliver the news to Phil and Vad the next morning. How to do it? I went back up to the room to catch a few winks because I knew that I'd have to phone them first thing in the morning. I placed a wake-up call for 7 a.m. and then hit the sack.

As soon as I got the wake-up call I washed my face, went back to the phone and called Phil.

Me: "This is Grapes. Phil, I want to talk to you, I'm comin' right down."

Phil: "Don, don't tell me."

Me: "I can't talk about it here, I'm comin' down."

Phil: "Grapes, tell me it didn't happen!"

(Years later Phil told me he thought *I* had been fired and wanted to come down to his room to talk about it; to get some anger off my chest.)

I dressed and, fifteen minutes later, I knocked on his door. Phil opened it and I walked over to a chair near the window and sat down. Phil sat on the bed.

Me: "Phil, I might as well give it to you straight; there's no use beating around the bush. Phil, you've been traded."

His body contorted. He was in physical and mental agony. He got up, sat down; got up again, sat down again. At least five minutes went by before he even said a word; then the words came blurting out.

Phil: "Grapes, please tell me, they traded me to *any team but the New York Rangers.*" (Funny how things work out. Much later Phil told me that the Rangers were the best team he could have gone to. He was made for New York.)

I looked out of the window and watched the raindrops course down to the window sill. Then, I looked at Phil and saw the tears filtering down his face. I couldn't hold it back any longer.

Me: "Yes, it is the Rangers."

Phil: "But, Grapes, when I signed my last contract with Harry I said I wouldn't ask for a 'no-trade' contract. All I asked was that Harry give me his word that I would go to any team *except* the New York Rangers. And we shook on that."

Me: (To myself) "You should have known that old Yogi Berra saying that verbal agreements aren't worth the paper they're written on."

Now I had to go down the hall and tell Vad. I knocked on his door and his roommate, Gary Doak, answered. I asked Gary to leave, then sat down and gave it right to Vad. He just sat at the edge of the bed and stared into space for what seemed like an eternity. Finally, he turned to me and said: "You know what, Grapes? I *can't* be traded during the season."

I asked why, and he said that it was written right in his contract. Sitting there in Vad's room, I got a little queasy so I phoned Harry to tell him what Vad had told me. Harry said that Vad was wrong and that he was at his desk and would pull out his contract just to be sure.

Sure enough, Harry pulled out the contract and began assuring me that there was no clause saying that Vad couldn't be traded. Suddenly, Harry fell silent and I could hear nothing but pages being flipped frantically but still no sounds from Harry. Finally, the flipping stopped but still no Harry. I was getting worried. All I could hear was heavy breathing. Vad asked what was going on so I hollered for Harry a few more times and still got no response so I hung up.

"Vad," I said, "I don't know what to tell you but sit tight and as soon as I find out, I'll tell you."

I went right back to my room and as soon as I turned the key in the keyhole the phone rang. It was Harry. As it turned out Vad *did* have a no trade during the season clause in his contract, but there was no way Harry—or the Rangers, for that matter—would let the deal fall through. New York wanted Phil and Vad. So the Rangers, who had lots of money to unload, came up with a bundle for Vad and that persuaded him to drop his objections.

Now that all the dirty work had been done, I finally had a moment to relax. I stretched out on the bed and turned on the radio just as the sports report was coming over the air. The first thing they mentioned was that Phil and Vad had been traded.

Apparently someone in the East had leaked the news. Can you imagine the position I would have been in if Phil and Vad had heard about it on the radio before I had had a chance to tell them?

Whatever, life had to go on and I had a team to coach. At least I *thought* I had a team. When the guys finally convened on the bus heading for the Vancouver Coliseum there was a deathly silence that carried over to the practice. As the guys glided around the ice, Bobby Orr, who had been side-lined with one of his injuries, sidled up to me and asked whether I had played a part in the deal. I admitted that I had. "Look," he said, "I don't want to sound as if I'm bragging or anything but why couldn't you guys have waited til I came back to see how the team would have played with me back in the lineup. Maybe we would have been all right." I told him that Harry and I felt that there was no time to waste otherwise the Rangers might have nixed the deal.

I left Orr and got ready to launch into the accelerated part of the skate. I blew the whistle, which meant the guys were supposed to move into high gear, but nothing happened. There was no reaction; as if I hadn't even blown the whistle. I blew it a second time and, again, it was as if my whistle were mute. Exasperated, I called them over to the corner of the rink. "Listen, you guys," I snapped. "Espo and Vad are gone and we all feel bad about it. I know how you feel. But if you guys don't smarten up, you'll be gone, too—and that means everybody! Now, when I blow the whistle, you guys had better get goin'."

I knew I was on the spot. If they didn't respond this time, it meant that I had lost the team. The whistle cut through the quiet of the Coliseum and they reluctantly sped up. They were a sullen bunch and I knew there would be trouble for a while because Phil and Vad had meant a lot to them. But we went on with the practice until there was a *real* downer: Phil and Vad came by the rink to pick up their sticks and skates and to make their goodbyes.

(I must add a postscript here about Vad. In 1967, the Rochester Americans had been given rings for winning the Calder Cup three years in a row. Anyway, the little glass chips in the rings were so cheap that they turned green.

One night, while we were with Team Canada in 1976, and remember, we had just traded Vad, he and I were in a jewelry store buying some stuff for our wives. I turned to Vad and I told him that now would be a good time to fix those glass chips. Vad took the ring from me, said something to the jeweler in French, and told me that the ring would be ready in a week.

A week later I went to pick up my ring, and when the jeweler gave it back to me I was stunned. There was an enormous diamond in the middle and two big diamond chips around it. I said to the guy, "Oh my gosh! How come you did this? I can't afford this!" He said that the job would cost me nothing. I said, "What do you mean nothing?" He told me that it was all taken care of by Carol Vadnais.

Vad, it seems, never wore diamonds, so he had had the gems removed from his two Stanley Cup rings and put into storage. He told the jeweler to put the big diamond and the two chips on my ring and to send him the bill. That's the kind of person Vad is.)

Needless to say there wasn't a dry eye in the place as the two veterans moved around the dressing room, shaking hands with everyone. My heart was with them, but my mind said the deal had to be made if the team was to be straightened out. That night we went out and were beaten by Vancouver. Right after the game I phoned Harry to give him the result. "I know you won't believe this," I added, "but I see some good things on the horizon. We're going to start winning soon and everything's gonna' be all right." As it worked out, we went from the basement to first place and stayed in first place for the next four years.

Harry said he would be on the next flight West and when we met the following day, he looked like he had just come out of the grave. He told me that the Boston papers had crucified him over the deal. Emile Francis was depicted as a burglar stealing Esposito and Vadnais from Boston while

Park was said to have a couple of bad legs and Ratelle was considered over the hill.

"Don't worry," I comforted him. "Wait til you see Park and Orr working the points together."

When all was said and done, the big deal saved my career. I give Harry full marks for a lot of guts on the deal. He knew we were in trouble and went out and did something, even though he knew it would be unpopular with the players, the fans and the media. Park, who was supposed to be out of shape and possibly at the end of his career because of his knee problems, played sensationally for me, as did Ratelle. Of course, at the time we had no way of knowing that it would work out so well, and a number of players on the Bruins suffered grave doubts. Phil and Vad were popular with their teammates and Park was high on the Bruins' hate list. He had written a book as a Ranger, called *Play the Man* in which he was severely critical of some of the Boston players, inspiring intense resentment among the guys. Nobody had feelings either way about Ratelle who was always considered a quiet and classy guy.

One particular player took the trade harder than most. The night the trade was announced, he was drinking quite heavily. Then he returned to his room, where the guys had a lot of beer and shrimp on the table. I joined them for awhile.

He had been very close to Phil and after a while he began ranting and raving about what a lousy deal we had made. I listened and listened and, after about an hour, I could take no more, so I got up and left. But I told some of the other guys to keep an eye on him, because I could tell he was going to get himself into trouble. They didn't heed my warning and a short time later he proceeded to demolish the room—literally. Had you seen the place, you would have guessed that a large bomb had been planted there, because there wasn't a single piece of furniture that wasn't in splinters.

It wasn't difficult for the hotel detectives to get wind of the ruckus but, the funny thing was, they wouldn't allow anything to be put back into place until photos were taken of the damage. The next morning, when we were about to leave, I phoned the player involved. He thought I was calling to bawl him out, or even to fine or suspend him for what he had done to the place. Instead, I said, "I left a red tie at your place last night. Can you check to see if it's still there?"

He asked me to wait a minute. I could hear furniture being moved, glasses falling. Then he returned to the phone and said, yes, he had found the tie. I said, "Good, bring it to the bus." Was he ever happy that I had only called about the tie!

Some people have criticized me for not disciplining him severely for his outburst, but I wouldn't think of it. For one thing, he wrote a cheque for a couple of thousand dollars in damages as he left the hotel. For another, over the years he had given his heart and soul to the Bruins.

When the going got rough, he was there. You couldn't ask for a better ally to be in the trenches with you in time of war.

In time, Park would make a similar contribution to the team although, at first, his teammates were extremely wary of the defenseman. Park was as unhappy leaving New York as Esposito was sad about leaving Boston. My first impression of Park was not good. He had a reputation in the NHL of being "The Pillsbury Doughboy" on skates and upon first look, it was well-earned. He was significantly overweight and I told him he would have to lose some pounds if he wanted to be in my good graces. He took my advice and became a one hundred percent Bruin. About two months afterwards I met him at Boston Airport and he said to me, "Grapes, look what you did to me!" He had lost fifteen pounds and his suit was two sizes too big for him (I like 'em lean and mean.). Fans who had booed him as a Ranger immediately took him to their collective hearts. One leather-lunged spectator in the balcony echoed the sentiments of the others when he chanted one night: "Hey, Pahk, welcome to the Gahden!" From that point on Brad knew that he was a genuine Bruin.

What most people haven't realized about Brad was that he was as quick-witted off the ice as he was patrolling the blue line. And he was especially good at feeding me lines to tell the reporters in the post-game press conferences. For example, one night we played the Minnesota North Stars and completely dominated them in every way. After the game Brad stuck his head through the door opening in my office and said: "All right, here's what you tell them: 'It was an up-and-down game. They got up and we knocked them down!' "

Much as I grew to admire Park, I can't say that I always was especially fair to him. One night we were playing the Washington Capitals when they were the doormats of the league. Late in the third period we were leading, 5-4, when Park coughed up the puck, a Caps player grabbed it and rifled it home to give them a 5-5 tie. What I should mention up front is that the incident took place just two days after Brad had returned to the lineup following knee surgery.

Of course the only thing on my mind was the blown lead and the culprit. I was so worked up at that time that I threw a water bottle and three towels at him.

Why did I do it? I imagine that I had reached a point in my coaching career where I expected almost the impossible from my players and most of them responded accordingly. Brad tried, but his knees wouldn't let him. Needless to say, Brad was hurt by my behaviour.

A day after the episode Park phoned me and said he wanted to meet right away at a bar. I agreed and we sat down over several beers, whereupon he proceeded to tell me how hurt he had been and how he didn't deserve the treatment he received the previous night.

"Grapes," he said. "Your throwing that bottle and towels at me hurt worse than any knife could have. I think a lot of you, but this has me thinking of quitting. I think I deserve an apology."

I laughed. He couldn't be serious—me apologize? Me, whose father had always said, "Never apologize; it's a sign of weakness." I looked closer; he was serious.

For some perverse reason—I don't know why—I was still in an obnoxious mood and instead of talking quietly with Park, I proceeded to lambaste him again. I told him that if he ever repeated the mistake again, I'd give him the same kind of crap, and if he didn't like it, he knew what he could do. I kept blasting at him until I suddenly looked up and realized there were tears in his eyes. This was a first all-star defenseman, tough as nails, one of the nicest guys you'd ever want to meet, who had returned to the team in seven weeks where most others would take six months, and here I was berating him. Here was a player who had likely saved my career and risked his own by returning prematurely to the lineup and I threw a water bottle at him, embarrassing him in front of his teammates.

I was close to destroying him; close to making him quit. When I left him at the bar, I began thinking about what I had done. I started questioning my desire to win at all costs and I began to move back closer to reality.

The next day I called a team meeting. I walked up and down the dressing room trying to get up my nerve and apologize—the hardest thing I ever had to do. I had almost made up my mind *not* to after all, when I saw Brad looking at me. Ah, well, here goes ...

My players sat there in stunned silence. I tried to explain that, sometimes, in the heat of battle I did things that I later came to regret and that this episode had been an example of that. At first they couldn't believe what they were hearing, but I think that moment brought me closer to the team than at any time during my entire stay in Boston.

In retrospect, I wonder whether I did it for Brad or rather to approach the team in a different direction. I looked at the guys' faces as I talked, and I said to myself, "These guys are really eating this up: Grapes in the humble role."

Shortly after I finished the talk, Park approached me, his eyes a little moist again and a look of gratitude across his mug. "Thanks!" he said warmly and walked away. I knew I had done the right thing.

Brad had two traits I didn't like: he would fight at the drop of a hat and he would continually lead rushes up the ice when he should have been spending more time in the defensive zone. Two of my major projects were trying to cure Park of these traits. I realized that neither would be easily treated, but I tried nevertheless. Now let me say right here: deep down, I loved it when Brad fought, but I had my designated fighters, and he wasn't one of them.

The fighting syndrome was particularly difficult because opponents understood how valuable Brad was to the Bruins and consistently tried to goad him into a fight, thereby getting him off the ice and making it easier to beat us. I finally got fed up during a game with the Detroit Red Wings. They had a pesky little forward named Dennis Polonich, who was always stirring up some kind of brouhaha or other. This time he needled Park until Brad finally went after him and, naturally, got thrown out of the game.

That did it. Instead of directly bawling out Park, I took another route. I contacted the newspaper guys and told them I was going to prevent Brad from getting into any fights in the future. Then, I told the same thing to the television people and, finally, I went to my own players. Furthermore, I added, that if Brad *did* get into a fight he would have to answer to me and he would be fined, to boot. What I *really* wanted to do was take the onus off Brad. I told the entire league, in effect, that Park was no longer permitted to fight so he, therefore, no longer felt obliged to display his toughness and we were all the better for it.

Next, I tried to contain his rushing tendencies. Perhaps it was selfish on my part, but I felt that if Brad did less rushing and concentrated more on defense, he would expend less energy and I would be able to play him up to forty minutes a game instead of twenty or twenty-five minutes. I also felt that the rushing would, ultimately, shorten his career. Eventually, I sat down and had a heart-to-heart with him. "Look, Brad," I said, "for the good of the team I'd like you to hold back more, stay in our half of the ice, don't rush so much. It'll cost you the Norris (best defenseman) Trophy, but you'll be helping the team a lot more than you think." He didn't hesitate. "No problem," he said, and that was that.

What made me feel bad was the fact that Park was, technically, good enough to win the Norris Trophy, but the writers who vote on the award always look at the scoring statistics of the defensemen and fail to take into account the players defensive strongpoints. To win the Norris Trophy, a defenseman has to *score* 25 to 30 goals in a season and there was no way Park could do that under my new instructions. But he accepted them and we all were better for it—except for his trophy case. He never has won the Norris which I think is a crime.

CHAPTER FIFTEEN

The Lunch Pail Gang And Some Good Referees

The Bruins were known as "The Lunch Pail Gang," courtesy of a column written by Boston writer Fran Rosa. He wrote, "They punch the time clock at 7:30 p.m. and never stop working." Somehow Harry took offense at this name because he thought it was demeaning. He thought it meant we had no talent.

I, of course, was proud of the name. To me it meant that we were proud but honest, and that we gave one hundred percent all the time. We did have the talent, as our first place finishes certified. Besides, who says being a "hard worker" isn't a talent?

In my estimation we had the toughest team ever in the league. Guys like Cashman, Schmautz, O'Reilly, Wensink, Jonathan and Secord would do anything to win.

In his book, *The Hammer, Confessions of a Hockey Enforcer*, Dave Schultz wrote that he couldn't sleep the night before playing the Bruins, out of fear of the consequences. We intimidated, to be sure, but we were "tough fair." That is, we never picked on a star—not a Marcel Dionne or a Guy Lafleur. We'd go after the opposition's biggest gunfighter and get him, not the star.

We expected this unwritten rule to be honoured by the enemy, and if it was disregarded, the foe had hell to pay.

Here's an example: our classiest—and most non-violent—player was

179

Jean Ratelle. Ratty was so clean-living that, to him, a terrible curse word was "damn!" When I went into one of my obscene tirades in the dressing room, I'd always do a double-take and feel like cringing when my eyes fell upon Jean. He sat there calm and unruffled and I felt as if I were confronting the parish priest. Just the sight of Ratelle made me stop the outburst.

As a rule, Ratty was treated with the same respect by the opposition, but there was one exception. His name was Gerry Hart and he was playing defense for the New York Islanders at the time. On this occasion Hart, who was relatively small for a defenseman, really messed up Ratty with a cheap shot. When Ratty got hit, everybody on the team felt it.

John Wensink, who was one of my main enforcers at the time, remedied the situation. He immediately grabbed Hart, took him by the scruff of his neck and rammed his head into the boards. As he held him there, he quietly whispered in his ear, "Next time you touch Mr. Ratelle, your head will go *through* the boards." Naturally we won the game, and Hart never laid a hand, glove or stick on Ratelle again as long as I was with the Bruins.

The ingredient that made our club especially fearsome was that we were tough from the goal out. They talk about Billy Smith of the Islanders being tough among today's goalies, but he's nothing more than an unoriginal facsimile of my number one goalie, Gerry Cheevers.

As Cheevers saw it, the goal crease was his eminent domain. Stray too close to that crease and you were apt to have your toes, ankles or knees chopped up by his big goalie stick. Although he carried up to forty pounds of equipment, Cheesie, as we called him, thought nothing of engaging the enemy with his stick. As goalies go, he was the original "puck's bad boy."

But he was also a good guy to have around the dressing room, and I speak from experience because Cheesie and I played together in Rochester under coach Joe Crozier. He was in his early twenties then, but he had the savvy of a veteran.

One of the things that impressed me about him was that he had the knack of losing more than twenty pounds *on a weekend*. Gerry would drink only beer—and eat nothing—from Friday night to Monday morning. Sure enough, at the Monday scrimmage he would be the shell of the man I had seen Friday afternoon.

Cheevers' midsection always had been a problem, going back to his early days as a pro in Rochester. And even though he had the ability to trim off large amounts of weight in a very short time, there were occasions when Cheesie simply did not want to take off any pounds. I shared that sentiment with him and, as a result, Gerry and I frequently would get into trouble with Crozier.

I should note at this point that there are two methods for losing weight; the first being the traditional method of cutting down on beer and the second being tampering with the dressing room scale.

Cheesie and I specialized in this department, employing an assortment of very practical techniques. We discovered that by putting pennies *underneath* the scales the poundage would be reduced by two. Another effective method was affixing a well-chewed piece of gum to the inside arm of the scale. That would subtract up to four pounds. Unfortunately, Crozier eventually caught on to each of those tricks. But one that always eluded him was the "grab-the-post" method. Whenever we were weighed on a Toledo scale, Cheesie and I would grab hold of the post as we were being clocked, and push down. That saved us five pounds, easily, many, many times.

Like so many goalies, Cheevers was eccentric. Put him in the nets and he was utterly fearless. He would stand in front of shots travelling 115 miles per hour without flinching, but if you asked him to room alone on the road he would quake in his boots. At first I found this hard to believe. Once, when we were neck-and-neck in a race for first place with the Buffalo Sabres, we had two critical games, back-to-back. The first was in Toronto against the Maple Leafs followed by the second in Buffalo against the Sabres. Instead of having Cheesie stay over in Toronto, I sent him ahead of the team to Buffalo so he could get some extra rest and relaxation. Little did I know.

Against the Sabres, he was just awful and it was only then that I learned that he was so afraid of rooming alone that he hadn't slept all that night and was a wreck by game time.

In time, I began rooming Cheesie with one of my favourite defensemen, Gary Doak. It was the perfect marriage of hockey player-roommates. Gerry said that Gary was the only guy he could room with and Doak said Gerry was the only guy *he* could room with; now Cheesie is coaching the Bruins and Doakie is his assistant.

Gerry had no fears when it came to partying and, in that regard, he can be thankful that his wife, Betty, was so understanding. Here's proof positive: we had lost a tough game at Boston Garden and Cheesie and some of the guys decided to go out and chase their sorrow with a couple of beers. And then a couple more and a couple more after that.

One day went by and then another and, still, Gerry hadn't returned home. On the third day, we had a practice and, sure enough, who trooped into the dressing room but Cheesie, unshaven, looking like a fugitive from Skid Row. I knew that Betty had been worried about him so the first thing I did was insist that he phone her. "Nah," he said, "I'll do it after practice."

"She's concerned," I demanded, "do it now!"

After a bit more cajoling and pushing, I got him into the trainer's office and handed him the phone. I sat there wondering what he could possibly say. After a couple of rings someone at the other end picked it up. "Betty," Cheesie said with great exultation, "it's me, Gerry. DON'T PAY THE RANSOM; I JUST ESCAPED."

Gerry bought a colt named Royal Ski, paying $20,000 for the horse. It turned out to be a big winner and made something like $800,000 for Gerry who, in turn, sold the horse for $1,700,000 to a Japanese horseman, who made a $500,000 down payment on it. Suddenly, Royal Ski took sick and the Japanese horseman decided that he wanted to back out of the deal. That was fine, but Gerry had the right to keep the 500 grand. Instead, he gave the money back and waited and hoped. Sure enough, Royal Ski got better and, this time, he sold him for $1,300,000.

The one time I remember Cheese getting teed off with me, believe it or not, was when I swung into a duet with his father, Joe, an Irishman through and through and one of Canada's best lacrosse players. We had lost to the Maple Leafs that night in Toronto and Gerry was quite upset about the game. His father came into the dressing room and he and I put our arms around each other and began singing "If You Are Irish Come Into The Parlour."

Gerry was upset and didn't want us to sing in the dressing room after a loss because he thought it would make Harry mad.

A week later, I got a phone call from Gerry, telling me he couldn't come to practice. I said, "How come you can't come to practice?" Gerry answered, "Joe died." I said, "You're kidding." Gerry replied, "Nope, and it's his first time, too." Gerry was devastated at Joe's passing and this was his way of covering up.

I had a real problem with Cheevers in practice. He simply would not try to stop shots and this invariably ruined our scrimmages. To remedy that I called a meeting of the players, minus Cheevers, and said, "During the scrimmage, if you can hit Cheevers' goalie pads, we'll count it as a goal." After three practices Cheevers came to me and said "Geez Grapes, have you noticed how great I've been in practice lately?" When some wise guy told him the truth he was absolutely furious, because he thought I had made a fool out of him.

Another winner on the Bruins was Terry O'Reilly, a big right wing from Niagara Falls, Ontario. We nicknamed him Taz, short for Tasmanian devil, a powerful carnivore that seeks its prey at night.

The first time I ever saw him in action, he was skating for the Boston Braves, then the Bruins' farm team in the American Hockey League.

It is safe to say that I had never seen a professional player fall down as much as Terry did. He seemed to be horizontal as often as he was vertical. When I next saw him, a year later, I couldn't believe that he was the same man. He had improved by about 180 percent. He had gone to power skating school and had diligently practised to the point that he had made a more significant improvement in his skills than any professional athlete I've ever known. Terry had only one problem; he played the game too honestly. At the beginning, he was the epitome of what fair play is all about.

If an enemy seriously fouled a player like Bobby Schmautz, that player, more likely than not, would be carved up *without warning*. But if that very opponent fouled Terry in the same way, O'Reilly would go after the guy, tap him on the shoulder, allow him to turn around, invite him to fight and then permit the enemy to strike the first blow. The Marquis of Queensbury would have been terribly proud of him. The problem was that O'Reilly's ritual hurt the team. Invariably, he would wind up with an additional two minute penalty for going after the guy and a five minute major for fighting. The other fellow would get away with just a five minute penalty.

Try as I might, I couldn't convince O'Reilly that he was being too nice, but one of the best fighters in the league cured Terry of his etiquette. We were playing the Los Angeles Kings, when Dan Maloney was the Kings' number one gun fighter. I had been cautioning O'Reilly that he had to stop permitting the enemy to take the first punch at him. I didn't want him to go around sucker punching the opposition but, on the other hand, I didn't want to see him getting hurt by being too nice. Well, on this night Maloney not only hit him first but he did a pretty good number on Terry. It was a painful experience but Maloney had done me a favour because, now, Taz made sure he got the first punch in before the other got started jabbing.

I found Terry to be a very paradoxical character. As tough as he was on the ice, that's how lamb-like he was when he wasn't in uniform. He was an avid antique collector. If he had one flaw it was a vicious temper.

Sometimes Terry pushed his courageousness too far. He and his wife Lourdes were vacationing one spring in Acapulco when Terry decided to go for a swim. As it happened, he misjudged the waves and the undertow and, before he knew it, he had drifted out far beyond the acceptable limit. Strong as he was, he still had a difficult time making headway with all the waves and the undertow. In time it became apparent that he was in trouble—big trouble. Just when it appeared that he might fade out of sight, a couple of lifeguards spotted him, swam like the devil through the waves, and reached him just in time. It took them a half-hour to haul him in, but they did and, thoroughly exhausted by the ordeal, they laid him out on the beach.

Apart from the fact that he had nearly drowned, O'Reilly also had pulled his ankle so badly in the rescue operation that he could hardly walk, but he finally pulled himself together and headed back to his cabana, limping all the way. As he walked along the beach he passed a bunch of guys who had hang gliders, surf boards and other gismos. One of the fellows noticed Terry and began goading him. "Hey, big fella, let's see ya do some surf gliding."

Terry politely shook his head, but the guy persisted. "No, thank you sir," Terry repeated, but the hustler wasn't satisfied. "How come," he snapped. "Are ya' yellow, or too cheap?"

The man who had just come this close to drowning and was hobbled by a bum ankle, looked over at his adversary and replied: "I'll show you who's yellow," and proceeded to grab the guy and bury his head in the sand. You just don't say things like that to Terry O'Reilly.

Of course, I've said a few things to O'Reilly, but sometimes my words went flying past him like a slapshot aimed wide of the net. The classic example took place one day when Terry, Dwight Foster, Mike Milbury, Peter McNab, and I were helping Terry move to his mansion in Georgetown. The address, by the way, is One Cherry Lane. (Terry says he's changing it to One Cheevers Lane.)

When it came time to load the fridge I said, "Terry, we better take all the food out of the fridge before we pick it up." "No Grapes," he laughed. "Remember, you're not my coach in the summer. I don't have to listen to you now. The stuff won't come out." There was not much I could say to that, so I watched as Terry, Mike, Peter, and Dwight lifted it.

A split-second later, the door flew open and everything poured out of the refrigerator. It looked like Fibber McGee's closet. After the last bottle of milk hit the ground, I patted Terry on the shoulder. "Taz old boy," I said, "you should always listen to your coach."

Terry really demonstrated the kind of friend he is during a family crisis. In 1979, our son Timothy had to have a kidney transplant. As you can imagine, we were all absolutely devastated. He was on a dialysis machine, and the whole ordeal was extremely hard to take. Rose and I were tested to see whether or not our kidneys were compatible for a transplant, but as it turned out, our daughter Cindy's kidney was almost identical to Tim's. Cindy was a miracle throughout the whole thing. She just said, "Take mine," without hesitation.

The whole experience was getting to be a little hard for me, so much so that I began to look forward to road trips so I could get out of Boston. I left the whole burden on Rose's shoulders.

Some people might wonder how I could leave my family at a time like this; how could I even function. Well, when you're a professional, you have to work all the time. You separate one aspect of life from another. I didn't realize the seriousness, the importance of the operation, until I saw both Cindy and Tim being wheeled into the operating room. Then, I finally realized the sacrifice Cindy was making.

Throughout all of this, the Bruins won twenty of our first twenty-two games. Someone asked Terry why we had gotten off to such a good start and he said, "Well, we had a meeting and decided that Grapes was having enough trouble, so let's give him one less thing to worry about." That's the kind of guy Terry is and that's the kind of guys they all are. They all went to donate blood so that Tim would have enough blood for the operation. Now you see why I loved them.

Stan Jonathan, a tough Tuscarora Indian from Brantford, Ontario was one of my favourites, too.

Of all my discoveries, Jonathan is the one in which I take the most pride. It happened this way: in 1975 our number one draft pick was Doug Halward, who earlier had been playing junior hockey for the Oshawa Generals. One day Harry Sinden suggested that the two of us take a look at Halward in Oshawa to see how he was shaping up. As bad luck would have it, Halward was injured early in the game so that part of our trip was ruined but, as the game progressed, I couldn't help noticing this rugged little Indian. He didn't play an exceptional game, but there was something about him that made me take notice.

I didn't say much about Jonathan to Harry, but I filed his name in the back of my mind for future reference and at draft time I called Harry aside and said: "Do you think you could get me one hockey player?"

Harry was not as impressed as I was and bypassed Jonathan on the first, second, and third picks. We finally got him the fourth time around and sent him to the Dayton Gems of the International League. A year later he made our team.

In Jonathan's first big fight he so thoroughly destroyed Keith Magnuson, the Chicago Black Hawks defenseman, that he gained notoriety throughout the league and my infinite praise. But beating up on Magnuson was not that big a deal because Keith, for all his tenacity and gutsiness, was a real catcher.

Stanley reminded me of my pet dog, Blue, a bull terrier. They were both relatively small but enormously tough. I liked Stanley so much that I took a beautiful painting of Blue from home and had it hung directly above Jonathan's locker. One day Stanley's father was visiting Boston and was introduced to me in my office. "You've got a great son there, Mr. Jonathan," I said. "He reminds me of my dog, Blue."

Old man Jonathan was aghast. Comparing his son to a dog. Well, this big Indian stared at me and stared at me until I thought I was going to get scalped. I had to do a lot of fast explaining there or I would have gone the way of General Custer.

If I had had the time I would have explained to Mr. Jonathan that Blue was not only my pet, but also my alter-ego. You don't have to take my word for it, just ask Jim Coleman, the noted Canadian sports authority. Coleman, whose column is syndicated across the country by the Southam News Service, once observed that Blue has been the real brains behind my success. "It is a matter of public record," wrote Coleman, "that Don never made an important long-range decision as a coach until he had consulted Blue."

What is Blue like? Superficially, she is a white bull terrier. That says nothing. Here's how Coleman described her: "Blue is a canine aristocrat, a highly cultured and highly intelligent individual who despises vulgarity and pretension." He might have added that Blue was tough, a discovery my Bruins made soon after she visited the dressing room.

One afternoon Wayne Cashman, as hard-bitten as any pla·er I've ever had, went after Blue with a hockey stick. She grabbed the sti :k from Wayne *and broke it in her mouth.* Cashman hadn't had enough so the next day he grabbed a blowtorch the players use for curving their sticks and stuck it in Blue's face, figuring that she would be afraid of the fire. Blue chased Cashman right into the stickroom!

Rose and I had to take Blue to the veterinarian one day, and while we were sitting in the waiting room a man walked in with a Scottish Terrier. The terrier began barking at Blue, as if it wanted to start a fight. The owner said: "This terrier is so tough he'll take on anything." With that, Blue looked up at me as if to say, "What do you think Dad?" And I looked over at Rose and Rose said to me: "DON, DON'T YOU DARE!!"

Another time we were at the vet because Blue needed some shots. Now I kid you not when I say that Blue is afraid of nothing, not even a needle. Well, this particular doctor—I don't know if he was a sadist or not—just jammed the needle into Blue extra hard and farther than he had to and Blue looked at him as if to say: "Now, you didn't have to do that." Before the vet knew what had happened Blue grabbed his watch band—a rather expensive one at that—with her teeth and pulled it back and finally released it so that it snapped back on his hand with great force. It was Blue's way of saying, "Next time, don't be such a wise guy!"

I used Blue as a role model for my players. I remember telling Stan Jonathan, John Wensink and Al Secord that they should maintain *eye contact* with the enemy the way Blue does. "After you hit somebody," I told them, "don't skate away with your head down. That's like saying, 'Hey, look, guys, I didn't do anything wrong; the coach put me out here and made me hit, so don't get mad at me, it's just hockey.' When you want to hit them, *look them in the eye* and say, 'Yeah, I hit you, what are you gonna' do?' "

Then I brought Blue into play and pointed out that even though I was her master and she loved me, if I had eye contact with her she'd come at me. I then proceeded to stare at her and she stared at me for ten seconds. Then, she started getting angry, glaring at me as though saying, "Hey, what's goin' on here?" Staring at eye level meant a challenge to her. At that moment Blue came at me and I turned away, letting her know I was only kidding around. But Jonathan, Wensink and Secord got the point; and from then on when they hit somebody, they'd stare into the eyes of their foe and, inevitably, the other guy would turn away. That meant they had conquered him.

Blue had a winning *attitude.* When my son, Timothy, was young I would tell him that life is a matter of *attitude.* It all depends on how you view things; if you accentuate the positive, you're likely to come out on top. I'll give you an illustration: Half a mile from our home on Wolfe

Terry O'Reilly scoring the winning goal at 1 a.m. against Philadelphia in overtime. Terry was put on by accident—one of my better moves.

Bobby Schmautz saying, "Another genius move," after the Boston crowd booed when I put Wensink on for a powerplay and he scored in 18 seconds.

Boston team photo, 1976-77. This picture appeared in the paper the next day with the caption: "Bruins going to the dogs."

A. ALTMAN

Record-setting group—eleven 20-goal scorers on one team. (left to right)
Wayne Cashman, Al Sims (who shouldn't be there), Bobby Schmautz, Gregg Sheppard, Bobby Millar,
Terry O'Reilly, me, Peter McNab, Rick Middleton, Stan Jonathan, Don Marcotte, and Jean Ratelle.
(Brad Park is missing.)

Island, near Kingston, some fellows had two enormous Great Danes. Well, one night I was out for a walk and was carrying a bushel basket. For no reason at all these Great Danes attacked me and I suppose I would have been dead if I hadn't been able to protect myself with the basket until the owners came and called the dogs off.

Three days later I was with Blue near our house when the two Great Danes appeared. They looked like the Hounds of the Baskervilles and, to be honest, I figured that one or both of them would devour Blue on the spot. There was no way she could beat these monster Great Danes. But Blue confronted them with the attitude "Hey, you two stiffs, what are you gonna' do now?" Guess what? They were absolutely terrified of her; they didn't do a thing. In fact, she walked right around them and they didn't even so much as snarl. It was Blue's *attitude*.

Jim Coleman claimed that Blue's attitude toward Denver was responsible for my demise with the Rockies. "The dog hated Denver on first sight," said Coleman. "She regarded the citizens of Denver as brash and pushy. Blue went on strike; she simply refused to give Cherry any help in making important decisions."

Even in distant Denver, Blue was in demand. I once received an offer to do a Miller Lite beer commercial with Blue. The advertisers had me come to New York and audition for the commercial with another dog—which, by the way, was a brilliant performer—and then said they were ready to shoot it with me and Blue.

"We'll fly Blue into New York from Denver next week," the advertising guy told me.

That floored me. I had assumed they understood that Blue doesn't fly. They hadn't known so I had to tell them. "I thought you guys were going to come out to Denver." No, nooooooo, they said. If I wanted the fifteen grand for the commercial, I had to bring Blue out by plane. (P.S. I'm the only guy in the world who turned down $15,000 because my dog wouldn't fly!)

It goes without saying that I'm very sensitive about Blue. One day a woman from a charity organization phoned my wife and asked if she would enter Blue in an "Ugliest Dog Contest." Rose told her she was lucky I was out of town. The woman diplomatically suggested that Blue be *the judge*, which is what Blue did. Unfortunately, some papers said that Blue had won the ugly dog contest, which was not the case and I'm setting the record straight right now.

All of which is another way of saying that when I compared one of my players to Blue it was like nominating him for knighthood; and that is precisely how I felt about Stan Jonathan.

Now, don't get the mistaken impression that I coddled Stanley, just because he reminded me of Blue. I never wanted to see any of my players get spoiled and, if I detected signs of that failing, I immediately took action. In Jonathan's case, he had a spell when he scored eight goals in ten games for the Bruins at one point and *I sent him down to our minor league affiliate in Rochester.* He couldn't believe it until I explained to him that I didn't want him to forget what had got him to the NHL in the first place; hard work and hitting, not goal scoring. "Stanley," I said, "you're starting to think you're a Guy Lafleur. Forget it, and be Stan Jonathan. I don't want you to fall into that ego trap." He got the message.

Perhaps such a drastic move on my part was unnecessary. At best, that's debatable. My concern was the welfare of the team which would have been best served by Jonathan hitting and intimidating the opposition. When he concentrated on that, he was virtually invincible and it was a lesson vividly dramatized for Scotty Bowman and the Montreal Canadiens during a Stanley Cup playoff series we had with them.

The Canadiens had a big defenseman named Pierre Bouchard, whose father Emile (Butch) Bouchard had been a great NHL blueliner on the Canadiens when Maurice Richard and Toe Blake were in their prime. Pierre was not as good as his dad. Scotty Bowman, who coached the Canadiens, kept him around as a fifth defenseman and used him occasionally as a regular. He had a reputation as a fairly clean player, but one who could really handle his dukes. He once flattened Teddy Irvine, a pretty big New York Rangers winger, with one punch at Madison Square Garden, and word got around the league that Bouchard was not to be trifled with, although Jonathan never paid much mind to that warning—or any warning for that matter.

Although Scotty has from time to time decried rough hockey, NHL history has clearly shown that when it suits his purposes he will ice as rough a bunch of skaters as any coach. He did it when he coached the St. Louis Blues in the late 1960s (the Plager brothers and Noel Picard were no blushing violets) and even with the Canadiens he had a knack for delivering a "no-nonsense" message from time to time. In this particular case he sent Bouchard, Gilles Lupien, a gigantic defenseman who could do little else but fight, and Rick Chartraw, a utility forward with a reputation for toughness, out on the ice.

Originally, I had the Peter McNab-Terry O'Reilly-John Wensink line out there but I sent Jonathan out to replace McNab. (Peter later told me getting off the ice at that point was one of the happiest moments in his life.) Anybody with half a brain knew that there was going to be trouble, although I was *not* looking for it; after all, I had a game to win. But for some reason Scotty *was* looking for it, else he wouldn't have loaded the ice with those troublemakers.

As soon as the linesman dropped the puck, the sticks came up, there was a flurry of action, a whistle for an offside and Jonathan and Bouchard were side-by-side, elbows at the ready. Stanley gave Pierre a little shot. All of a sudden they dropped their gloves and started swinging. Pierre got in the first good blows, but Stanley was virtually impervious to pain and he took the best shots Bouchard had to offer and kept swinging.

By this time, no matter who would eventually be the winner, I knew that I was watching the best hockey fight of my life. Even though Stanley was considerably shorter than Pierre he traded punches evenly with him. Then, without any warning, Jonathan, who was leading with his right hand, switched to his left and caught Bouchard off guard. He pounded Pierre's face with a series of lefts until Bouchard crumpled to the ice, his nose and cheekbone broken, and his face covered with blood.

Bouchard's reputation as a fighter was destroyed by that bout and, if the truth be known, he was never the same as a big-leaguer after that. As for Jonathan, he instantly became the undisputed middleweight *and* heavyweight champion of the NHL. Yet, in some ways, Stanley wasn't as nasty as one of his teammates, Bobby Schmautz.

Built along approximately the same lines as Jonathan (although somewhat more on the wiry side), Schmautzie was one of the most feared NHL players because of the manner in which he used his stick on the foe. The enemy called him "The Surgeon," and not because he was genteel with his scalpel. Bobby, himself, liked to be known as "Doctor Hook." Whatever the label, Schmautz was so vicious when it came to carving up the opposition that even *I* would caution him. He'd always reply: "Grapes, I'm small and the stick is the old equalizer."

His teammates used to kid him a lot about it. We used to say that at Christmas, instead of using a knife, Schmautzie carved the turkey with his hockey stick. I once phoned him in the off-season at a hunting lodge out west and his daughter answered the phone. "Did your Dad kill anything?" I asked her and she said no, he hadn't. "Well," I suggested, "he should have taken his hockey stick, then he would have killed something!"

While his stick may have been "the great equalizer," Schmautzie got his comeuppance every so often. Once, he got into a row with Larry Robinson, the towering Canadiens defenseman, whose arms were almost as long as Bobby was tall. Robinson got ticked off one night because of Schmautzie's stick work and grabbed him around the neck right in front of our bench and proceeded to pound him in the head with the other hand.

My players wanted to go over the boards to rescue Schmautzie, but I wouldn't let them go because I felt that if they did pour over, Bobby would be embarrassed. He could take on anyone, no matter how big and even though he was getting his lumps this time, he was showing a lot of courage. "Don't worry guys," I told the team, "Schmautzie is all right." What Schmautzie got was a good pasting and later, he took me aside and said, "Grapes, when I heard you tell the guys not to come, I was saying to myself, 'You SOB, Grapes, let them come!'" Well, you learn something new everyday.

True, Schmautzie was ruthless with his stick against others, but he was also ruthless with himself when it came to playing hurt. His knees were so beat up that he actually skated with a brace on each one. There was a time when he was suffering through an awful scoring slump and we were approaching the playoffs. He suggested that I bench him for the good of the team. I said, "No, sir, I don't care how badly you play, Schmautzie, you and I will go to the end together."

I kept him in the lineup for the series against the Los Angeles Kings and he scored eight goals on eight shots. Another time he went down to block a shot and the puck smashed into his nose, breaking it in five places. My only comment to Schmautzie about his broken nose was, "It hit you in the face, how could it miss your nose?" He also took ribbing from his daughter. She asked her mother if Daddy's nose was going to look like Rick Smith's. (Whose nose was like a winding road. Sorry, Rick!) Against Toronto, Schmautz tried to split the Maple Leafs' defense and was hit so hard by their defenseman, the late Scott Garland, that the metal brace on his leg was bent. Three months later, we played them again, he tried the same play and this time he split the defense and scored.

Schmautzie was trouble for the opposition but he also was trouble for me. We were in Minnesota for a game with the North Stars and Bobby was out one night drinking. He later walked into the hotel's coffee shop and broke the crêpe machine. Just like that. The hotel socked him with a bill for $1,000, so I took up a collection for him. But Schmautzie refused and wrote out a cheque for the damages.

I was still furious with him because I could not tolerate that kind of behaviour from my players in the hotel, even though he had gotten carried away that night. My revenge was to play him to death against the North Stars. I played him on a regular shift, on the power play, killing penalties and even on other shifts. I wanted him to look bad in front of everybody, although I knew he was dying from a hangover. I didn't relent and when we got a penalty with five minutes left in the game I threw Bobby out as a penalty-killer. The score was tied 2-2 at the time and, wouldn't you know it, he got a breakaway, scored the winning goal and then collapsed in a heap in the corner of the rink.

We had another toughie, Al Secord, who was terrific with his fists. For some reason, though, he never was a favourite of Harry Sinden's. That proved to be his ruination with the Bruins. While I was there, though, I tried to use him as much as possible. Although Al was born in Sudbury, Ontario, and had played his junior hockey in Hamilton, like so many Canadian kids, he looked upon Maple Leaf Gardens in Toronto as the cathedral of the sport.

We were headed for Toronto one night when Secord asked me, as a special favour, if I would let him start the game at left wing. I realized that this would be a special thrill for him but I asked for a favour as well. I told him that I would start him if he took off his helmet.

I didn't like Secord in his helmet and I thought he would be more intimidating without it on. So I said to Al, "If you take off your helmet, I will not only start you in Toronto, I will play you on every power play." So Al took off his helmet and started the game. On his first shift he picked a toughie, Dave Hutchison, to get into a fight with. I said to myself, "Oh no, please help him, Lord, to not get his clock cleaned." But he did a sweet number on Hutchison.

There are players who fight because they must to stay in the league and there are players who fight because of personal pride. But there are few players who fight because they like to. Al was one of them. I came into my office at 8:30 in the morning once and there was Al showing his family the tapes of his best fights.

Sinden always liked fighters, which is why I couldn't understand why Secord didn't make a hit with him. After I left the Bruins, I ran into Al one day in Boston and he was really depressed. "I don't understand what the Bruins are doing to me," he said.

"I'm on the bench. I asked why I wasn't playing and they told me, 'Because you're not playing your game, you're not aggressive and not hitting.' So naturally I go out and be aggressive and start hitting and naturally I get a few penalties. Then they bench me again. I say, 'Why aren't I playing?' They say, 'Because you're getting too many penalties.' My head is all screwed up."

I could see the kid was falling apart, so I grabbed him by the lapels and looked straight in his eyes. "DON'T CHANGE, AL." He looked at me. "There are twenty teams in this league that will take you. Just don't change your game."

Sure enough, the Black Hawks got him in 1981 and he became a big scorer—though still fighting—overnight. Besides, he made Chicago stronger and braver, as a team, just with his presence. He finished the season with 47 goals, tops on the Black Hawks, and 303 penalty minutes.

One player who listened to me was Mike Milbury. Like Terry O'Reilly, Mike seemed to have minimal talents at first, but he developed rapidly because he was simply determined to make good. He was a Boston boy who originally had been a football player at Colgate University, but had then tried his hand at hockey. I first met him at my hockey school in Rochester.

By this time he had his heart set on a professional career as a defenseman, but I was very skeptical about his chances. I told him straight out that one of the first things he would have to learn was how to turn into the corners to get the puck. For some reason, all young American defensemen seem to have the same problem, turning and going into the corners.

He took my word and, I remember, one morning I showed up at the rink before seven and there was Mike, with his pregnant wife, Debbie, out on the rink. She was standing at center ice, in the cold, damp arena, dumping pucks from the red line into the corners. And there was Mike, chasing down those pucks, turning in the corners, working his tail off, practising his turning and picking the puck up, making himself a better hockey player, and eventually a big-leaguer with the Bruins.

Mike and I had a curious relationship in that, while I loved him like a son, we disagreed on many topics. (Sort of an Archie Bunker/Meathead relationship.) And we had plenty of time to disagree, because we lived only five doors away from each other in North Andover and drove back and forth to practice.

We were talking about our favourite people one day and I mentioned that I was very fond of John Wayne. When Milbury told me that he didn't particularly care for John Wayne, I nearly went through the roof. "How could anyone not like John Wayne?" I demanded. "Not like the Duke? You gotta' be crazy." Then I asked him who his favourite actor was and he told me Woody Allen. As soon as I heard that name I called him a college freak and a hippy. Then, we moved on to the next topic.

Mike was sent down to Rochester after a great camp, as I told you earlier. I knew his heart was broken and sometimes when a young player has his heart broken like that he never recovers. I heard that he was playing poorly, not hitting, without enthusiasm. This was a sure sign of a broken spirit. Well, I talked Harry into bringing him up for a couple of games, near the end of the season. We had first place locked up, so I figured, let's see what this guy will do in the playoffs. He came up and he was a complete pacifist. During the game, in between every shift, I screamed in his ear, "You hippy, liberal pacifist, you'll never make the big time." Harry was going to send him back to Rochester.

I talked Harry into keeping him for one more game, against Toronto. Bobby Schmautz spelled it out for him, "You want to stay here, hit, be aggressive, and a fight wouldn't hurt."

The night before a game in Toronto I wandered by a bar (The Stable) and who should I find standing outside the bar a few minutes after curfew but "Muldoon" Milbury. I politely asked him what he was doing there and he answered that he couldn't sleep. When I answered him the paint started to peel off the walls of the bar. "You big stiff! You're hanging by a string! I'll kick your ass all the way back to Rochester if you don't play well tomorrow night. Let's go!"

He walked five paces in front of me like a little school boy. I cursed at him all the way back to the hotel. Needless to say, he played an aggressive, tough game the next night and has never looked back since.

Mike and I got so close that he asked me if I would be the godfather to his child, Luke, and naturally I accepted. Not long after that, Mike was interviewed on television and was unusually nervous. The questioner asked him if he was fond of me and Mike, said yes, he was.

"I think so much of Don Cherry," Mike added, "that I made him *father of my child!*" Thus ended one of Boston's most embarrassing sports interviews.

Only Mike and I could fall in love with a lowly weed, but this actually happened during our drives to and from Boston Garden. As we were motoring along the highway one day, I noticed a single weed, about two feet high, growing through a crack in the concrete at the side of the road. Suddenly it dawned on me that this weed had great symbolic value. Although it was ignored by everyone and maligned as a mere weed, it had managed to survive storms, salt, spraying, blizzards and whatever else might have been dumped on it. Still it managed to stand tall and I offered this bit of insight to Mike.

He immediately understood how I felt about this weed and I instantly knew that he, too, felt for the little shaft of green. "Mike," I said one day, "that weed shows character. Any plant that can grow out of a crack in concrete and survive all the climactic indignities has to be something special. Our team has to have character like that." Milbury agreed and, each day, we would acknowledge the weed as we headed for Boston.

But one day a terrible thing happened. As we were driving to the Garden we noticed that a highway clean-up truck was grooming the side of the road *and was heading straight for our favourite weed.* "Mike," I shouted, as if a human life was in danger, "they're going to get our weed!"

He slammed on the brakes, jumped out of the car and ran—dodging the rush-hour traffic—back in the direction of the weed. Several times I thought he was going to get killed as he raced to beat the cleaning truck to the weed. Sure enough, he got to it just in time, plucked it from the concrete crack and then zigzagged back through the traffic again until he safely reached the car. As he slammed the door, he said, "Grapes, they aren't gonna get *our* weed. No way!" When I got home I took some fertilizer and planted the heroic weed in my backyard.

Two days later, Rose was weeding the garden and came to our weed. She looked at it and thought, "What's this old weed doing here?" She uprooted it and threw it in the garbage. I suppose there is a moral here, but I haven't figured it out yet.

There are some people I wouldn't treat as nicely as I treated that weed. People like referees.

Major league baseball umpire Ron Luciano once said that managers argue with umpires for three reasons. "One, they believe the umpire has made an error in judgment and should be so informed. Two, they are trying to prevent a player or players from being dismissed from the game. Three, temporary insanity."

As a hockey coach, I would say that temporary insanity was the primary reason for arguing with the referees. Start with the fact that officiating a hockey game flawlessly is an impossible task. There is only one man who is trying to keep an eye on ten skaters going up to 25 miles per hour with half of them behind the referee's back. There's no way one person can detect all the infractions. When a ref missed one—or two, or three—I would get insane. It was part of the business of coaching.

I did learn *something* about handling referees from all my experience as a player and a coach. The important thing was not to embarrass the official. Referees don't even mind if you swear at them, but you have to do it the right way. The best way to do it is skate over to the official and look as if you're adjusting your stick, or taking a piece of tape off the blade, then hand it to the ref while speaking your mind about his lousy call.

My problem was that the moment I became a coach I started embarrassing referees. I would stand on the boards and rant and rave, making the ref feel like two cents. Once, when Andy van Hellemond made a particularly (in my eyes) awful call, I screamed bloody murder at him. But Van Hellemond very wisely stayed so far from the bench he couldn't hear me. He finally sent Brad Park over to the bench and Brad said that if I had a message for the ref to give it to him and he, in turn, would transmit it back to Van Hellemond. "Tell him," I said, "to go f--- himself."

I meant it as a joke, but damned if Park doesn't skate right back to Van Hellemond and deliver the message exactly as I had said it!

Some referees could accept a situation like that with a sense of humour. John McCauley was one of them, and that's why he was my favourite.

McCauley was handling one of our games when a fan tossed an egg from about 200 feet up in the stands and it hit him right in the middle of his forehead; dead-center. I have never seen a shot like that before or since and I wondered how McCauley would handle it. He skated over to the bench and was handed a towel. As he wiped the yolk off his face, he turned to me and said: "Nice shot, wasn't it, Grapes?" You've got to like a man for that.

Another good one is Dave Newell. He was handling a Bruins-Maple Leafs game in Toronto. I let him have it almost from the opening face-off and how I escaped without a bench penalty I'll never know. Finally Newell reached what I thought was his breaking point. He called time for a moment and skated over to our bench. I figured I really was going to catch hell. It was Saturday night, the game was on network television; there were 16,000 fans in Maple Leaf Gardens and everybody was watching me and Newell as he headed for the bench.

Before he actually got to me, I tried to anticipate his diatribe. "Yeah, okay, Newell," I snapped as he arrived at the sideboards. Dave took his forefinger and pounded me on the chest with it and then said: "Grapes, this is the sharpest suit I have ever seen!"

As I live and breathe, this was the first time in my career that anyone pulled so perfect a squelch on me that I was actually speechless. Then, to cap the great line, Newell slowly skated back to center ice and added: "And don't you forget it."

The fans thought he was really giving me the going over, and they were hollering, "That's the way Dave, don't let that stiff get away with that." Even the TV commentators said, "Cherry has been severely reprimanded by Newell." But the players loved it because they finally saw me at a loss for words.

For some reason a ref we had a great deal of trouble with was Ron

Wicks. I once chased him down the rink after a game in Washington, not meaning to do anything but yell, but I couldn't put on the brakes in time and banged right into him. I was called on the carpet by NHL President Clarence Campbell for that one.

Another time we were playing a big game against the Islanders and Wicks was (in our estimation) calling an atrocious game. At the end of the second period, the ref headed for his dressing room and Harry was there waiting for him to step off the ice. Instead of actually lunging at him, Harry calmly stood next to the wall and as Wicks headed for his room, he said: "Nice game, Wicksie." When we arrived back on the ice for the start of the third period the public address announcer was reading off a penalty against us for unsportsmanlike conduct. It was the one and only time I ever heard of a team being penalized because a g.m. told the ref he was calling a nice game.

My hassles with the refs did not wear well with Clarence Campbell. Clarence was a Rhodes Scholar, a lawyer and as distinguished an individual as ever graced the NHL. He was a man of few words, but I had the misfortune of hearing those words quite often. Shortly after I would be involved in an incident with a referee I would get a message that Mr. Campbell wanted me to call him. Our conversations went something like this:

Mr. Campbell: "Campbell here!"

Me: "This is Don Cherry, Mr. Campbell!"

Mr. Campbell: "Explain your actions in Washington."

Me: "I didn't think the referee was calling a very good game and I got carried away etc. etc."

Mr. Campbell: "Unacceptable." (Click of telephone.)

A few days later I would receive a letter from NHL headquarters informing me that I had been fined $500. In five years of dealing with the NHL President the only words I remember are "Explain your actions . . ." and "Unacceptable."

On one of the other "Unacceptables" that cost me $500, Mr. Campbell followed up the fine with a visit to Boston Garden. Rose and Timothy were at the game. Rose said to Tim, "Mr. Campbell is up there in the crowd." Tim said, "Gee, I'd like to meet Mr. Campbell." Rose said, never thinking that he would go, "Well, why don't you go up and introduce yourself?" So Tim went up to Mr. Campbell and said, "Hello, Mr. Campbell, I'm Tim Cherry." Clarence didn't make the connection to Cherry, coach of the Bruins, so Tim said, "Mr. Campbell, my Dad just wanted to know if you got his cheque." Mr. Campbell, who almost never lets his hair down said, "Oh, you're *that* Cherry." Then he burst out laughing and told Tim, "tell your Dad I got the cheque, and tell him thanks a lot!"

CHAPTER SIXTEEN

Triumph And Disaster

The Boston Bruins club had become a formidable force in the NHL, though still not the champions, and I had been named the league's Coach of the Year. Such recognition was a balm for my ego which was further enriched when I was invited to be one of the coaches involved in the Team Canada 1976 organization. This was quite a feather in my cap because the members of Team Canada would be selected from among the best professionals in the dominion. I was highly elated.

The tournament would be played in September 1976 and earlier in the year, the key men behind Team Canada—Al Eagleson, Sammy Pollock and Scotty Bowman—officially gave me their blessing to help run the club. Now I was really in select company.

As head of the players' union, an attorney and an agent as well, Eagleson was the most powerful man in hockey; more powerful, even, than the President of the league or even the Chairman of the Board of Governors or even some of the power brokers among the club owners.

The Eagle runs the Team Canada operation. The Canada Cup was basically his idea, and he is the guy who makes all the arrangements, from choosing the coaches, right down to selecting the sites and making it all go.

Sammy Pollock, architect of the Montreal Canadiens dynasty, was a logical choice to oversee the operation. He was a no-nonsense guy who seemed to have an intuitive knack for doing the right thing at the right time. His record as general manager of the Canadiens proved that. Pollock always favoured the gung-ho "firewagon" style of hockey practiced by his Flying Frenchmen, so it was no surprise that Sammy put the accent on players who were the best skaters, the best shooters and, of course, the best scorers. There was no argument about that—he simply wanted the best offensive hockey players in the league and wanted to blow the opposition out.

Scotty, who had had a successful run as coach with the St. Louis Blues, had gone to work for Sam and the Canadiens. He was a stern, opinionated individual whose sense of humour was not very apparent. Although there were other coaches aboard—Al MacNeil, Bobby Kromm and myself—it was evident to us that Scotty would be the number one man behind the bench, as it should be.

Kromm had been an effective coach of Canadian amateur teams in international competition and MacNeil had coached the Canadiens to the Stanley Cup in 1971. I didn't suffer any illusions about my role. Scotty would be *the* coach of Team Canada and the rest of us were there to share the blame if anything went wrong—and maybe to help, a little.

If there had been any doubt about who was dictator of the operation, that was removed at our very first meeting at the Queen Elizabeth Hotel in Montreal.

One of the fellows who was feeling a little stronger than he should have been was Bobby Kromm. While we were sitting around, Bobby announced "I'm gonna tell the reporters a few things about the team ..." Before he could finish, Eagleson laid him out cold: "NO YOU WON'T!!" There was never any doubt in my mind about The Eagle's power after that. Bobby just sat there stunned. Like everyone else in the troupe, he was awed by Eagleson. The man was a bundle of energy. When he entered a room he absolutely annexed the place. He made everyone, no matter how many people happened to be there, feel as if they were his most personal friends. And the weird thing about him was his knack of being able to handle his enemies almost as easily as he does his friends. He would joke with them and act almost as if they weren't his foes at all, even though everyone—especially The Eagle—knew that they were.

Our high command was a curious mixture of the young and old. I was still a little wet behind my ears in terms of NHL experience and there I was sitting with Toe Blake, who had once coached the Canadiens to five straight Stanley Cups, and Keith Allen, who had managed the Philadelphia Flyers to Cup wins in 1974 and 1975. Keith and Toe were there to help Sammy, and the bunch of us convened for our first formal dinner in the very posh Beaver Room of the Queen Elizabeth Hotel. The scene was right out of a movie. Violinists played in the background as the waiters—each table had its own special waiter—presented one of the most lavish menus I had ever seen.

Al MacNeil, who is a native of Sydney, Nova Scotia, ordered some exotic fish. When the dish arrived at our table, the maitre d' instantly appeared with a magnificent sauce that could only be obtained at a high class restaurant such as the Beaver Room. "Would you like some sauce?" the maitre d' asked MacNeil.

With that, Al replied very matter of factly, "Nah, just bring me some ketchup." It was as if a bomb had just been dropped. The maitre d' was consummately embarrassed yet he was obliged to pass along the order. He leaned over and whispered Al's request to the waiter who immediately turned red. The poor waiter had to go to the kitchen for the ketchup and when the chef learned what Al wanted to put on his coveted item he almost ran out and chopped Al with a cleaver. What did Al care? He was a Maritimer who happened to like ketchup on his fish.

Now that we were getting ready for the start of camp, there was a lot of talk about whether or not the National Leaguers could keep up with the highly-trained Russians and Czechs. I had no fears, but there were some in our group who felt that conditioning would be in the Soviets' favour. With that in mind the Canadian government spent a lot of money to send some physiotherapists and physical instructors to work with our professionals. The minute I got word of that I cringed. I remembered an experience when instructors from the Royal Military College had come to our Toronto training camp to help whip the players into shape. They had been more interested in doing scientific experiments than producing a winning hockey club. I didn't like the idea of the government people coming in at all, and my worst fears were soon realized. The minute I saw these instructors I confronted them. "What are you doing?" I asked. They said they were running tests.

"Running tests for what?"

"For everything."

I walked into the training rooms and found out out what "everything" meant. They had players doing marathon sit-ups and, already, the guys were pulling their stomach muscles. Another instructor had players riding a stationary bike. He would increase the pressure to see how long the players could continue without collapsing. The problem was that three guys had already suffered groin pulls.

What these instructors didn't comprehend was that they were dealing with superstars who were so proud that they would not quit any challenge and, as a result, they kept going and going until their muscles couldn't cope with the demands and, consequently they were injuring themselves.

The real topper was an order that the players should run up to the top of Mount Royal, the mountain that sits in the middle of the city of Montreal, just off the downtown area. Once again, the players tried to meet the challenge and some of them fell by the wayside. Literally. Gerry Cheevers, one of our goalies, hurt his knee trying to run up the mountain and the knee was never the same after that. Bobby Hull, physical nut that he was, tried to outrun everybody, hurt his back and wound up in the hospital. These physical education experts were doing more damage to Team Canada than the Russians and Czechs could ever do.

Not that all of the players were as gung-ho as Hull. Cheevers was a problem when it came to working out, especially on the ice. He never liked practice to begin with and he certainly wasn't crazy about the idea of having the NHL's best shooters taking aim at him every day. The way things turned out, Gerry was probably the only goalie in the history of hockey to be yanked from an intra-squad game for indifferent play, and *I* was the guy who did the yanking.

Steve Shutt of the Montreal Canadiens, one of the hardest shots in the business, let one go and Cheevers just stepped aside and let it into the top corner of the net. I skated over to him and said, "Cheesie, you better get out of there; that puck almost hit you." Sure enough, he skated straight to the bench and was tickled not to have to practice anymore. This, naturally, ticked off a lot of people in the camp. Toe Blake was going crazy about him and so were some of the other players, but it really didn't matter that much in terms of our goaltending quality because we also had Rogie Vachon and Dan Bouchard, two pretty good goalies, who were more willing to take practice seriously.

Some of the upset players were irreplaceable. Picture this. Guy Lapointe of the Canadiens, who was the best defenseman in camp, was about to be cut from the squad because he refused to run up to the top of Mount Royal. I pleaded with the high command, but they still wanted him to go up Mount Royal. I finally swung a compromise solution; I got the high command to call off the Mount Royal run at the end of the week and then persuaded Guy to dash up the mountain during the couple of days we had left before the end of the week.

To the average hockey fan, the sacrifice being made by these superstars may not seem to have been much, but I can assure you that it hurt them a lot more than one might think. For example, they already had a full 80-game schedule to contend with, not to mention a playoff season that extended to the end of May. So, if you have a guy like Lapointe, whose team would make it all the way to the Stanley Cup finals, you have a man who was playing ten months of hockey without a break. Unfortunately, there were some opinion-moulders who failed to understand the sacrifice they were making. One of then was Christie Blatchford of the Toronto *Globe and Mail*.

Ms. Blatchford, who now writes for *The Toronto Star*, was then one of the few women sportswriters in Canada. Her column in the *The Globe and Mail* was widely read.

According to Blatchford, the "sacrifice" being made by the players really didn't amount to much. She called it a "crock," pointing out that Team Canada stayed at the best hotels, ate the best food, and was generally treated like royalty. When the players read the column, they were furious and bitter, especially since the criticism came from a Canadian. The players felt that they were in a no-win situation. If they won the tournament, well, they were expected to come out on top. And if they lost they were nothing but a bunch of choke artists.

My gripe was that journalists like Blatchford didn't bother to get all the facts because, if she did, I think her viewpoint would have been rearranged by about 180 degrees. I don't think she was tuned into people like Dan Maloney of the Toronto Maple Leafs. Dan was a big left wing who was not exactly twinkletoes, but an asset to the club anyway. He was in his prime at the time of the Canada Cup. About five days after the start of training camp we put a call in to Maloney, asking him to come to our camp. I'm not sure what the powers-that-be had in mind by inviting Maloney, because he certainly wasn't in the same class as Bobby Hull, Bobby Orr, or Denis Potvin. But I imagine that they wanted a lot of players there to make the auditions as competitive as possible. There was only one problem; at the time they decided they wanted Maloney, Dan was off with his family somewhere in Alaska.

Somehow they tracked him down and extended the invitation. Dan must have realized that there was no way he would make the team, yet he said, no problem—I'll be there. He grabbed the first available flight and was in camp a day later. Watching him practise that first day, I knew that he didn't have a chance to make the team—and he knew it as well. But he busted his gut every time he got on the ice, as if this was the most important challenge of his entire professional life. He worked and he worked, until that most difficult of all times came along; the day when the roster cuts had to be made. And Dan, when told he was cut, replied, "Thank you for inviting me, it was an honour." Of all the things I remember about Team Canada, I think Dan Maloney's class stands out.

Ever since I became a coach I've always been puzzled over the "best" method for telling a player that he's not good enough to make the team. It always reminds me of the "Kowalski" story. There was a tough Marine sergeant who got word that the father of one of his men had passed away. At roll call he snapped: "Hey, Smith, your father died!" The Marine fainted on the spot. A week later the sister of another Marine died, and the sergeant once again called his men together. "Jones," he yelled out, "your sister died last night!" The Marine burst into tears. Finally, word got back to the general about the sergeant's insensitivity, and he was called on the carpet and told to be less direct and gruff when one of his troops suffered a tragedy. Sure enough, a week later the sergeant was notified that one Private Kowalski had just lost his mother. Remembering what the general had said, he lined up his troop and demanded: "Everyone whose mother is alive, please take one step forward—NOT SO FAST, KOWALSKI!" In retrospect, some coaches cut their players in the same manner.

I suggested that the guys be taken aside and told quietly—nice and easy. Spare them the humiliation. But these street-smart hockey players were away ahead of us, anyway.

The players found out that the cuts were to be made on Tuesday. So early Tuesday morning they went down and asked the hotel clerk for the Wednesday and Thursday room lists. The lists, obviously, would only include those fellows still with the team, so it was easy enough to deduce who the losers were. Of course the high command didn't realize this, and that afternoon the entire group was summoned for lunch, and after lunch we read the names of those who *made* the club. To this day I'm not sure whether the guys who were cut were more angry because of the method employed, or simply because they weren't considered good enough to make Team Canada.

One such individual was Jean Pronovost, a damn good goal scorer who figured he was good enough to stick with the team. I ran into him in the hotel lobby an hour after the public cut had been made and told him I was sorry he was out. "Nice try, Jean," I said.

He murmured something about not understanding how players who had scored 20 goals less than he had were still on the roster and yet he was a goner. I extended my hand for the token goodbye handshake and he stunned me. My hand was relatively limp. He grabbed it and squeezed, harder and harder, almost crushing my hand in his anger. Then he let go, turned and walked away. The more I thought about it afterwards, the angrier I got. So I waited for him in the lobby the next morning. When I spied him, I made a bee line for him and shook his hand again. I was going to put him to the floor, but this time *his* hand was limp. So I said, "Jean, you almost crushed my hand yesterday. I hope it was nothing personal, because if it was, we'll settle it right here."

By the time the words had come out, I knew he had acted out of despair the day before. Now he had cooled down, and sure enough, he apologized. This time we shook like normal people and each went his own way.

It would be nice to say that that was the last of the bruised egos, but we had a few more. Invariably, there were personality clashes. Scotty Bowman and Phil Esposito, among others, couldn't get along for some reason. Phil's high scoring didn't impress Scotty as much as it did others.

One of the things that bothered Phil was that Scotty had him wearing black sweaters during the workouts. Phil didn't like black because, from time immemorial, a black jersey connoted players who were fourth-stringers; otherwise known in hockey circles as the Black Aces. There are few lower insults in the business than to label a hockey player a Black Ace. Funny thing was, I asked Scotty about the black sweaters, and he said he didn't know a thing about them—the trainer just happened to have passed them out that way!

I was pleased with the team, particularly Bobby Orr. If Orr had been a selfish person, he wouldn't have even tried out for Team Canada; he would have remained at home, taken it easy and conserved his damaged limbs for the upcoming NHL schedule. But, as those of us who knew him realized, Orr had an unquenchable thirst for combat and, once again, he proved that he ranked among the most glorious warriors in hockey history (I know, I know; I'm getting carried away again!).

With Orr leading the way, we breezed over Finland, 11-2, in the opener and then took the measure of Team USA and Sweden. To our surprise, the Soviet club was not as overpowering as had been expected, and we beat them too. Naturally, there was a media alibi for why we beat them—it was never that we were simply good, or, God forbid, even great. No, it was always that the Russians were breaking in new players, or weren't taking the series seriously. No matter what, it was a no-win situation, even if we won!

But the Czechs were just dynamite. Before we were up against them, I was chatting with Red Fisher, columnist for *The Montreal Gazette*, about the upcoming matches.

"I'm not all that worried about who we dress or don't dress," I mused. "Goaltending's what bugs me."

"Goaltending?" asked Red, somewhat baffled. "You mean you're down on Rogie Vachon?"

"No, no, no!" (I didn't want this misquoted) "not *our* goaltending. *Their* goaltending. I've been saying since the first day we came to camp, the only thing that can beat us, is if somebody else's goalie gets unconscious."

I still carried around in the back of my head the nightmare of the 1975 playoffs, when my Bruins had hammered the Chicago Black Hawks, 8-2, in the opening game of the best-of-three preliminary round. But the Hawks had rebounded to beat us, 4-3, in overtime of the second game. In the decisive third game we should have clobbered Chicago, but it didn't happen.

We threw everything at their goalie, Tony Esposito—something like 63 shots—but he was having one of those games. When the game was over it was the Hawks, not us, who went on to the next round.

Now we were ready to play the Czechs at The Forum in Montreal. Our record was three wins and no losses; their record was two wins, no losses and a tie. By the time the night was over the Czechs were the only undefeated team in the tournament; a chubby goalie named Vladimir Dzurilla saw to that. He drove us crazy with a miraculous performance that was so good, the partisan Canadian fans at The Forum gave him no less than three standing ovations.

Needless to say it wasn't Dzurilla alone who stopped us. As our players grew increasingly frustrated in the Czech zone, we became lax in our end of the rink and Rogie Vachon produced a number of sensational saves to keep us in the contest. Unfortunately, Dzurilla was playing as if he had the entire four-by-six-foot cage boarded up and the final was 1-0 for the Czechs.

I didn't mind the fans cheering Dzurilla for his fine play, but what did bug me was another occasion in Toronto when we faced the Swedes. Prior to the match players from each team were introduced. Lanny McDonald and Darryl Sittler, both regulars on Team Canada, were then with the Toronto Maple Leafs and each drew applause from the Maple Leaf Gardens audience. But when the Swedes were introduced and the public address announcer mentioned the name of Borje Salming, the crowd went wild. A standing ovation. I was in the press box at the time and there were journalists there who got up and began cheering. I couldn't figure that one out; I mean here they were, Toronto writers, cheering a guy who was going to be skating against their own team and country and not even giving the same applause to Sittler and McDonald.

I stood up in the press box (where Al MacNeil and I worked, phoning down observations to Bobby Kromm who was behind the bench) and bellowed that anyone who dared to cheer on a Swede against Canada once the game was on, purely and simply, sucked. In fact I carried on so much along this theme that my companion in the next seat became terribly upset. He happened to be "Gentleman" Joe Primeau, a Hall of Famer who centered the great Maple Leafs' "Kid Line" of Busher Jackson and Charlie Conacher. One of the nicest guys of all time, Primeau kept soothing me: "Don, you'd better sit down. Don't get so carried away—it's only a game."

Apparently the Canadian players got carried away as well. They didn't care that much for Salming (nor some of the other Swedes, for that matter) and were running at them all night, with Bobby Hull leading the hitting (now figure that one out!).

Bobby Orr's knee was still bothering him, but he never let on and you'd never have known it—he was simply sensational (Scotty told me off the record that of all the guys on the team, we could least afford to lose Orr). Bobby had told me that the one thing he wanted to do before he retired was play the Russians and, boy, was he turning it on. Game after game he was selected as the best player of the game, and it was a popular decision with the players—only they knew the pain he was going through just to skate.

The only player who disagreed with the decision was Denis Potvin. Denis always resented the fact that people always called him a "Second Bobby Orr" when he was young. Actually I could never really understand the resentment: would a baseball player resent being called another Babe Ruth? He said he did not like being constantly measured against Orr and I guess I can't blame him for that. But they measured him against Orr nonetheless, and when Bobby ultimately was named the Most Valuable Player in the tournament, Potvin burned. He could not understand why he had been picked and even went public with his thoughts in the *Toronto Star Weekly*. Needless to say, he was not too popular with a lot of people when that piece hit the newsstands. Truthfully, I always thought Rogie Vachon was second to Bobby in the "Most Valuable" category.

The individual stars of one game were given hand-carved seals, sculpted by the Canadian Eskimos. Denis beefed about not getting one of the seals and the players picked up on the complaint. One day the players called a meeting on the ice and naturally everyone figured something terribly serious was about to happen. Just then a couple of players skated on to the ice carrying a huge stuffed toy seal and presented it to Denis!

Bobby Clarke, the Philadelphia Flyers center, was injured quite a bit during the series, but still gave 100 percent. Clarke's reward for his efforts was delivered on his birthday after a scrimmage. His teammate and old pal, Reggie Leach, made the presentation and, quite frankly, I had never seen anything like it before.

Another meeting was called on the ice whereupon Leach skated out with an enormous white cake with the inscription, HAPPY BIRTHDAY, BOBBY, on top. Before the presentation was actually made the boys swung into a chorus of "Happy Birthday" and Clarke seemed truly touched by the gesture; so much so that once the singing subsided he began to utter a few words of gratitude. Leach wound up and hurled the entire hunk of pastry in Clarke's face. Reggie threw it so hard—remember, Bobby's mouth was open at the moment of impact—that the cake was driven right down his throat and into his eyes and damn near knocked him right off his feet. Imagine, a guy nearly choking to death on his own birthday cake!

Clarke took it graciously, accepting the humour of the situation and, for me, it was a pleasure to be associated with players of such high calibre. Their classiness was detectable in a lot of different ways. Orr, Clarke and Guy Lafleur, for example, displayed their devotion by coming to the rink extra early. For an eight o'clock game, Orr would be in the dressing room at two in the afternoon, puttering around with his sticks, chatting with the trainers and just plain getting himself "up" for the game. Clarke would arrive an hour or so later and Lafleur might be in the room by four, pacing back and forth like a caged tiger, chainsmoking cigarettes with half of his equipment on.

By contrast, Peter Mahovlich, Frank's kid brother and potentially one of the best players in the business, would drive Scotty Bowman nuts.

Peter, essentially, is a loosey-goosey guy who likes a good time as much as he cares about good hockey. Which is fine and dandy, until the priorities collide. Mahovlich would drive Bowman crazy with his nonsensical yelling in the dressing room. (Scotty would be standing outside in the hallway saying, "Just listen to that jerk. He's doing that just to bug me.") Another time, we were having a team dinner the night before a big game and, according to protocol, the players were to sit at their tables and the high command was to eat at their own table. Now, I don't know why Peter did this, but instead of sitting with his teammates, he plunked

After we won the Canada Cup in The Montreal Forum. (left to right) Al Eagleson, Bobby Kromm, Toe Blake, me, Keith Allen, Al McNeil, and Sam Pollock. (Imagine me with no tie!)

Team Canada, 1981.   JAMES LIPA

Larry Robinson, Guy Lafleur, and me, after Guy had been injured.

Lanny McDonald, Timothy, and me.

himself down at management's table. I knew that he hadn't been drinking that much, but he pretended that he had for some reason and that just made Sammy Pollock and Scotty Bowman furious. But that was Peter and maybe that little scene helps explain in capsule form why a fellow with immense ability never was able to harness it and, in effect, threw away what could have been a great career.

Team Canada prevailed to the final game, neck-and-neck with Czechoslovakia for the championship. The Russians had already been disposed of and, on paper at least, it appeared that we should romp to the title.

But the Czechs had shown us in the 1-0 upset that they were not only capable of playing tight hockey, but that they had a great goaltender in Dzurilla. I figured that if we could solve that guy between the pipes we'd be able to top them.

Conservatively speaking, I would say that the final match between Team Canada and the Czechs was one of the finest I have ever seen or played in, anywhere, anytime. Rogie Vachon was magnificent in the nets for us, but that sonofagun Dzurilla was proving that his shutout in the earlier game was far from a fluke.

The score was tied with about a minute left in regulation time when one of the Czechs broke through our defense and it looked like curtains. But Vachon came up with one of the greatest saves I've ever seen and we went into sudden-death overtime. The Czechs were playing almost flawless hockey except for one thing. Dzurilla seemed to betray one weakness that I thought our guys ought to know about so I sent a message down to the dressing room from my private spotter's box: "He's moving further and further out of his net. I think you can fool him if you get a chance. Anybody who breaks in on him should delay his shot a bit. Dzurilla will keep coming. You might wind up with a lot of room to shoot at."

Sammy Pollock ordered me downstairs to give the message directly to the guys. So, I went down and talked it over with Cheevers and Bowman. "Whether they're coming down the left or right side," I explained, "have them fake the slapshot, then keep going wide and slide the puck along the ice."

It seemed like a good idea, but as I made my way back to the booth, I wondered whether the guys would ever get the chance to use the ploy and if they did, what would come of it. Fortunately, it didn't take very long for me to find out. The sudden-death period began and not too far into the period Marcel Dionne, the Los Angeles Kings center, got control of the puck and gave a pass to Darryl Sittler who was moving down the left wing. Sittler couldn't have made a better move if I had been manipulating him with strings from above. He faked the slapshot, took an extra stride or two and then pulled the trigger. By this time Dzurilla had obliged by sliding way out of position and Sittler finished the play by sliding the puck into the net. While the capacity crowd was screaming, I sat there, more dumbfounded than anybody.

When I finally made my way down to the dressing room, I expected to find the kind of jubilation normally associated with winning the Stanley Cup. There was, of course, an aura of happiness, but not nearly the intensity I had anticipated. Instead there was more a feeling of relief that, at last, the pressure was off. Then someone mentioned that now the guys had to get ready for the NHL training camp. We had just played a season against the Russians, Czechs, Swedes, Americans and Finns, and now we had to start the NHL trek from September to, with luck, May.

Personally, I felt great. I was one-for-one as an international hockey coach and had actually come out of it without getting into trouble once! As I left for the Bruins training camp, I assumed that I would never experience anything like international hockey again. Little did I realize that just five years later I would be leading a club featuring Guy Lafleur into the world championships at Stockholm, Sweden; only this time I would be hellbent for disaster.

As an international hockey coach, I was batting a thousand. Of course, the record was a mere one-for-one but, what the hell, serving on the staff of the Canadian entry in the 1976 Canada Cup victory had been a feather in my cap. A lot of people remembered my Dzurilla strategy (my mother and Blue) so it really wasn't all that surprising when my name came up as a coaching candidate for Team Canada in the 1981 World Championships in Sweden. Do you really want to know the reason I was chosen? I was the best unemployed coach still being paid by an NHL club. The NHL liked that because they wouldn't have to pay me. I was supposed to be doing this for the "glory." (I told you my brother had all the brains in the family.)

The Eagle was running the show again. He called me and asked me if I wanted the coaching job. At first, I was hesitant. Instead of giving him a yes-or-no answer, I countered, "O.K., but my son Timothy comes along as assistant trainer." (Somebody in the Cherry family was going to enjoy themselves over there!) The Eagle said it was okay, so I agreed to take the job although I still suffered some doubts.

My brother, for one, told me that I was dumb to accept. He, too, pointed out that I'd be in a no-win situation. If the club did all right, so what? And if they lost—which was what figured to happen—I'd come out looking like a chump.

Another thing that worried me was the effect it might have on my television career, such as it was. I had spent a successful year as a commentator with *Hockey Night in Canada* and now the Stanley Cup playoffs were about to begin, the best part of the season. On top of that, I'd have to forego banquets which, surprisingly, bring in a lot of money.

I realized that I'd be at a disadvantage, because there would be so little time to prepare. That didn't bother me half as much as the ridicule being heaped on our club by our own people. We hadn't even assembled the squad and already we had been dubbed Team Terrible and Team

Losers. I was quietly encouraged. I loved to take a bunch of players and tell them that nobody believed in them—but me. From a motivational point of view, it was ideal. I figured that with their pride at stake the pros would come through.

I also figured that, no matter who was beaten in the first playoff round, I'd wind up with a star or two. The best bet was that the Canadiens would knock off the Oilers meaning that Wayne Gretzky could join our club and give us terrific power at center.

My superior in this venture was John Ferguson, who had been the "policeman" on some of the great Montreal Stanley Cup-winning teams and later was coach and general manager of the Rangers. Now Fergie was general manager of the Winnipeg Jets and co-manager of Team Canada 1981. Before I left for Europe my brother once again provided me with the deathless message: Get along with the boss.

"You can't afford to fight with Fergie," he said, "or get him mad. For Heaven's sake, get along with him." Richard's voice kept ringing in my ear as we jetted across the Atlantic. Meanwhile, I was getting excited about the tournament and mulled over a number of strategies. A factor I had to keep in mind was the rink size. European rinks are considerably larger than the ones we are accustomed to in the NHL so I decided it was imperative that we work out on a big rink as soon as we could arrange a scrimmage. When we finally regrouped in Stockholm and headed for our first workout, the Swedish hockey authorities gave us a small rink. Obviously, they had every angle figured.

I did get a few good hockey players. Lo and behold, the Oilers upset the Canadiens in three straight games of the first Stanley Cup round which meant that some very good talent would be headed my way. Larry Robinson, the big, rangy defenseman, and Guy Lafleur, were both enroute to Sweden. Frankly, I didn't believe Lafleur would show up. He had suffered through one of the most miserable seasons any athlete could endure. First of all, he had been hurt for a large part of the hockey season; then he had fallen asleep at the wheel of his Cadillac only a month earlier and had almost been killed. Finally, his club had been humiliated by the upstart Oilers.

The day Guy arrived in Stockholm, I could see that he was fatigued beyond belief. I told him I only wanted him to play when he was ready. He replied that he would play whether he was tired or not. Our next game was against the West German team which had a few German Canadian players who would have liked nothing better than to cork Lafleur. In fact, before the game I mentioned to my assistant coach Andre Boudrias "This game bothers me, some of these Junior B Canadians would love to get their names in the paper back in Canada by hurting Guy." (Robinson was too big, they would never come near him.) I hesitated using Guy because I saw no point in getting him unnecessarily banged up just after arriving; but he insisted on lacing up the skates so, like a fool, I relented. On the very first shift Lafleur was fed a sucker pass at center. A German-Canadian player—from Toronto—noticed that Guy had his face down and elbowed him right in the face. What a shot; Guy was flattened while blood poured from his head. The thing that hurt him the most was the dumb helmet everybody has to wear over there. It came down and cut him on the nose.

Our players had to help him off the ice and I was beside myself. If I could have gotten hold of that player I would have killed him; Guy said, "I can't win. I fall asleep driving my car and I fall asleep on the ice."

My frustration was showing and I continued to betray a certain impatience as the series progressed. Who wouldn't? When we went up against the Russians the first time around we decided to play a cautious, close-checking game and we got our butts whipped. So, we altered our tactics against the Czechs and decided to play offensive hockey and we got our butts whipped, again, because our goaltending fell apart in the first period.

Next came the Swedes and naturally, a reporter asked: "How do you plan to cope with them?" I told him he should have asked me three weeks ago when we were still in Canada. At that time they were billing me as a hockey expert. Now, three weeks later in beautiful downtown Gothenburg, I was just another dumb hockey coach whose team was playing .500 hockey. Although we were playing only .500 hockey, I noticed a strange thing. The games were fast and furious and we were playing to the largest and most boisterous crowds. I would watch the Russians play the same team the following day to small crowds and it was about as exciting as watching paint dry. Please don't tell me they play exciting hockey; I know they are great and technically super, but I sure wouldn't want to watch them for 80 games. The people flocked to see *us*, and their booing of the opposition was great.

In terms of the play itself, our worst fears were realized. Lack of practice time for our club to jell hurt us right from the start. By contrast, the team play of the Russians and Czechs was giving us a good lesson. The Czechs and Russians had six-man units. The goalie, two defensemen and three forwards knew instinctively where every man was going to be, every split second. These six-men units had been practising and playing together for 800 hours getting ready for the tournament. Our guys had been working together for only two weeks. We were breaking down occasionally because our defense pairings hadn't had time to get accustomed to the forward lines they were playing with.

Despite the adversity, I was proud of our guys, especially Lafleur. He was giving it his best shot and so was Larry Robinson, except that Larry fell victim to one of his own little pranks and we all were the worse for it. In a giddy moment after a practice he decided to play Martian. He gathered a bunch of extra-long Q-Tips and inserted them in his ears and ran around shouting, "Look, I'm a Martian!" It got a few laughs until he tried to remove the Q-Tips from his ears. Apparently, Robinson forgot that they were extra-long and when he reached for one of them, instead of grabbing it, he accidentally drove the thing *into* his ear, right into the ear drum. Blood spurted out of his ear and the doctor had to be called.

Robinson was given pain-killers and sent back to his hotel room to recuperate. Unfortunately, he couldn't recuperate fast enough for us. He missed three games but, worse than that, the poor guy was suffering excruciating pain. (He told me that during that first night he had never been in such agony in his life. "If I had had a gun," he told me, "I would have shot myself.")

Eventually, Larry recuperated and played superbly. Hockey players being what they are, provided him with a warm welcome on his return to the dressing room. Everyone stood at attention—with Q-Tips in his ears. It produced the required laugh but, I must admit, my sense of humour took a few dips around this time. One of the problems concerned Morris Lukowich and Dave Babych, a forward and defenseman, respectively, from the Winnipeg Jets, employees of John Ferguson.

Babych had just completed his rookie year with Winnipeg while Lukowich had been around a few years. Each was a good player in his own way but they had been playing badly in this tournament. (For some reason—probably the coaching.) The way I run a team, if a guy is screwing up and there's someone around who could do a better job, the one who could help the team most gets the nod. To be true to myself and the team I had to bench Lukowich and Babych. But the minute I made that decision I began to hear my brother's voice—"Don't get Fergie mad at you."

I have to admit I had second thoughts. I began talking to myself. ("Don, when are you going to learn to be a politician? Play the 'game.' Save yourself some grief. Do what'll make Fergie happy.") But deep down, I knew all along what I was going to do.

Needless to say, I paid the price for my decision. Fergie was never the same with me after that. Not that he fired me or second-guessed me in the media. (At least not *then*.) But there *was* a certain detectable coolness that didn't exactly make me the most comfortable coach in Scandinavia. I figured the only way things would straighten out would be if we could somehow come up with a win over the Russians. But how? One theory was: you can't out-Russian the Russians; play your own game, take the man, finish the check.

The plan worked—to a certain extent. We had a 3-1 lead and were outplaying them by a long shot, outshooting them two-to-one. But, the Soviets came from behind and tied us. In a sense, it was a moral victory so, that night, for the first time since I had arrived in Scandinavia I went out and had a good time. I found myself a cozy bar and just nursed a few drinks well into the night. Before I knew it the clock had struck two in the morning and I was the only one left in the joint. Time to return to the hotel.

I picked up a beer mug with a Swedish emblem on it—my souvenir—and began making my way back to the hotel. The streets were completely deserted; creepy is the word for it. No cars, no people, and not much light. I headed for the river, where the hotel was located. Suddenly I looked up and, a few yards ahead of me, saw a large figure leaning against a street light, smoking a cigarette. The hotel was eight blocks away and there was no way I could get to it without actually walking past this guy. Whatever street-wise toughness I might have developed in Kingston had vanished in this scary moment. I began imagining headlines: DRUNK CANADIAN HOCKEY COACH MUGGED IN STOCKHOLM.

Closing my right hand on the beer stein, I prepared for the worst. I took another few steps while the stranger took a long drag on his cigarette. I took another step and now we were eye-to-eye. The man took another puff on his cigarette and, in almost perfect English asked: "How's Blue?" That was almost as good as beating the Russians.

So we finished in fourth place, losing the final game 4-2 to the Czechs. I wasn't all that discouraged.

I was very proud of our effort although I realized that the people back home wanted at least a medal. Still, I had managed to get behind the bench again, and that felt good. Even John Ferguson was friendly toward me when we sat together on the flight home from Sweden. When we arrived in Toronto I shook hands with Fergie and figured that any differences we might have had over Lukowich and Babych had been resolved. Three days later a story broke out of Winnipeg. Some reporter had asked Ferguson about the job I had done. He told the fellow that as a coach I make a good television commentator. (Nice, here we go again!) I talked to Fergie about it. He assured me that he had never said what had been printed, that he was quoted out of context and he was sorry about what had made the papers.

"John," I said, "that reminds me of the guy who's accused of rape and gets front-page headlines because of it. Then, when he's found innocent the story is buried on page 60."

My gut feeling is that Fergie *was* misquoted. When we returned home somebody asked Guy Lafleur whether I'd be a good choice to coach the Montreal Canadiens. He said he thought I'd be ideal for the job. Which only proves that Lafleur is not only a gentleman, a scholar, and a fine athlete but also a great judge of coaching talent.

I have been asked why Canada sends a team over to the World Tournament without our best players, fully aware that they're going to get stiffed. (A good example was 1982. Canada could have won a silver medal if Russia had beaten the Czechs. Naturally the game ended in a 0-0 tie.) The real reason we send a team is that if we don't go over there, they will not come to Canada and participate in the Canada Cup. Somebody has to go and pay the price.

Before the last Canada Cup Eagle was in a dilemma. He felt

obligated to have me as one of the coaches since I had been one of the sacrificial lambs in the earlier World Tournament. But Eagle was having a tough time with some of the g.m.s.

"Quite simply," said Eagle, "it's this way. I want you, Scotty wants you, but some of the g.m.s. don't like your attitude, or you."

I let Eagle off the hook. I said, "That's okay, Eagle, but do me a favour. Tell them I don't like them or *their* attitudes."

Another little piece of gratitude I received a year later when they were considering the coach for the next World Tournament in 1982. It was said in the newspapers that "we want somebody employed by the NHL to coach, not like Cherry. He was too independent and couldn't be controlled." (I liked that.)

EPILOGUE

If I had a dollar for every guy who stopped me on the street and said, "Don, you should be coaching again," I'd be as rich as Gretzky. Sometimes, though, I can't tell whether they say that because they want me back in coaching, or whether they want me *out* of TV!

At one point in my life I wanted very much to coach in the NHL, but I have almost cured myself of that affliction; and I *do* mean it's a sickness. Think about it: if a coach is worth his salt, he has to devote 24 out of 24 hours to his job, whether his family likes it or not. There have been over sixty coaching changes in the last four years in the NHL.

I would not only take the game home with me—because I used to take every loss personally—but I'd drive my family nuts. No, I don't miss that hassle at all. What I do miss is the camaraderie—the morning skates at the practice rink, the fooling around after practice, having fun with the young players, and, of course, the friendships that developed over the years with both the players and the media alike.

Perhaps I wouldn't be so offhand about it, if I hadn't gotten very lucky during my last weeks with the Colorado Rockies. Even though it wasn't certain that I would be fired, the handwriting *was* on the wall. My radar told me that I would be out of a job, so the time had come to find another means of earning a living. It was just about then that I got a call from the people at *Hockey Night in Canada* asking if I'd be interested in doing some television work. The idea was for me to host a feature called "Coach's Corner," in which I'd discuss various aspects of hockey technique.

I was pretty tired at the time, and as I was about to say no, they said, "Come on down to Toronto, do a few tapes and see your mother in Kingston." Well, when they put it that way, I thought, why not? I did four tapes of "Coach's Corner" and flew back to Denver. I had barely gotten back when they called to say that the show had gone over well and they wanted me to do eight more.

The next thing I knew I was a TV personality! In no time at all I realized I was enjoying a lot of the benefits of coaching without any of the headaches. I was still around hockey people, I still had a certain amount of preparation to do, but best of all I was *involved* with the game. The producers not only allowed me, they encouraged me to express my opinions.

A lot of thanks has to go to Ralph Mellanby, executive producer of *Hockey Night in Canada*, for his encouragement. After my first Stanley Cup finals as a commentator, Ralph said that he didn't want me to change, the only promise he wanted from me was that I would never "turn professional." If any of you readers have seen me, you know I've kept that promise! So thanks to Ralph and my friend and advisor, Gerry Patterson, my TV career suddenly took off. I wonder where I'd be today without them?

The TV experience proved very enlightening and quite a balm for the ego of a twice-fired NHL coach. Look at it this way: I played sixteen years of professional hockey and won four championships in five years. Then I'd go home and my mother would say,"Where did you play *this* year, Don?" When I coached the Bruins, a few people knew me. Since I've become a television personality, everybody on the street seems to know me. I've been invited to do commercials, I've been invited to more banquets than there are rubber chickens and my ego became so inflated at one point that it required a quick puncture which, fortunately, happened before I became totally unbearable. It happened at Toronto's International Airport, where I was waiting in line for a ticket. An old gentleman and his wife were standing in front of me. They turned around and looked me over, whereupon the old gentleman said to his wife, "Do you know who this is?"

"I sure do," replied his wife, "I see him all the time on TV." (By now I'm feeling pretty good, as usual.)

"Well," asked the old gent, "who is he?"

"Why," his wife replied, "he's the Friendly Giant!" (For the uninitiated, The Friendly Giant is host of a Canadian children's TV show, and has been for 25 years. I'm surprised they recognized me without my giraffe!)

Another deflation occured at the Nassau Coliseum during the Islanders-Nordiques semi-final series in April, 1982. I was in the broadcast booth, when a voice blared out of the crowd: "Hey, Cherry, when are you gonna' get yourself an honest job?" I looked up and who should my heckler be, but Mrs. Mike McEwen.

I shot back, "How come Mike's got you up here in the cheap seats? Did he scalp his good ones?"

Whether Mrs. McEwen cares to believe it or not, I think I have a better feel for hockey now than I did at any time in my career. I talk to the referees, to the managers, the owners, the press and most important, I talk to the players. When I coached, I didn't have this opportunity or scope, because I mostly devoted my time to my own team. My contact with the players has really touched me.

For example, after one of the Islanders-Nordiques games, I was talking to some fans at the Nassau Coliseum parking lot, when, at a distance, I noticed Islander left wing Bob Nystrom (whom I've never met and always admired) getting into his car. Our eyes met. He waved to me and then gave me the thumbs-up sign.

You may wonder why I've made such a big deal over such a trivial gesture, but it meant a lot to me. Nystrom epitomizes the good, honest grinder. I like to feel that I'm a good, honest grinder. Being acknowledged that way by Nystrom was better than winning any lottery. It told me that he liked me just the way I am.

That incident, in turn, reminds me of an evening I once spent alone at our home on Wolfe Island, just across the St. Lawrence River from Kingston. The house is located on an isolated part of the island. Rose and Tim had gone back to Denver; it was September, late in the tourist season and that part of the island was deserted. It was just me and Blue and a few pints, watching a storm rage over the river, late at night.

I was feeling low. The Soviets had beaten Team Canada and I was suffering doubts about my future. I thought about brother Richard's lectures on conformity and others who had suggested I change my ways "for the better," whatever that meant. Suddenly, I flashed back to a talk I had had with an old gentleman who thought it would be wise for me to take the straight-and-narrow path and not antagonize so many people. As I mulled over the old man's message, I peered over toward the lighthouse beacon that pierced the black night. Then I recalled the old fellow's very words: "Keep fighting the world, Mr. Cherry, and you'll wind up being a lighthouse keeper on that island of yours."

So I sat there in the silence with Blue sitting beside me, sipping my brew, watching the waves crash over the docks. I began to think that, maybe, the old guy had been right. Maybe I wouldn't have blown hundreds of thousands of dollars by being stubborn, if, in fact, I had bent with the wind. But, as I cracked another pint, I said to Blue: "Ah, to hell with it, Blue. It's too late for me to change now.

"And I'll tell you another thing, Blue: if I do end up a lighthouse keeper on this island, I'll run it my way and it'll be the best damn lighthouse this island ever had."

Blue looked up at me and clearly said: "Damn right, Grapes, Damn right!"

EPILOGUE'S EPILOGUE

It's August 1993, beloved Blue is gone. No more walks in the moonlight to straighten things out in my life. Our chats helped me when I had no job in Rochester, when I coached the Americans and the Bruins, they even helped me on "Coach's Corner." Baby Blue just doesn't seem to care, she's off chasing a rabbit or something. Things aren't the same.

I'm doing OK now, but when I look back to 1982, which is when *Grapes* ended, I was struggling big time, with no more money coming from the Colorado Rockies. I was doing colour for "Hockey Night in Canada" but I was also a dog and pony act travelling all over Canada doing banquets for $500 to $750 trying to survive. (I remember one time I travelled all over Saskatchewan for a chemical company doing six banquets in five different cities in five days. On our safari I stopped at a diner for lunch and a trucker said that the truckers were having a meeting, so I went along and was glad to go. On that same trip, we went to a school auditorium one afternoon. As I went into my act, I noticed the men all had beards and the women were wearing bonnets. Kind of strange, says I, but I gave them my best stories about Wayne Cashman. The silence was deafening, not a laugh, a giggle or a smile; somehow the company had brought me to a group of Mennonite farmers and believe it or not they weren't impressed with stories of Cash getting drunk and going to jail and ordering Chinese food.)

Well, you get the idea, life was not a bowl of cherries as they say and a lot of people were unhappy with me for various reasons. Even my mom was upset with segments of "Coach's Corner," especially the one about Dr.

219

Randy Gregg of the Edmonton Oilers when I said, "How would you like this guy operating on you with those hands when he missed an open net in the semi-finals between Edmonton and Chicago?" I got it force 10 from Mom. She said, "It's one thing to get on somebody about their hockey life but it's totally unfair to bring in personal things." As usual Mom was right and I've never done it since (I think). Also at that time I wrote this book and I'm ashamed to say, it was sprinkled with the "F" word. When Mom saw the draft, she said, "I'm very disappointed in you, that you would put that word in the book. There are going to be a lot of children reading it. This is not a book your father or I would be very proud of with that word in it." I went back and took the word out, and the upshot of this story is that my brother Richard, who is the principal of a public school, said the book was a favourite in the public library but if that word had been in it, no way it would be in the library. Mom was right again. She is gone now, and another guiding hand is no more.

So between a million banquets and doing "Hockey Night in Canada" I was surviving, but I had rubbed too many people the wrong way as usual and a lot of people at the CBC were not too happy with me — something about how they owed it to the English-speaking children of Canada to get rid of me. Executive producer Ralph Mellanby was in my corner so I was okay for a while, but to tell the truth, folks, the future did not look good. It looked like dark clouds were forming for old Don.

I finally got a break around 1982. My friend Gerry Patterson and Ralph Mellanby thought up the idea to have a sports interview show on TV on CHCH Hamilton. They came up with the name "Don Cherry's Grapevine." Now, I'm not bad doing "Coach's Corner" or colour commentary because I don't have to think, I just react. But when I tried to do a cold opening for the show I was terrified (I swear Ralph literally had to hold my hand I was so scared). Still, hunger is a great motivator and I kept plugging away, but to tell you the truth I was so embarrassed by those early shows, especially the cold openings — the terror in my eyes was something to behold. Finally, at his wits' end, Ralph said, "Look get a big picture of Blue and let on you're only talking to Blue and not the cameras." So I got a big picture (actually the cover of the first book) and it worked. I would forget the camera, look in Blue's eyes, and say, "Blue, tonight on the Grapevine we have the greatest hockey player who ever lived — Bobby Orr." It wasn't Dave Hodge but I got by. People seemed to like the show and a funny thing happened — I got asked all the time where the bar was. When I told them it was only a set at CHCH studios in Hamilton, they always answered, "Gee, that's too bad, we would go to it; it looks like a dandy bar." So that's how the idea of the "Don Cherry's Grapevine" restaurants was born; Gerry Patterson and I looked and looked for over a year till finally we found an old restaurant in Hamilton that had been closed for months. Everybody thought I was nuts but I loved it, the place looked like an old Boston bar. But I couldn't find the

right guy to be partners with me. (I was very wary as I had had a few buddies who went into partnership with another guy and lost their shirt; as I
knew ZIP about the restaurant business, the guy who would be my partner had to know what he was doing and be somebody I could trust.) To
make a long story short I met a young fellow named Rick Scully and we
teamed up. He supplied the brains and know-how and I supplied — come
to think of it I don't know what I supplied — but we're doing all right.

Things were not all right with "Hockey Night in Canada" back then;
it seems I was on the carpet almost every week about something. I didn't
want to get fired from TV because it looked like I had been blackballed
from ever coaching again and jobs were scarce, so I had to watch myself;
but controversy seemed to follow me everywhere. Finally a producer said
the management was upset because I never pronounced names like
Holgrem and Gilles correctly (I remember the names like it was yesterday) and that I definitely had to stop cheerleading for the Boston Bruins
when doing the colour for their games. They said I had to be neutral.

So I was doing OK minding my Ps and Qs, till one night in a game
between the Habs and the Bruins. I was doing the colour with my buddies
Dick Irvin and Danny Galivan and the Bruins were beating the Canadiens
4-3 with a minute to go. The Bruins' Craig MacTavish got the puck in the
corner, spun around and snapped it in the top corner for a 5-3 lead. I
jumped up and yelled, "We're beating them to-night." So long colour job. It
was my last, and the only thing left between me and the unemployment
line was "Coach's Corner" and the knives are being sharpened on that one.
It was getting down to decision time for old Don, I was getting it from
everywhere and it hasn't stopped right up to this day. I'm being ripped up
in the papers pretty good; listen to this one from a Pittsburgh writer named
Gene Collier. Here is part of the column he wrote after I called Jaromir Jagr
a slug and there was talk of me going to Pittsburgh to do TV on KBL which
does the Penguins' games: "In the vast glossary of Cherry's vitriol 'slug' is
a rather benign entry. When Don really gets mad, his hockey analysis bor-
ders on hate speech. If Cherry isn't bigoted, the precepts of his commentary
are. They are essentially that hockey, to be played correctly, must be con-
tested by hard-working English-speaking Canadian boys, their virtue obvious and inversely proportionate to their number of teeth. French
Canadians and Americans, as you might expect, are barely tolerated... .
Europeans are openly despised, explaining the Jagr remark and the fre-
quent attacks on Ulf Samuelsson. (He's your worst nightmare; a foreigner
in a shield.) When Dale Hunter mugged Pierre Turgeon out of the playoffs,
there was one man on the planet who took Hunter's side... . When nine
Russians turned up in the NHL in 1989 and one, Alexander Mogilny, con-
templated retirement because his fear of flying was so acute, guess who
said, 'One down, eight to go?'

Bill Craig, the boss of KBL, said in the column: "I don't want the
broadcasts to stay sterile and perfect, I'd like to see us involve the fans

more... . If Don Cherry thinks Mario is No. 3 behind Bobby Orr and Wayne Gretzky, I want him to say so."

Gene responded: "Well, that *could* involve the fans more. The climactic scenes of 'Frankenstein' come to mind." (Remember when the citizens chased Frankenstein and burned him to death.) Gene continues, "I can't decide [which is more ridiculous]. Is it that Cherry is a journalist or that he has a craft? His 'craft' is the verbal equivalent of ripping the head off a live chicken." By the way, the headline of Gene's column was, "Let's Learn to Love to Hate Don Cherry." Hey, as my Dad said, "If you're going to dish it out, you're gonna have to take it."

I particularly like the column of a lovely lady named Jane O'Hara who is an editor for the Ottawa *Sun*. Here's part of Jane's little tribute to me: "I used to think that Don Cherry was an amiable clown. Big collars. Big mouth. Big thumb, always pointed up to signal his pleasure at the most recent dirty hit or near decapitation on some ice surface somewhere in the world... . A case can be made that Cherry has a place in hockey. He appeals to guys who want their hockey tough, their beer cold, their Russians back in Russia, their Finns back in ballet school. He makes sense, in the way that cartoons do, to guys who think the world's become too complicated, too correct. Just let 'em play is one of Cherry's favourite themes. And it doesn't seem to matter to the doughheads who are watching whether he's talking about hockey, the House of Commons or the Gulf War." Ms. O'Hara continues, "It says something about a country when its most recognizable TV personality, its most bankable advertising mug, is a guy like Cherry." Also she says the CBC has turned into the DCN, Don Cherry Network — TV for guys talking to guys about how to be bigger and better guys.

Well, you get the idea, a lot of alligators after my behind. And I'm told by a lot of guys who I respect in the TV business that I'd better cool it, lay off a little, back off 30 percent, no more knocking the foreigners, smarten up and I could go on forever on TV. And I keep thinking back to that old fellow who told me, "Keep fighting the world, Mr. Cherry, and you'll end up being a lighthouse keeper on that island of yours."

I know these people are right; they mean well and have only my interest at heart. Maybe they are right, they make sense, grab the dough and run. When I'm gone do you think anybody will care? Who needs the heat — but I know even as I try to convince myself that I'll never change, I'm too far down the road and there's no sense in turning back.

I've got to keep doing what I do and if I have to go, it will be too bad because I really have fun and love doing "Coach's Corner" now that I've straightened out MacLean. But all good things must come to an end and if the powers that be say "See ya later, Grapes," it's OK by me, I never thought I'd last this long. I can look back and say, "Thanks a lot, I really enjoyed it, it's been a good ride"; but if I gotta go, I'm goin' down punchin'. As my father used to say, "If you're gonna be shot, better to be shot as a wolf than a lamb."